WITHDRAWN
UTSA LIBRARIES

White Society in Black Africa:
The French of Senegal

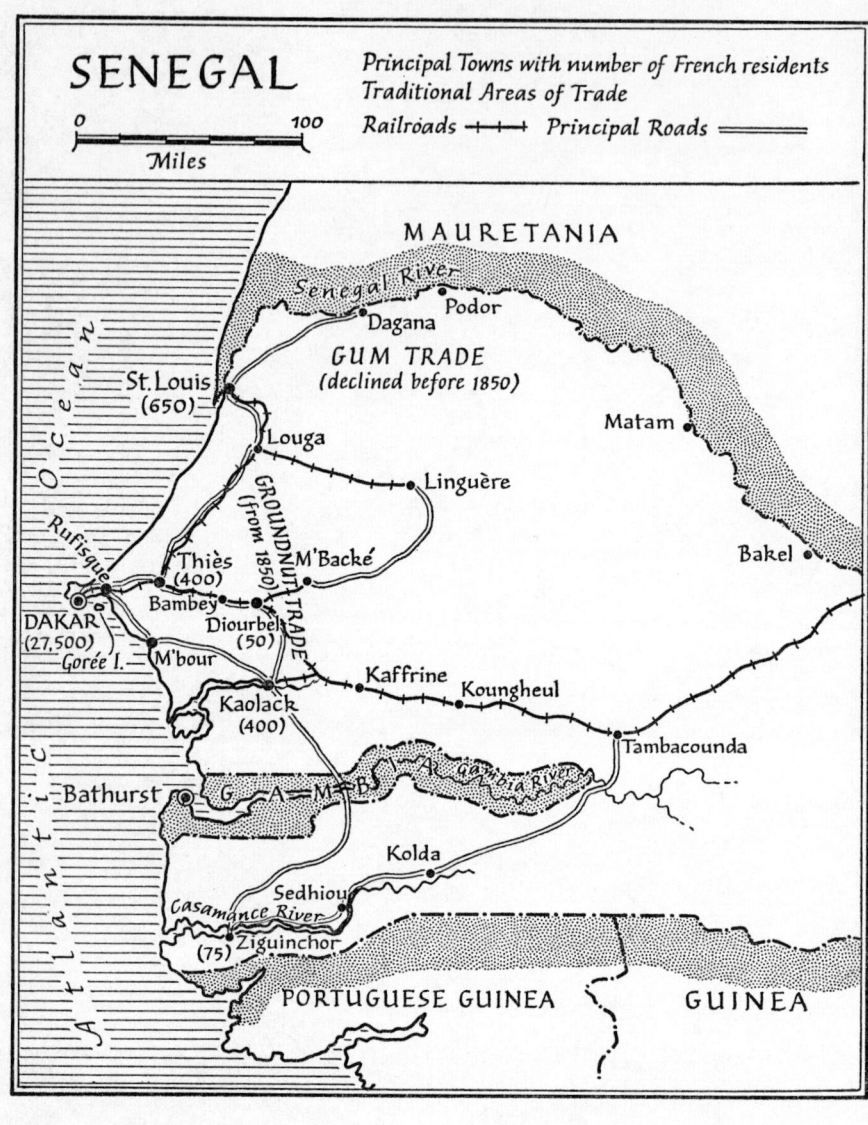

White Society in Black Africa:
The French of Senegal

by RITA CRUISE O'BRIEN

Northwestern University Press
Evanston, Illinois

*First published in the United States of
America, 1972, by Northwestern University Press,
1735 Benson Avenue, Evanston, Illinois 60201*

ISBN 0-8101-0374-5

Library of Congress Catalog Card Number: 74-183533

© *Rita Cruise O'Brien, 1972*

To Donal

Acknowledgements

For his encouragement in the early stages of this study, as well as his continued interest I owe a great debt of gratitude to Professor Michael Crowder, whose knowledge of Senegalese history and recent development is considerable. In preparation for research, access to library and archival materials were provided by the staffs of the *Bibliothèque Nationale* in Paris, the *Archives de la République du Sénégal*, and especially kindly and efficiently by the staff of the *Institut Fondamental d'Afrique Noire* (I.F.A.N., Dakar). I was greatly assisted by funds for research provided by the Central Research Fund of London University and by the Jackson Lewis Fellowship, awarded by the London School of Economics, which helped finance the first stages of analysis and writing up towards the completion of my doctoral thesis in Sociology. The final survey was analysed at the Computer Unit of the L.S.E., where the staff were particularly patient and helpful.

A number of French and Senegalese social scientists were of assistance to me. I would like to thank in particular André Hauser, Research Fellow in Industrial Sociology for the *Office de la Recherche Scientifique et Technique Outre-Mer*, whose interest and guidance throughout my fieldwork in Dakar greatly facilitated research. Many thanks are also due to Paul Mercier of the *Ecole Pratique des Hautes Etudes, Sixième Section* in Paris who took an interest in the initial stages of the study, to Jean Le Plat of the Statistical Service of the Senegalese government, and Yves Mersadier of I.F.A.N. Professor Pierre Fougeyrollas and Mlle. Fatou Sow, formerly at the Centre of Social-Psychology, University of Dakar, were of great help in discussing methodology and procedure for the survey and putting me in contact with interviewers (from among their students). I was very grateful for the efficiency and effectiveness of those who helped me administer the questionnaire: Françoise Hemy, Monique Ferraro, Bernard Potterat and Ibrahima Seck.

To Mlle. Janine Blanc I owe a particularly large debt of grati-

Acknowledgements

tude, not only for her kindness in giving me access to the facilities and staff of the *Institut de Science Economique Appliquée* in Dakar when she was acting director, but for her deep personal interest, encouragement and good humour throughout my research. Indeed without her hospitality, sociability and friendship, my stay in Dakar would have been very much less enjoyable.

My thanks are also owed to the countless Frenchmen in Dakar who overcame their initial suspicions of '*le sociologue anglais*' and gave freely of their time in order to share their ideas, experiences and problems with me both in connection with the survey and in informal conversation. The staffs of a number of institutions in Dakar made my organizational tasks much easier: the French *Mission d'Aide et de Coopération*, the Senegalese *Service de l'Assistance Technique*, as well as the French Consulate. In particular I wish to thank the Secretary-General of the Chamber of Commerce in Dakar, and the Administrative Secretaries of the two large employers' associations, SCIMPEX (commerce) and UNISYNDI (industry).

Professor John Hargreaves gave scrupulous attention to the chapters on early history, and made very useful suggestions concerning historical interpretation therein contained. An especial debt of gratitude is owed to the two professors who supervised my doctoral thesis, Ron Dore and Daryll Forde, whose critical suggestions on content and presentation, and meticulous attention to the manuscript were unusually thorough and invaluable. None of these people, of course, is to be blamed for any errors of fact or interpretation, all of which are my own responsibility. Elaine Barwell and Andrea Walker at the Institute of Development Studies, University of Sussex, did an excellent job of retyping the manuscript for publication.

My research experience in Senegal was deeply enriched by being able to share it with my husband, Donal. It was his encouragement and understanding through my first worries about conducting a survey in French and his astute suggestions through to the last page of the manuscript which made it all seem feasible and worthwhile.

Institute of Development Studies, R.C.O'B.
University of Sussex July 1971

Contents

	page
Acknowledgements	9
Illustrations and Tables	13
Introduction	15
1. The Origins of French Presence in Senegal	29
2. Colonial Society, 1900–1945	48
3. The *Petit Blanc*, Changing Economic and Social Structure, 1945–1960	66
Appendix to Chapter Three: Letter from an 'Old Colonial'	88
4. Race Relations, Politics and Decolonization, 1945–1960	92
5. Changing Patterns in Commerce and Industry	110
6. Expatriate Employment and Africanization	133
7. Technical Assistance	163
8. Expatriate Politics and Political Influence	190
9. Expatriate Social Structure and Social Life	214
10. Race Relations	239
Appendix 1: French Population of Dakar, and of Senegal, 1909–1970	275
Appendix 2: Sample of Frenchmen in the Technical Assistance and Private Sector	277
Appendix 3: Questionnaire and Frequency Distribution	281
Bibliography	304
Index	314

Illustrations

MAPS

1. Senegal   *frontispiece*
2. European Residential Areas, Dakar, 1955   *page* 94
3. European Residential Areas, Dakar, 1967   216

CARTOONS

1. Cartoons from *Les Echos d'Afrique Noire*, April 1952   70–1
2. Anti-Lebanese weekly strip cartoon from *Les Echos d'Afrique Noire*, 1954   75
3. Anti-Lebanese cartoons from *Les Echos d'Afrique Noire*, April 1952 and April 1954   77

TABLES

1. Education, Non-African Population, 1955   90
2. Categories of Employment, 1955   91
3. French Attitudes Towards the Lebanese, 1967   131
4. The Senegalese and Economic Development, 1967   132
5. Distribution of Senegal's Labour Force, 1964 and 1965   157
6. Distribution of the Labour Force, 1962   158
7. Distribution of the Labour Force, 1964   159–61
8. French Attitudes to Africanization, 1967   162
9. Technical Assistance Personnel, 1963–1971   188
10. Planning Commissions of the First Economic Plan   213
11. Planning Commissions of the Second Economic Plan   213

Introduction

'Why have you come to Africa to study whites?' I was asked by a Senegalese shortly after my arrival in Dakar. The answer may seem self-evident even to the casual visitor observing the working day in the capital city and the seeming omnipresence of the French. In the local cinema newsreel, *Actualités Sénégalaises*, one watches the summary of a week's events only to wonder what African independence really means: the Minister of Finance (a Frenchman with Senegalese nationality) signs an accord with United Nations representatives; at a school track meet, French teachers control the start and finish; at a drawing of the National Lottery, the French director calls on a French child to select the winning numbers. At the national independence day celebrations a French army officer can be seen directing and placing the schoolchildren, scouts and other groups in preparation for the parade. The mere conspicuousness of French presence is not, however, an answer to this query: it only provides the setting.

Post-colonial French policy in its first phase was not at all concerned with the economic independence of its former African colonies. Awarded the political attributes of nationhood, these countries were bound structurally, politically and financially to the metropolitan system. Self-sufficiency was an irrelevant consideration. The maintenance of substantial French personnel in Senegal today is the calculated cost to the French taxpayer of ensuring the security of French aid and capital investment and/or of providing the necessary stability for Senegalese economic development within the franc zone and the French Community. For most of France's former dependencies in Africa, close co-operation with the metropole was the logical political successor to dependent status. This allowed for at least formal political autonomy, which in the

Introduction

case of Senegal was rendered questionable in practice by the extent of its continued economic and financial commitment to France.

It is obvious that in the decade since political decolonization in many African countries, the role of the European has remained crucial. Expatriates have served in a wide variety of contexts, even in countries noted for their anti-colonial ideologies, and yet their activities and attitudes as a group and their influence in these early stages of political independence have been little examined. The first independent government of Senegal, under the leadership of Leopold Sèdar Senghor, has held to the conviction that the immediate future of the country is best served not only by retaining close ties with France, but by relying heavily on French personnel. Not least important of these is perhaps the 2,200 French troops stationed just outside Dakar whose presence has a clear political significance.

The basis of Franco-Senegalese relations has been referred to by President Senghor as a dialogue, although the real situation does not in fact reveal the reciprocity implied by the term, either in institutional or behavioural terms. The dominant aid programme is French, and French companies process the groundnuts which account for some three-quarters of Senegal's exports. Frenchmen are close political advisers of the President, represent Senegal abroad and even provide the background advice to Senegalese teams negotiating with the French government. More crucial than their obvious presence in high places, however, is the apparent depth of Senegalese dependence on Frenchmen individually and collectively. Steeped in the French tradition, the ruling élite in Senegal seems to retain the conviction that Senegalese development may be defined as the improvement of local performance within basically French structures. So long as this is the case, Frenchmen remain the natural leaders of this process.

It was possible for President Senghor to chastise the National Council of the ruling single party (*Union Progressiste Sénégalaise*) in 1967[1] with the words: 'The truth is that we have not yet decolonized either our mentalities or our habits.' One of the

[1] Reprinted in *Dakar-Matin*, 16 May 1967, p. 3.

The Background

themes examined in the following chapters will be that the difficulties inherent in the transformation of a colonial structure to one of assistance or co-operation lies not only in a transformation of institutions (which may be imperfectly achieved), but also in the area of roles and attitudes which have been built both on the side of colonizer and colonized throughout the period of colonial rule and afterwards. Such a general argument is particularly applicable perhaps in a country which has for a long time had such a large resident French minority.

Historically, Senegal was never a colony of European settlement, chiefly because groundnuts were not sufficiently lucrative to support European plantations. Unlike white settlers elsewhere in Africa who became identified with the country as Algerians or Rhodesians, the French of Senegal never loosened their ties with metropolitan France. That they were never owners of the land or rooted from generation to generation to live, bear offspring and die on African soil made them expatriates rather than settlers. Regular leave and plans for eventual retirement to France always helped to sustain their roots with their families and regions of origin. There are no old people among them; they are a working population in which both men and women take advantage of the opportunities for augmenting the family income at inflated rates of pay.

'Why go to Dakar to study Frenchmen? Why not go to Nice or Marseilles?' I was asked in Paris in early 1967. It is this question which the succeeding chapters try to answer, by looking at the interaction of the white minority with an African people against the backdrop of structures and attitudes from a former colonial phase.

THE BACKGROUND

Ten years after independence there were approximately 29,000 Frenchmen in Senegal, the great majority of whom (27,500) were resident in the capital city of Dakar.[1] During the height of the colonial groundnut trade which was directed by companies from Bordeaux and Marseilles, French agents filled the *escales*

[1] Estimates from the French Embassy in Dakar, 1970.

Introduction

of the interior, but since the interior trade was withdrawn from private control in 1961, company employees converged on the capital. The services of the French technical assistants are also largely concentrated on the capital. The origins of French minority presence lie deep in the history of Senegal and its contact with France. A preface to the analysis of the role of the French in contemporary Senegal is to be found therefore in a description of the circumstances in which Dakar became the capital of French presence in sub-Saharan Africa. Local French residence had a considerable influence on the interpretation of colonial policy in Senegal and the relationship between colonizer and colonized in this context. Dakar was from the early twentieth century the administrative capital of the Federation of French West Africa, as well as the centre of maritime trade and light industry for the eight colonies of the Federation. For these reasons, plus that of its thriving groundnut trade and, above all, its exceptionally pleasant coastal climate, it became an obvious centre of European residence. Around its principal administrative and commercial installations spread European shops and services, making Dakar the most European city in West Africa, wherein the French carpenter and barmaid became an integral part of the local environment.

This enclave of provincial France in the tropics existed alongside the most advanced experiment of the French colonial policy of assimilation in Africa. Based on the principles of the universal rights of man, and on a faith in ultimate human improvement, it advocated the assimilation of an educated African élite to French civilization, on the same terms as educated Frenchmen. If one assumption of this policy was that Frenchmen in Africa became the interpreters of civilization to the uncivilized African, most of the local French population of Senegal seemed to provide a contradiction to the intent of the policy-makers in Paris. Despite the rather specific and limited circumstances of assimilation policy in Senegal, the framework of colonial rule was based on a series of clearly formulated roles and structures which basically involved the domination of the African by the European, and which tended to be generalized to group or individual relations between Africans and

Procedure and Methodology

Europeans. Even within the special framework of the Senegalese communes (urban enclaves wherein African residents had the political rights of French citizens), this remained the case for nearly all interaction. The Frenchman expected to direct and the Senegalese to be directed. The extent to which relations among Frenchmen and Senegalese can now be thrust beyond this framework into a collateral relationship between technical assistant and African civil servant or colleagues in the private sector is the crucial test of the somewhat ideal French formulation of *coopération* in the postcolonial context or its Senegalese corollary, *le dialogue*. It is often only with difficulty that the European technical adviser becomes more than just the successor to the colonial officer, or that the European employee of a European-owned firm treats his African colleague as more than just an auxiliary. In contrast with the clarity of roles provided within the colonial framework, the present interaction of European and African is rather more complex. Here lies a major part of the answer to the query: 'Why have you come to Africa to study whites?'

PROCEDURE AND METHODOLOGY[1]

Since little attention to date has been accorded to the analysis of the role of the expatriate in ex-colonial Africa, the present study was purposely designed to be very wide in scope, covering nearly all aspects of French presence, for I felt that it was essential to examine the entire framework within which interesting problems could be located. One such problem is the transformation of a colonial framework to one of genuine assistance, within which the role of the technical assistant and the precise

---

[1] This book is based on a longer presentation of the subject submitted as a Ph.D. thesis in Sociology, University of London, 1969, 'The French of Senegal: The Behaviour and Attitudes of a White Minority in Africa'. I have cut some of the more detailed historical and statistical material, as well as numerous detailed annotations and illustrations. I refer specialists interested in the subject to this text, and have indicated specific references in some instances below. A much more detailed presentation of the methodology and procedure of data collection and sampling for example is to be found on pp. 8–22 of the thesis.

Introduction

definition of assistance in both administrative and technical terms are crucial. A second is to be found in the field of labour relations and manpower training within the framework of a predominantly foreign-owned and directed private sector. Each of these themes could be assessed in much greater depth in Senegal itself, or expanded to a comparative analysis of several different countries with differing economic and political backgrounds. The present study in my estimation only begins to answer some of the questions which it is possible to raise in this context.

I first became interested in Senegal during a brief stay in Dakar in 1963 from which my lasting impression remained of the obviousness of continued French presence in this then recently independent country. An article by the French sociologist, Paul Mercier, entitled '*Le Groupement Européen de Dakar*',[1] came subsequently to my attention. The author, who spent many years in Senegal himself, had raised some interesting questions concerning the stability, life style, status and racial attitudes of Dakar Europeans in a study conducted some time before independence (in 1952–53). The coming of independence to Senegal naturally required the disbanding of the colonial administration and the administration of the Federation of French West Africa, as well as a certain amount of restructuring of the local economy and a reorientation of markets. The resulting alteration in the size and structure of the local French group caused a substantial change in their life style, although it remained heavily influenced by patterns of behaviour and structures established during the nineteen-fifties and before. It is for this reason that a prelude to understanding the present French minority lies in an analysis of their historical role in Senegal, and, in particular, the changes which took place in the Fifties.

The fieldwork for this study was carried out from September 1966 to June 1967 in Dakar and five provincial towns in Senegal. It concentrated on interviews with 250 French residents working both in the official technical assistance programme and in the private sector which were based on a standard questionnaire (to be found in Appendix 3). Those interviewed were selected

[1] *Cahiers Internationaux de Sociologie*, Vol. 19, 1955.

Procedure and Methodology

from a stratified quota sample of the working population including the following broad categories:

Technical Assistants—60 interviews[1]
  30 teachers
   4 technical advisers of senior grade
  21 regular technical assistants in administrative posts
   5 university personnel

Private Sector—175 interviews in six sectors of the economy
  19 directors
  47 executives and professionals
  55 foremen, supervisors, technicians
  48 clerks, secretaries, accountants
   6 skilled labourers

Non-French expatriates were specifically excluded since the focus of the study lies in any case not just in a portrait of the present European minority, but on a consideration of the dominant part played by the French in the country both historically and currently.

My first contacts were made among certain noted personalities in the French community, whose own recollections and family histories provided the background to documentary information collected from historical sources. All the subsequent interviews conducted as part of the survey itself were carried out personally (by myself and three interviewers) and responses were recorded directly on the questionnaire. This was invaluable not only for obtaining a commitment for certain delicate areas of questioning, but also in order to become acquainted with the milieu in which I was working, and to try to locate aggregate groups of attitudes. It was also useful for insights into differing individual nuances lying behind the expression of ostensibly similar opinions, and for obtaining information beyond the fixed schedule of questions.

In the absence of a sample frame for the global French population or the possibility of establishing one (owing to the lack of reliable statistics and the limits of time and finance), a set of quotas were first established for the French employed

[1] For a more detailed breakdown of the sample, see Appendix 2.

Introduction

in the private sector. These were defined by three characteristics: type of firm (industrial, commercial, etc.), occupational grade, and sex; the number in each quota being such as to make the sample representative of the total number of wage and salary earners in at least these three respects. The assignment schemes were fixed according to these three inter-related controls, and the numbers in each sub-group designated for interviewers. Age was a variable which it was found impossible to control, but interviewers were instructed, when filling in their quotas, to try to secure a wide spread over different age groups.

Since the number of Frenchmen serving in non-governmental technical assistance programmes is probably in all only about 100, and since they are spread over a wide variety of organizations, it was felt best for the purposes of interviewing to concentrate only on those in the official French programme. Personal statistics and records were available for this group from the *Mission d'Aide et de Coopération* in Dakar, and introductions through their offices facilitated initial contacts. With information provided by them, I constructed a second set of quotas defined by the characteristics: ministry or department in which employed, and grade, differentiating between ordinary technical assistants and technical advisers (*conseillers techniques*). By far the largest group of technical assistants, about two-thirds of all French personnel employed in the public sector, are to be found in teaching posts. With detailed lists of personnel in various educational institutions, obtained from the Ministries of Education and Technical Training, the quota of expatriate personnel in this sector was further broken down according to type of school (technical, lycée, etc.) and its geographical location (Dakar or provincial town).

The limitations of time and resources allowed for no more than a very brief test period of the questionnaire, through which only the most obvious weaknesses of questionnaire layout, and clarity or adequacy in the formulation of questions were eliminated (see Appendix IV, R. Cruise O'Brien, D.Phil., *op. cit.*). Interviews were conducted with the assistance of three part-time interviewers who were French students in social psychology at the University of Dakar. Interviews lasted between thirty and ninety minutes, and were entirely private;

the questions were posed orally and the answers recorded directly on the questionnaire. Only part of the interview schedule was precoded, which included mainly biographical and other factual questions. Most of the attitude questions allowed for open responses, which were invaluable as illustrations of analytical material presented in the text. (For an indication of the distinction, see first page of Appendix 3.)

The difficulty of securing access to subjects for interview during working hours gave the only method of selection which seemed feasible a significant, if unavoidable, bias. Approach in the private sector had to be made through company directors and business or shop-owners, who were usually themselves interviewed (to relieve suspicions about the nature of the questionnaire), and then asked if they could provide an introduction to a few of their employees for interview (of which their grade or type of work and sex were stipulated by the interviewer). Most directors were very helpful and often called selected employees immediately and provided a private place for the interview. Since the director had the opportunity to choose the employees, however, this provided an obvious bias towards the most well-balanced or reasonable respondents. This method of approach, on the other hand, gave the interview a kind of legitimacy which made respondents less suspicious and more open than they might otherwise have been.

Contact with French teachers was made through their schools, their names having been selected at random from Ministry lists. Interviews were conducted in a free hour or at home at a later time. Contact with technical assistants was usually made through the technical adviser or senior technical assistant in each ministry or department. This person was asked to provide an introduction to a specified number of French colleagues, usually only one or two in each ministry. As with the company directors, there was a natural tendency to suggest the most responsive subjects or those with the longest experience in Senegal who 'would know far more than those recently arrived'. Standard insistence was made by the interviewer against this latter bias, though it was not entirely overcome. Because of the method of introduction to subjects, almost no one refused to be interviewed: the French seemed

Introduction

either anxious to show that 'they had nothing to hide', or were mildly amused and flattered that they had been chosen for interview. Those few outright refusals which were met or cases of reticence on certain subjects touched on in the interview (notably on race relations) were found among the owners of small businesses and their employees, who of course remain in a marginal economic position.

A small group of fifteen housewives was also contacted through door to door requests in the predominantly white residential areas of Dakar. The group reflected neither its appropriate proportion in the global population nor did its selection make it representative. Its inclusion was only an attempt to have some information on attitudes formed entirely outside a working environment. Although the French population resident beyond the capital city of Dakar is quite small, interviews were conducted with technical assistants and company employees in the provincial centres of St. Louis, Zinguinchor, Kaolack, Thiès and Diourbel. Rather than an attempt to increase the representativeness of the sample, the purpose of these contacts was to become acquainted with the general activities, working relations and pre-occupations of Frenchmen in this provincial milieu.

In retrospect, I think it might have been better, and have yielded more information about the determinants of attitudes, if I had—at the expense of making the sample less representative of the total working population—over-weighted certain categories, of which there were only small numbers in the total population, in order to be able to make statistically significant comparisons between important sub-groups. At the time, however, I did not have enough information to establish clear hypotheses as to *which* characteristics of *which* sub-groups would prove to be crucial determinants of attitudes, and in the circumstances a sample which aimed at a rough representativeness of the total working population seemed to be the best available. The questionnaire survey did then provide for a systematic collection of data on this population, as well as a useful basis for a comparison of attitudes.

A BRIEF SENEGALESE SURVEY

While the main focus of the study was on the French and their views, it would have been unnecessarily one-sided without some attempt to describe Senegalese attitudes on the same matters. This therefore was the purpose of conducting interviews with twenty-five Senegalese, who were chosen on a non-random basis among middle-level employees and civil servants living in a Dakar housing estate. The civil servants included a statistician, a community development (*animation rurale*) officer, an archival clerk, a librarian, a primary school teacher, a typist, a municipal clerk, a court clerk, two policemen and two post office employees. The employees in the private sector were slightly more difficult to grade, although they were predominantly salaried office employees. They included accounting and administrative clerks, typists, a transport agent, an electrician, a chemist, and a junior executive. They worked exclusively for French companies, including shipping lines, airlines, oil and sugar refineries, trading houses, department stores and banks. Interviews were conducted in French because the types of informants sought were of a certain minimum grade of employment which demanded that they were literate and fairly fluent in French (all in fact had at least primary school certificates). The age range of those interviewed was from twenty to forty-nine, although all but two were under thirty-five. The results of these interviews and the attitudes therein contained are integrated into the various chapters where relevant. A complete exposition of the results is to be found in Chapter Eleven of the original thesis and the questionnaire in Appendix VI of the same.

By way of introduction to the general themes of the survey, informants were asked to consider whether or not the general participation of Frenchmen in the public or private sector was in the interests of their country. Half responded affirmatively ('they teach us progress, the way to work, and train our leaders'); while the other half had mixed feelings, depending on the varied competence of individual Frenchmen, and whether or not their posts could be Africanized. Certain

Introduction

respondents felt that although French presence provided obvious benefits for the country, most individual Frenchmen came to Senegal only for the purpose of making money. A government statistician was more politically inclined in his opposition:

> The ex-colonies serve as outlets for employment. The French are here because of the economic interests of France and in order to protect them. This implies considerable influence as well. French aid is not disinterested—France gives away nothing free.

Although the actual number of French expatriates currently in Senegal is less than 30,000, half of the Senegalese respondents estimated the size of the minority to be over 50,000, and half over 100,000. The discrepancy may be explained either by a general difficulty of estimation or by the fact that in Dakar, where the interviews took place, the French seem more numerous or more obvious than they really are. Those who considered French presence to be generally favourable mentioned the technical and financial assistance provided by the co-operation programme, and the provision of jobs by French companies as the chief examples of this. Those who were generally critical of French presence (ten informants) felt that there were perhaps too many Frenchmen or that their presence was not very discreet, which rendered their efforts at assisting the Senegalese less effective ('neo-colonialism is too apparent').

THE PRESENT AND THE FUTURE

Those Frenchmen interviewed in 1966–67 seemed to view their immediate future in Senegal with guarded optimism. They were confident in the leadership of President Senghor and his government, but wary of 'that younger generation which is much less attached to France than the older one, those who fought with us in the war and were much more devoted to French culture'. Most of them hoped to remain in Senegal as long as possible, although they were much less certain about the long-term future of Europeans in Senegal, as elsewhere in Africa.

The Present and the Future

Since the completion of the study, several factors must have been hardly reassuring to them. In May 1968 and again in March and April 1969, there were a series of strikes and demonstrations in Dakar which involved students and trade unionists and disrupted life in the capital city for some time. Each of these had decidedly anti-French manifestations as a part of more general grievances. In France itself, the demise of General de Gaulle might have been expected to bring about a change in aid policy towards France's former African dependencies. Without the nationalist sentiment which fostered support for a greater France overseas, the financial calculations of the 'bankers in Paris' of the cost and returns of aid to Senegal in contrast with certain richer and more lucrative franc zone countries might have caused a cutback in spending. This has not yet happened, but as Senegal remains one of the less attractive areas for additional investment, subsidies through the aid programme may no longer be so favourable. Any one of these things may alter France's relationship with Senegal and influence the future of the French resident minority. It would appear that the realism expressed by those Frenchmen interviewed in the study would, therefore, still be valid after a consideration of intervening events: most concluded that the *beaux jours* of the colonies had passed and that one remained to enjoy the few good years which were left and to profit from inflated expatriate salaries which would eventually provide for a better life in France.

1. The Origins of French Presence in Senegal

EARLY TRADING POSTS

The early history of French presence in Senegal can be organized around four inter-related themes: the development of mercantile trade, the construction of trading posts and towns, the structure of company rule and colonial society, and the relationship between trader-colonizer and African. French interests in the area were first established at three trading posts along the coast—Gorée, St. Louis and Rufisque. Except for a few explorers who penetrated the interior, the history of early French presence is confined to these coastal strongholds. The local term for these Europeans, which remains even now very much part of daily parlance in Senegal, was *toubab*.[1]

From the mid-fifteenth century onwards, trading and pirate ships of European maritime nations visited the coast of Senegal. Gorée, a small island just off the Cape Verde peninsula, was mentioned in the logs of Portuguese ships in the fifteenth century. Rufisque, several miles east on the mainland, was observed in 1635 to be 'a meeting place for men of all nations and all religions—Capuchins, Catholics, Calvinists, Lutherans, Puritans, Armenians, Jews and Turks'.[2] The potential river trade along the Senegal and the site at St. Louis were not developed until the second half of the seventeenth century. Before this time there was no serious French company interest in the area. Until the award of royal charters, trade in these ports was open to the ships of all nations, so long as tribute was paid to the company controlling the fort.[3]

Although one of the first West African centres visited by

[1] For a discussion of the origin of this term, see R. Mauny, *Glossaire des Expressions et Termes Employés dans l'Ouest Africain*, Dakar, Institut Français d'Afrique Noire, 1952, p. 66.
[2] Alexis de Saint-Lô, *Relation du Voyage du Cap Vert*, Rouen, 1637.
[3] Gorée changed hands many times in two centuries, among the Dutch, British and French.

Europeans, Gorée did not survive the abolition of the slave trade. Its geographical location and isolation from the mainland, while favouring its early development as a slave *entrepôt*, eventually made it unsuitable for the gum-arabic, and later the groundnut trade in the eighteenth and nineteenth centuries, which required direct mainland outlets for export.

St. Louis was founded in 1659 by an employee of the *Compagnie du Sénégal* who was sent to explore the commercial possibilities of the Senegal River. From 1664 to 1763, the fort at St. Louis, when held in the name of the French king, was governed by a chartered company. Granted a monopoly in the gum trade, the company installed at the fort began to penetrate the river, protected by its own gunboats and troops. As they were responsible for the administration and justice in the fort and for maintaining it against outside invasion, the companies provided the first form of European local government in the area.

The European personnel of the trading posts was recruited from among some of the most marginal elements of society in the French coastal towns of Dieppe, Bordeaux and Marseilles. Their 'moral and intellectual weakness' contributed to the failure of French enterprise in Senegal in the eighteenth century, according to André Delcourt in his painstaking study of company rule from 1713–64.[1] Blamed by company officials for their 'prevarication, malversation, incapability, clannishness, indiscipline and bad faith,' it is obvious that they were little constrained by the company regulations against 'cursing, or blaspheming the holy name of God, debauchery, drinking, quarrelling and fighting with arms'.[2] Insufficient supplies, disease, and death constantly menaced European survival. The motivations which brought men to these miserable outposts were often quite specific—to flee creditors or other personal

[1] *La France et Les Etablissements Français au Sénégal* (1713–1764), Dakar: Institut Français d'Afrique Noire, 1952, p. 181. For the later period, see Leonce Jore, 'Les Etablissements Français sur la Côte Occidentale d'Afrique Noire de 1758–1809', *Revue Française d'Histoire d'Outre-Mer*, Tome LI, 1964, and Françoise Deroure, 'La Vie Quotidienne à St. Louis par ses Archives (1779–1809)', *Bulletin de l'Institut Française d'Afrique Noire*, Tome XXVI, Ser.B, nos. 3–4, 1964.

[2] A. Delcourt, *ibid.*, pp. 95, 131. See also G. Hardy, *Histoire de la Colonisation Française*, Paris, Larose, 1931, p. 61.

and financial troubles at home.¹ The free and pioneering spirit of the adventurer-trader and the heroic superiority of colonial society were romantic inventions of a later generation. In this period, all employment was contracted through the chartered company. The best an employee could do was to hope to make money on illicit trade, for the dubious promise of being promoted by the company as an 'old coaster' upon return to France was little compensation for the perilous living conditions.

The European employees of the company fell into three categories: managerial and administrative personnel, naval and army recruits and labourers both for domestic and general purposes. The earliest trading settlement was a nearly self-sufficient European enclave, with butchers, builders, tailors, gardeners as well as labourers to make the necessary repairs on ships locally.² Employees with skills pertinent to the terrain were very difficult to find. Many of the experienced sailors and river pilots were bribed away from British and Dutch companies in the area. It early became apparent to the company that the way to cut labour costs and to ensure a certain stability of personnel for the trading post was to train the local inhabitants to fill these posts. They became artisans as well as pilots and navigators in the river trade. There were other jobs such as interpreter and river boatman which were designated for the local people.

In the second half of the eighteenth century, those free Africans living in St. Louis and Gorée who were 'sufficiently influenced by French culture' became known as *habitants* or free residents, which gave them certain rights and privileges under French law.³ A large number of them were company employees. And most were *métis*, the sons of white company employees and local women. They occupied an important place in the life of the trading post and later the colony. This early

---

[1] This practice of using service in the colonies as a way of fleeing creditors remained important throughout French colonization.

[2] In a few instances Governors and company directors continued to bring their faithful servants and cooks from France throughout the century. F. Deroure, *op. cit.*, p. 419.

[3] See J. Hargreaves, 'Assimilation in Eighteenth Century Senegal', *The Journal of African History*, Vol. XI, No. 2, 1965, esp. pp. 180–1.

form of *assimilation*[1] became official French policy for the creation of a loyal élite when the colony was established in the nineteenth century. These *habitants* rarely returned to their villages, their new status being inextricably bound to the French settlements along the coast. Because of their presence and particularly their established relations with the peoples of the interior, the success of company investment became dependent upon them. A certain interdependence between European and African in these small settlements was essential. Co-operation was a necessity of life. This often meant collusion in illicit trade, against which the company was constantly on its guard. It was difficult for white attitudes to be drawn on strictly racial lines, because, for the Europeans, the Africans did not constitute an undifferentiated racial group. They included slaves, villagers supplying the fort, soldiers, servants, wives, confidants, employees, and trade associates.

A group of European employees (clerks, labourers and sailors) had their own ways of coming to terms with the environment. By participating in curious magical ceremonies demonstrating their affinity for the local people, they became *fils de terre*. 'They felt themselves closer to the peoples who welcomed them than to their compatriots',[2] according to a company administrator, and were much used by the company because of their valuable local contacts. They also may have used this intimacy to establish private trading agreements. The tenuousness of European survival and the desire to make money by whatever means dictated the forms of contact between European and African. Before the imperial conquest of Africa and the institutionalized distinction of ruler and ruled, the French trading agent was not therefore resigning a responsibility by 'going native', as he would have been later accused.[3]

The trading season cut the life of a town like St. Louis in two: from January to June after the trade was over the town was

[1] For a discussion of assimilation, see below p. 45.
[2] Cited in A. Delcourt, *op cit.*, p. 48.
[3] In a reflection of many earlier official French sources, the most complete statement is to be found in R. Maunier, *The Sociology of Colonies: An Introduction to the Study of Racial Contacts*, edited and translated by E. O. Lorimer, London, Routledge and Kegan Paul, 1949, esp. Vol. I, pp. 111–12, Vol. II, p. 537.

Early Trading Posts

full and money plentiful. The distractions and leisure activities of the European agents and soldiers included musical and dancing exhibitions by the local people, to which were eventually added a number of cafés and restaurants where men met to drink together, discuss and play cards. Hunts along the river were also organized for the more affluent who kept horses for pleasure. While the celebration of French victories and other national holidays was a favourite local distraction, the isolation from news of Europe must have made events seem hardly perceptible in this environment.[1]

In order to combat desertion from these outposts, the company recommended marriage with local women. The absence of European women in the trading post and colony until well into the twentieth century had an important effect on inter-racial relations. The African mistresses and wives (*signares*) of Europeans resident in the trading post had a certain social status as consorts. The eighteenth-century social élite, insofar as it existed at all, revolved around these influential, often wealthy women. A soldier or company employee sometimes set his *signare* up in business to augment his own salary, and if he left the post definitively, his business and property were left to her and her children. *Métissage* became for the makers of colonial policy of a later era a calculated effort to ensure a loyal local élite with French blood flowing in its veins, and yet a natural immunization against diseases fatal to Frenchmen.

Certain *métis* held municipal office in St. Louis and Gorée, at first by appointment of the chartered company. In 1789, a group of *habitants* led by *métis* office holders sent a *cahier* to the Estates-General in Paris demanding an end to company monopoly. While it might have been defended by the slogans of the French revolution, this act is less important as a revolutionary measure in French colonial history than as a testimony of the importance and potential power of *habitants* in the economic life of the trading post.

The substance of the *habitant cahier* of 1789 was in fact identical to the demands being made by a group of Bordeaux businessmen. From 1783 a battle was being waged in the

[1] F. Deroure, *op. cit.*, pp. 422–5.

The Origins of French Presence in Senegal

Bordeaux Chamber of Commerce against the monopolistic practices of the charter company for Senegal by a group of young speculators. Hoping to break the mercantile system of the monopoly companies, the group also advocated the abolition of the slave trade, one of the main links in the system.[1] In an attempt to win a place in the profitable gum trade these shipowners (*armateurs*) were joined by the *habitants* of St. Louis. The alignment of their interests was successful, for the demands were met: certain company charters were withdrawn and slave trading was formally abolished in St. Louis. Although company rule had officially ended in 1763 with the appointment of a royal governor at Gorée, it was not therefore until the end of the century that the power of the chartered company was broken and trade was open to all.

Gorée and St. Louis were again occupied by the British in 1800 (who had held both from 1756–63 and St. Louis until 1779). French official interest in African outposts at the time was very limited. Above all, 'wartime rivalry with England was still high, and the French administration was not willing to risk a new antagonism for the price of a West African territory'.[2] The coastal settlements were returned to France after the Treaty of Paris in 1815, which marked the beginning of serious French interest in the area.

FRENCH COLONIAL EXPERIMENTATION

In the period between 1817 and 1830, the failure of agricultural experimentation in Senegal proved decisive for the entire future direction of the colony and its resident white population. After several unsuccessful attempts to initiate plantation cultivation with the hope of encouraging a European settler

[1] See Delcourt, 'La Chambre de Commerce de Bordeaux et la Traite Africaine dans les Dernières Années de l'Ancien Régime' (1783–91). In *Commission de Recherche et de Publication des Documents Relatifs à la Vie Economique de la Revolution*, Assemblée Générale de la Commission Centrale et des Comités Départmentaux, Paris: Tepac, 1939, Tome II, pp. 427–9. As with most of the anti-slavery movements in Britain and France, humanitarian overtones often disguised claims of rival trading groups.

[2] Phillip Curtin, *The Image of Africa, British Ideas and Action, 1780–1850*, Madison: University of Wisconsin Press, 1964, p. 146.

group,[1] the colony was eventually returned to its original commercial base. The Ministry of the Navy, which maintained the forts and was in charge of colonial administration until the close of the century, was at this time eager to reserve its meagre funds for the protection of trading interests. Private enterprise was initially encouraged to take up the challenge of agricultural exploitation. Two ill-fated expeditions in 1816 and 1817 by French colonial investment societies tried to establish a European settlement on the Cape Verde peninsula. Within a year after their arrival almost all the disillusioned men and women who had been recruited by the promises of plantations in lush tropical lands had returned to France with vivid memories of the scorched earth of Senegal.[2]

Except for the narrow strip of land on either side of the Senegal River, the land to the south in the central part of Senegal is savannah and unsuitable for growing anything except groundnuts and millet, which were already cultivated by the local people, and uneconomical for a European plantation system. Not until 1859, however, during the early settlement of Algeria, was the definitive instruction against European settlement laid down by the Ministry:

> Nothing similar to Algeria could be undertaken in Senegal. The climate is against it. The land should therefore be left to the Africans... at least as a general rule. The land cultivated by them will provide produce which will become the object of lucrative trade for the European, the only kind of work he can undertake in this climate.[3]

During the eighteen-twenties and eighteen-thirties, the traders of St. Louis were encouraged to continue their travels along the river, for the administration hoped to extend existing rule beyond the stronghold at its mouth. News of the lucrative gum trade reached France and many young men set out to

[1] See Georges Hardy, *Mise en Valeur du Sénégal, 1816–1854*, Paris, Larose, 1921, pp. 36–100.
[2] For an account of these efforts, see Claude Faure, *Histoire de la Presqu'île du Cap Vert et des Origines de Dakar*, Paris, Larose, 1914, pp. 17–23 and 35–6.
[3] André Villard, *Histoire du Sénégal*, Dakar, Imprimerie Viale, 1943, p. 131.

seek their fortune. Among these were Hilaire Maurel, Philippe Lafarge, Louis-Hubert Prom and Jean Anselme Delmas, the founders of Bordeaux trading companies which were to dominate the subsequent history of commerce in Senegal. Many of these men came from the south and southwest of France where they were small peasant freeholders.[1] Sometimes they set out with a few goods of their own, but usually they began as employees in already established companies. Once they had established a base, they set themselves up at St. Louis or Gorée and brought out younger members of their families to join them. By the eighteen-sixties they had become the 'notables of the colony' and the advisers of the administration.

Trade in the Twenties and Thirties remained on an uncertain base. Administrative attempts to regulate it continually provoked the animosity of the local traders. The origins of the difficulty were first, the lack of sufficient military strength to protect French traders and second, the number of new traders arriving in Senegal each year. The extent of the trade had outpaced the construction of forts, and its limited volume was divided and subdivided among many, resulting in its complete breakdown.

An investigating commission was designated by the Ministry of the Navy in 1850 to look into the problems in Senegal, for it was generally feared that the colony would return to its unimpressive origins as a minor trading post. The commission gave the first official recognition to the groundnut which it observed 'grew almost naturally'.[2] It was this new trade which ultimately transformed Senegal into an active commercial centre. Yet, according to the traders, this could not proceed until the safety of their agents travelling through the interior could be ensured or until an effective colonial administration was established.

---

[1] The Delmas family, for example, whose name means 'free peasant, owner of the land' came from Provençe. For a history of the family, see Robert Delmas-Guichenne, *Notes et Documents Recueillis pour Servir a l'Histoire du Sénégal Jusqu'à l'Indépendance*, Dakar, Private printing, 1964. Vol. II, pp. 270–1.
[2] G. Hardy, *Mise en Valeur* . . ., *op. cit.*, p. 337.

ESTABLISHMENT OF THE COLONY

Senegal, or at least the coastal trading posts, became an official French colony in 1848. The conquest of the interior and the establishment of a regular administration throughout the country did not begin until 1854 under General Faidherbe, and continued until much later. In keeping with the spirit of the Second Empire, the soldier preceded the trader into lands hitherto unvisited by Frenchmen. The appointment of Faidherbe was suggested by a group of local traders led by Hilaire Maurel, who emphasized 'the necessity of naming a Governor who would remain at the head of the colony for sufficient time to establish a programme of colonization and effective occupation'.[1] Through Maurel's friend, the Minister of the Navy, Napoleon III was requested to raise Faidherbe's rank so that he could be named Governor. In no other single instance in the history of Senegal is the influence of trading interests on colonial administration so apparent.

As important as the creation of a regular administration for the colony was the spread of knowledge of Senegal throughout France under Governor Faidherbe's personal direction. General information about Senegal and its commercial possibilities appeared in official metropolitan bulletins and the local *Le Moniteur du Sénégal* provided practical suggestions. As a result of such activities, trade in Senegal trebled by the end of his governorship.[2] After its grave crisis at mid-century, commerce had recovered vigorously. And Hilaire Maurel and the other French traders had been rewarded for their efforts.

The resurgence of commerce under Faidherbe was naturally reflected at St. Louis which he made an effective colonial capital. Gorée at the same time was becoming too confining for its active trading group. They hoped to interest the administration in the occupation of the adjacent mainland. Problems with the middlemen at the Dakar market prompted

---

[1] E. Baillet, 'Les Etablissements Maurel et Prom', dated 30 September 1923, typescript, pp. 6–7, obtained from the present company director of Maurel et Prom in Dakar, 1967.
[2] G. Hardy, *Histoire* . . ., *op. cit.*, p. 194.

indignant letters to the Commander of Gorée from several traders in 1854, in which they entreated him to turn his attention to 'this curious violation of the liberty of commerce in a land belonging to France'.[1]

Dakar was eventually occupied in 1857, apparently not at the behest of the traders but because of a shift in colonial policy. Its eventual growth as a major export centre was based in part on its excellent deep-water port, and in part on the conscious efforts of a group in the colonial administration. Despite its official favour, Dakar had very sparse early activity, while neighbouring Rufisque, long established as a terminus of caravan routes from the interior, was thriving on the new groundnut trade with nearby regions.[2] Faidherbe and the colonial élite at St. Louis resisted the creation of a rival centre at Dakar, but the traditional colonial capital inevitably lost its commercial importance. Trade was eventually shifted from the Senegal River basin to the groundnut growing areas of the south, for which Dakar, Rufisque and Kaolack were the natural maritime outlets. The latter two were later insufficiently equipped to carry the trade, and the bulk of processing and transport fell to Dakar.

New companies interested in the groundnut trade were rewarded for their efforts by the successive introduction of representative institutions in Senegal. Beginning in 1840, a form of 'guided local democracy' was initiated in which the Governor named a group of sixty electors who chose a council from among their number. The participants in this local council of notables were administrators, traders, property owners and merchants (European, African and *métis*).[3] In 1848, the new republican government in France introduced universal manhood suffrage in St. Louis and Gorée both for local councils and for the election of the colony's first deputy to the National Assembly. This coincided with the abolition of domestic slavery in the colony, which therefore created an

[1] Jacques Charpy, *La Fondation de Dakar (1845-1857-1869)*, Paris, Larose, 1958, p. 78.
[2] See R. Pasquier, 'Villes du Sénégal au XIXeme Siècle', *Revue Française de l'Histoire d'Outre Mer*, XLVII (1960), p. 106.
[3] *Arrêté*, No. 141, 16 November 1840, Archives du Sénégal, Dakar, 20/G/1.

unsophisticated and illiterate electorate. From this time, political battles in the colony seemed to follow a predictable pattern. Europeans and Africans voted in the single-college-system, since Senegal was intended to be the model of racially integrated political development—wherein all Africans living in St. Louis and Gorée could exercise their political rights on the same basis as local traders, and indeed as Frenchmen in metropolitan departments. All Africans by virtue of their birth or residence in the colony were eligible to vote. The result of this was that local notables—European and *métis* traders—formed a series of competing political clans, each vying for the majority of African votes in the coastal towns.

The electorate was not difficult to control because many of them were employees, and thus in a direct client relationship with their companies, while the other local inhabitants seem to have been organized by local bosses who received gifts and patronage in return for votes. Occasionally the administration also joined the competing clans, attempting to secure the political allegiance of a candidate or to ensure the election of a faithful servant.[1]

1848 was only a brief interlude, however, for the local franchise was withdrawn under the Second Empire, a regime which looked with little favour on democratic institutions. Colonial administrators were usually hostile to local representative bodies which they regarded as centres of potential opposition to colonial policy. After the conquest of the groundnut region, the trading community was much less enthusiastic to support the acquisition of land for the 'glory of France', or her military rulers. It meant increased taxes and would certainly have been opposed, had the traders had the power to do so.

In 1871, the right to elect a deputy for Senegal was restored and although the next election did not occur until 1879, the companies competed with renewed vigour in each election to secure the victory of a loyal candidate. The larger Bordeaux houses were particularly keen on having a spokesman in Paris

[1] When the administration supported a particular candidate it investigated scrupulously the electoral practices of his opponents. For the election of 1889, see Archives du Sénégal, Dakar, 20/G/6. For a later election, see Pierre Mille, 'The Black Vote in Senegal', *Journal of the Africa Society*, Vol. I (1901), p. 76.

The Origins of French Presence in Senegal

where colonial policy was made. Running an election became more and more costly, so that this battle was left to the most well-established houses while the newer independent traders tried to influence the local councils. Politics in Senegal in the colonial period remained exclusively urban, confined to the coastal enclaves of St. Louis, Gorée, Rufisque and Dakar. These four towns were *communes de plein exercice*, a status giving them local self-government, corresponding to the communes in metropolitan France.

A General Council for the colony, elected on the basis of universal suffrage, was introduced in 1879. This was the same governing body as existed in the French *départements*, but it had more financial autonomy in Senegal. The large companies already had a certain influence on colonial policy through the deputy, but participation in local councils was essential to ensure that licences, franchises and the expenditure of the local budget were also in their favour. Many of the clients who initially served the companies on these councils were *métis*, who themselves became company owners and notables and drew political organizations around their own interests. Influence and intrigue spread to municipal councils, where contracts and local expenditure were settled. The political cliques surrounding the deputy maintained their organization down as far as these local councils.

FROM TRADING POST TO COMMERCIAL CENTRE

The Chamber of Commerce, with its branches in the major trading towns,[1] provided a forum for the discussion of commercial conditions in the country. Its potential as a lobby to challenge the administration was successfully curbed by its built-in 'official responsibility'. More than half of the budget was supplied by the administration, and its composition dictated from official sources. Membership of all those licensed to sell or trade was compulsory. Opinions and advice were

[1] First founded in St. Louis and Gorée in 1869, they were later established in Rufisque, Dakar, Kaolack and Ziguinchor.

exchanged with the administration on such matters as the regulation of transport, arrangements for brokerage and the creation of commercial tribunals for adjusting disputes.[1] The Chamber was thus a service to the colonial government, a channel through which information was passed from the public to the private sector.

Trade had been considerably regularized by the final pacification of the interior of Senegal in the last two decades of the nineteenth century. The commerce of *traite* or barter was declining in favour of cash exchange in guinea pieces, although the term *traite*, to describe the marketing of groundnuts or gum, remained permanently in the colonial vocabulary.[2]

A series of newspapers appeared in St. Louis from 1885, which were used by independent trading interests to 'muck-rake' against the collusion of the administration and the large trading houses. Without satisfactory representation in the political spheres, these outsiders used the press to publicize their grievances. Certain newspapers were solely anti-administration, which explains the brevity of their existence.[3] Others accused the administration of allowing 'abusive monopolies' to run the groundnut trade, by awarding exclusive franchise on trading rights in a given area.

The companies which were comfortably installed at St. Louis in turn tried to use their influence to restrict the influx of traders who were encroaching on the profitable trade. These companies were run by the same families who had fought for their place in the gum trade in the Twenties and Thirties, but who had now become the commercial élite of the colony. Too many things thus divided the trading community for them to act as a unanimous block *vis-à-vis* the administration. There remained a contradiction of interests between large and small

---

[1] Exposition Universelle de 1900, *Le Sénégal, Organisation Politique, Administration, Finance, Travaux Publics*, Paris, 1900, p. 275.

[2] See R. Mauny, *op. cit.*, p. 67.

[3] One of the reasons why a local press did not appear until this time in Senegal was that the newspapers in the port towns of France, notably Bordeaux and Marseilles, were read along the coast of West Africa because they contained much commercial news relating to the colonies. See R. Pasquier, 'Les Debuts de la Presse au Sénégal', *Cahiers d'Etudes Africaines*, No. 7, 1962, p. 481.

companies, as well as between those in different branches of trade or different geographical areas, not to speak of the effects of direct competition. The variance of relationships with African rulers, as well as different views on the expansion of the colony and the establishment of an interior administration throughout the nineteenth century remained potential sources of conflict among traders, depending how each served their individual interests and opportunities for profit.

Lebanese and Syrian immigration, which began in a small but steady stream about 1890, was later to have a profound effect on the trade circuits of the colony. The first Lebanese, a M. Issa, actually arrived in Senegal in 1860, but he was the sole member of this group for many decades. Numbering only ten in 1897, the Lebanese had a near monopoly of petty trade in St. Louis, just after the turn of the century.[1] Even though initially few in number, their presence was already noted by independent French traders, keen on maintaining Senegal as an exclusive reserve.

The increase of trade and the acquisition of lands throughout Senegal in the latter half of the nineteenth century had a considerable impact on the structure of colonial society. There were now many more Frenchmen serving in military and civilian functions throughout the colony. This resulted in a growing antagonism between the administrator and trader, owing to their divergent views of colonial purpose and their differing loyalties and recruitment. Although there remained many conflicting interests among the traders themselves, it was the promotion of good relations between the military and commercial sector which was a subject of much administrative attention. Military officers received requests without enthusiasm to aid traders, 'suspecting that these *petits bourgeois* might be trying to use the French flag to further their base commercial intrigues'.[2] Frenchmen were, however, reminded of the need to set an example of the superiority of European civilization: 'The rivalry between the civil and the military element, odious

---

[1] Anfreville de la Salle, *Notre Vieux Sénégal*, Paris, Challamel, 1909, n.p.
[2] J. D. Hargreaves, *Prelude to the Partition of West Africa*, London, Macmillan, 1963, p. 93.

in France, becomes criminal in the colonies because it compromises the success of our common work.'[1]

A Ministry of Colonies was established in 1894 under civilian administrative authority. This was a reflection of the growing pains of colonial establishment. Naval rule was appropriate when the Empire was a series of scattered coastal enclaves, while the development of an internal administration and viable economic structures demanded a new kind of administration. But although this succeeded in ridding the colonies of a serious metropolitan antagonism, it served only in the local sphere to change the object of hostility of the trader from the military officer to the civilian administrator.

St. Louis had a population of 20,000[2] in 1889, and remained the centre of social life in the colony. The commercial élite stayed in town while their agents and the new independent traders travelled the routes of the interior. The distinction between those who remained along the coast and those who went to the interior was thus a real economic one. In the colonial service this coastal-interior distinction was less clear. It has been suggested that there was a personality distinction concealed in the geographical one, between those officers who wished to create a synthetic France on the coast of Africa, and those who plunged into the interior in order to leave France behind. Thus, there was the bureaucrat 'who brought to the service an anti-feudal passion which he (did) not hesitate to turn against the *commandant de cercle* (local administrator) who thought of his station as a fief where civil servants had no place'.[3] To romanticize the styles of colonial service in this period is to minimize the precariousness of survival and the rigours of life especially in the interior, which made naval officers, for example, reluctant to serve in West Africa:

> Compelled by a tour of service or by the necessities of career, they have, with regret, lived or more precisely

[1] le Dr. Barot, *Guide Pratique de l'Européen dans l'Afrique Occidentale*, Paris, E. Flammarion, 1902, p. 313.
[2] Gen. L. Faidherbe, *Le Sénégal*, Paris, Hachette, 1889, p. 18. He estimated the population of Dakar and Gorée at about 2,000 each at this time and Rufisque at about 7,000.
[3] R. Delavignette writing on nineteenth-century colonial society, in *Service Africain*, Paris, Gallimard, 1946, p. 48.

vegetated and left with joy, happy not when they can conserve their health intact (this is too rare), but with the hope of finding themselves once again under the sky of France.[1]

In literary form, the crudeness and boredom of nineteenth-century colonial life is vividly portrayed in the novel, *Roman d'un Spahi* by Pierre Loti, who lived for a number of years at St. Louis. The novel slowly unfolds the phases of depression and delirium, the enervation and anxiety of a colonial soldier. His story is one of the destruction of a personality under the pressure of the environment,[2] and has little affinity with the later interpretation of the colonial as a hero, whose personality before his subjects was 'so strong that it seemed as if only he possessed one'.[3]

The introduction of a colonial ideology, a widely accepted body of ideas based on a confidence in the superiority of French civilization, and used to justify French presence, followed the reorganization and firm establishment of colonial rule in West Africa. It is particularly explicit in the *Guide Pratique de l'Européen dans l'Afrique Occidentale*,[4] published in 1902, which illustrates both the high moral tone adopted by senior colonial administrators, the originators and guardians of these ideas, and the quality of actual recruitment to the colony.

It begins with a warning of the heavy demands of colonial life, together with vigorous criticism of the 'new type' of Frenchman attracted to the colonies. The idealized colonial hero persists throughout literature of this kind, as the embodiment of the colonial ideal. 'Colonials by vocation', its authors lament, are increasingly rare . . . and that which is embellished with the pompous name of colonial amnesia is nothing but vulgar idleness. We need strong and healthy men in the colonies who work hard.'[5] And although the Ministry advised the

[1] Anne M. Raffenel, 'De la Colonie du Sénégal', Etudes Historiques et Commerciales, *Revue Coloniale*, June 1850, p. 321.

[2] P. Loti, Paris, Calmann-Levy, 1881, especially p. 91.

[3] R. Delavignette, *op. cit.*, p. 56.

[4] le Dr. Barot, *op. cit.*

[5] *Ibid.*, p. 159. A section on moral hygiene advised that 'work is the best safeguard against the quite common tendencies of alcoholism and all its depravities: moral perversion, sexual immorality, cruelty, criminality' (p. 310).

companies to provide agents 'industrious, up to the task and animated with the spirit of French territorial and intellectual expansion', it found those who 'only come for un-elevated motives among which the payment of debts takes first place'.[1]

ASSIMILATION AND ASSOCIATION

The lofty ideals of France's policy of assimilation in Senegal were often less than well represented by the local Frenchmen who became the vehicles of its interpretation. In its earliest form, assimilation was essentially the outgrowth of the revolutionary thinking of 1789 and 1848, which assumed that there was no racial or cultural barrier that French education, and participation in French institutions could not eliminate. This provided for a very few Senegalese in the nineteenth century the personal status of *assimilés* or *evolués*. In addition to this personal status, however, the policy of assimilation also referred to the political and economic integration of France's overseas territories into metropolitan institutions, exemplified particularly in the four communes of Senegal. This attempt to give full implementation to the ideas of assimilation, by making all residents of the communes French citizens, remained a unique experiment in French colonial policy in West Africa. The apparent anomaly it provided was the creation of a mass of illiterate black French citizens who had as little in common with Frenchmen as other Africans born immediately outside the commune boundaries.

It became obvious towards the close of the nineteenth century, as France acquired a West African territory eight times its size, that assimilation as a political or administrative programme was unviable.[2] Actually, from mid-century, when

---

[1] The *Guide Pratique* was published just a few years after a number of books on the more sordid aspects of French colonial life at the time, such as Debiefs, *La Vice en Algérie*, Paris, 1899, and le Dr. Jacobus, *L'Amour aux Colonies Observée Durant Trente Années*, Paris, 1893.

[2] See Michael Crowder, *Senegal: A Study of French Assimilation Policy*, London, Methuen, 1967, especially chapter one, and Raymond Betts, *Assimilation and Association in French Colonial Theory, 1890–1914*, New York, Columbia University Press, 1961.

45

The Origins of French Presence in Senegal

a colony had been officially established in Senegal, the privileges of the communes were not extended to the interior, wherein a system of administration which was strictly authoritarian and certainly non-assimilationist was in force. In the last two decades of the century the relative merits of assimilation or 'association' (as the new administrative policy for the interior came to be called) were under close scrutiny. But while the distinction in official policy towards natives or colonial subjects of the interior and citizens of the communes was gradually clarified, the actual behaviour and attitudes of colonial officers and other Frenchmen did not always recognize this distinction.

The difficulties of administering the policy of assimilation in the Senegalese communes had already been apparent to local administrators. Various governors found it onerous to be saddled with elections and democratically elected local councils, and as late as 1912 there were attempts to deprive black citizens of their vote. It may have been essential for colonial administrators to have at least formally recognized the differences in legal status among various blacks and mulattoes in the colony, but administrators were concerned above all with efficient government, which often involved a degree of contempt not only for democratic institutions but for those they ruled, regardless of their official status. The traders and merchants, on the other hand, who were untrammelled by loyalty to official policy, were involved in a type of work which demanded that they develop personal relationships of considerable interdependence with black and mulatto clients, employees and colleagues.

Certain relationships between European and African at the turn of the century were not therefore dissimilar to those which existed at the time of the trading post. But the existence of a colonial ideology built on the notion of French cultural superiority did provide the Frenchmen arriving in the colony with automatic membership in a superior group. Despite the nominally non-racial policy of the communes and the existence of an assimilated élite, therefore, there remained a tendency for Frenchmen to identify superior status with skin colour. The assimilated élite remained small because of limited educational facilities, and dominated by *métis* who considered themselves

Assimilation and Association

Frenchmen on the basis of their lighter skin colour. The existence of this group served to reinforce the racial component of status definition in the colony within the policy of assimilation.

The year 1900 marked the close of a period of imperial expansion and the beginning of a rapid increase in commercial activity in Senegal. The continued expansion of trade and the founding of a federal administration for French West Africa based at Dakar[1] meant the arrival of many more Frenchmen in Senegal. This tended to accentuate the cleavage between the public and the private sector, and to introduce new stratification patterns within the European group. Both business competition and professional antagonism generated tensions as commercial activities continued to expand. The administration was committed to defend the most efficient form of commerce in the colony, which generally meant increasing co-operation with a few large companies. The group which seemed entirely left out of this new colonial design was the European shopkeepers and independent traders, whose efforts to defend their own position added a new dynamic to life in the colony.

---

[1] For a description of its structure and functions, see Colin W. Newbury, 'The Formation of the Government General of French West Africa', *Journal of African History*, I, I, 1960.

2. Colonial Society, 1900-1945

TRADE AND COMMERCE

At the beginning of the twentieth century, the pre-eminence of Bordeaux trading firms made Senegal seem like a Bordeaux colony. The names of Delmas, Prom and Maurel[1] were prominent in the Chamber of Commerce in that city and the discussions of investment and administrative policy for the colony dominated its commercial affairs. This traditional relationship was not, however, to remain unchallenged between 1900 and 1945, by the end of which Senegal had a highly developed export structure.

There were several important changes in the organization of the economy in the first half of the twentieth century which considerably affected the political and social life of the European residents. First, the world demand for groundnuts brought several new companies to Senegal which challenged Bordeaux hegemony. Second, the availability of new types of investment in light industry compelled traditional trading companies to reorganize their structures and interests. Third, the general prosperity of the colony and the restructuring of trade in the interior brought a substantial Lebanese minority and new European shopkeeper class to the fore. Fourth, the depression drove the less efficient investors back to France and made new French shopkeepers and independent traders aware of the precarious nature of their economic position.

The background for these changes was that the export of groundnuts from Senegal rose from less than 15,000 tons in

---

[1] E. Maurel was for twenty years on the Tribunal of Commerce of Bordeaux, and H. Prom was President of the Chamber of Commerce, 1885–90. E. Baillet, 'Les Etablissements Maurel et Prom', typescript dated 30 September 1923, p. 18, from the company archives. Members of the Delmas family have been members of the Bordeaux Chamber of Commerce almost continually since this time (private communication).

Trade and Commerce

1898 to more than 500,000 tons in 1930.[1] French commercial trusts such as the *Compagnie Française d'Afrique Occidentale* (*C.F.A.O.*) and the *Societé Commerciale de l'Ouest Africain* (*S.C.O.A.*) began to interest themselves in investment not only in the groundnut trade, but also in the establishment of groundnut oil refineries and light manufacturing industries[2] for the West African market. The Bordeaux companies were quick to take up the challenge, and began to invest in the new economic projects. They had in their favour long local experience and a knowledge of dealing with the administration.

The enlarged volume of the groundnut crop and the geographical area it covered made the old system of direct purchase from the peasants unworkable. The companies were obliged to use *traitants* or middlemen who would buy from the peasants at their fields and transport the produce to a provincial trading centre. The Lebanese immigrant filled this function admirably. Only 100 in Senegal in 1900, they numbered 2,560 in 1936.[3] They were aided enormously in taking over certain key posts in the trade, by replacing Frenchmen who returned to Europe to do military service during the First World War. Along the trading circuits of the interior, the Lebanese and Europeans were, however, not initially competitors. The isolation, poor living conditions and necessary mobility of the *traitant* were as unattractive to French expatriates as the meagre profits of the trade. That the Lebanese were better adapted than the European to the mode of living and commercial demands found in Africa was apparent. They were poorer and in greater need than the corresponding European group who migrated to the colonies. Europeans demanded a minimum housing standard, and periodic vacations in a temperate climate,

---

[1] H. Deschamps, *Le Sénégal et la Gambie*, Paris, Presses Universitaires de France, 1964, p. 72.

[2] See J. Suret-Canale, 'L'Industrie des Oléagineux en A.O.F.', *Cahiers d'Outre-Mer*, No. 11, July 1950, pp. 280–1. In the period preceding the Second World War, the administration was opposed to the establishment of industries in the colony, yet from 1920 to 1932, five oil refineries were established in Senegal, employing a total of about 160 Europeans and more than 1,000 Africans. See Institut de Science Economique Appliquée, *Les Industries du Cap Vert*, Dakar, 1964, pp. 7–8.

[3] J. G. Desbordes, *L'Immigration Libano-Syrienne en A.O.F.*, Poitiers, Imprimerie Moderne, 1938, p. 19.

standards which could only be maintained at a certain salary level.

The prosperity continued in the post-war years and encouraged both European and Lebanese company employees to strike out for themselves once they had earned some capital and made some contacts. European and Lebanese independent traders initially developed similar types of links with family or friends in other trading towns and tried to form small commercial circuits on this basis, gradually bringing members of their extended families from home to join the business. Most of this activity remained marginal, however, for ultimately it was difficult for them to compete with the organization of the major companies. Except for a few independent European traders who benefited from special local conditions, most of them eventually gathered their savings and went to become shopkeepers in the towns. For those less fortunate in this venture, there was always the opportunity of being re-employed by one of the companies.

In addition to the movement of European traders from the interior, an artisan and shopkeeper class had been encouraged as early as 1900 to migrate directly from France: 'Although the climate prevents Europeans from engaging in many types of work, a certain number of artisans, good shoemakers and good tailors would have a chance of success if they wish to be content with modest but sufficient profits.'[1] In Dakar, where the civil servants in the federal administration and African employees provided an ideal clientele, many services and a variety of shops were owned by Europeans. This development was noted with surprise by some who compared it with other non-settler colonies in Africa:

> The visitor to the market of Dakar will see European women selling fish to natives; if he enters a restaurant or store, he will see European women waiting on natives and Europeans alike. Both the French and the Belgian colonies have imported a large number of artisans and unskilled European workers who labour side by side with blacks, and

[1] France, Ministry of Colonies, *Le Sénégal et Dépendances: Notice à l'Usage des Emigrants*, Paris, Imprimerie Administrative, 1900, p. 23.

perform work which in a British territory is performed by Indians or natives.¹

This urban shopkeeper class came into direct competition with the Lebanese merchant who was often aiming at the same market and willing to compete at a lower profit margin.

Lebanese immigration to Senegal was not looked upon with disfavour during the period of economic expansion and prosperity, but the depression, which made the European shopkeeper and independent trader aware of his precarious position, provided a situation which was ripe for an anti-Lebanese campaign. This latter group of Europeans had no leverage on local institutions and no spokesman in France. Unable to impress the administration with the importance of their case for protection and powerless in any case to suggest a satisfactory solution, they found an obvious scapegoat in their closest competitor—the Lebanese.

The background to this situation is provided by the fall in the world price of groundnuts between 1929 and 1931.² Credit could no longer be extended to the *traitants* and there was little circulation of capital to sustain the independent trader or shopkeeper. Faced with this problem, the Chamber of Commerce tried to make the plight of Senegal known in France by reviving the colonial mystique: 'the civilizing mission of France in these regions of Senegal and Soudan, soaked with the blood of our pioneers, is of late being not only compromised but irremediably destroyed'.³

The romantic aspects of colonial lore were no longer the exclusive reserve of the senior colonial administrator. Its rhetoric was employed not only by the Chamber of Commerce but by any vocal white minority against whatever group in the colony was not behaving according to 'France's mission', as they defined it. The depression brought out its use with great

[1] R. L. Buell, *The Native Problem in Africa*, New York, Macmillan, 1928, Vol. II, pp. 79–80.
[2] G. Hiernaux, 'Le Rôle du Grand Commerce Dakarois', Université de Dakar, Faculté des Lettres, Diplôme d'Etudes Supérieures de Géographie, June 1961.
[3] Pierre Faucheux, 'Premier Voyage à Dakar', *Lyon Colonial, Bulletin de Reseignements Economiques et Coloniaux*, No. 80, Nov.–Dec. 1930, p. 161.

Colonial Society, 1900–1945

force; a group of European traders and shopkeepers campaigned against commercial trusts which were 'ruining the colony' and the Lebanese who were not equipped for the 'civilizing mission'. On the influence of the big companies, a local newspaper pleaded in 1932:

> Aid the small planter and merchant! The French are hardly interested in the Colonies anymore... Too many shady affairs are going on between the administration and certain companies.[1]

And on the negative role of the Lebanese, the President of the Chamber of Commerce at Dakar in 1935 wrote:

> In order to provide (the civilizing mission) one must oneself have a sufficient degree of civilization. Outside the Libano-Syrian élite—there are a number of Syrians in Senegal who have descended to a level not very far from the natives among whom they live.[2]

The ideology of protest was that to protect the 'colonial mission' in the colonies was to guard against the selfish profits of big companies, the dishonesty of the Lebanese and put trust in the independent trader and shopkeeper who were the best guardians of this effort.

The organized anti-Lebanese campaign was mounted during the nineteen-thirties but was successfully ignored by the administration and the major companies. It may in fact be interpreted as an extension of hostility to them on the part of the shopkeepers because it was the companies, after all, which had given the Lebanese their start in Senegal and the administration which permitted their immigration unchecked. The introduction of a new system of credit in 1935 under the rural credit organizations, the *Sociétés de Prévoyance*,[3] was regarded by the independent groundnut trader as a severe

---

[1] *L'Indépendant Colonial*, No. 1, May 1932, p. 2. See also Jean Paillard, *Périple Noir*, Paris, Les Oeuvres Françaises, 1935, p. 52, for a discussion of harmful interlocking directorates in which Unilever becomes 'Public Enemy No. 1'.

[2] Letter from J. L. Turbé cited in *Les Echos d'Afrique Noire*, 19 February 1953, in the context of a later anti-Lebanese campaign. (See Ch. 4 below).

[3] See K. E. Robinson, 'The *Sociétés de Prévoyance* in French West Africa', *Journal of African Administration*, Vol. II (1950).

Trade and Commerce

blow to his interests. Favouring the larger, better-organized commercial firms, it seemed to confirm the collusion of all the 'enemies' of the independent trader and merchant (the administration, the companies and the Lebanese), and touched off the period of most profuse distrust against the weakest among them—the Lebanese.

The anti-Lebanese campaign was organized by a group called the *Syndicat Coopératif Economique du Sénégal*. Despite its misleading title, its members co-operated on little else except publicizing the Lebanese menace. The S.C.E.S. had overlapping leadership with the Chamber of Commerce, which had since its foundation consistently excluded the Lebanese. Its written appeal was made through several existing newspapers, but relied particularly on the monthly *France-Afrique Noire* (1935-37), 'Organ of the Defence of French Interests in French West Africa', which was founded for the purpose of alerting all concerned to the 'Libano-Syrian invasion' and its dangers. *France-Afrique Noire* published statistics showing the population, patents and shops of the Lebanese outpacing those of the French, which were intended to sow discontent.[1] The effort behind the publicity was that of a Basque journalist, Jean Paillard, whose documentary collection of the campaign with the evocative title, *La Fin des Français en Afrique Noire*, was intended to mobilize the administration into restricting Lebanese immigration. Propaganda against their extra-legal business practices was widely circulated and a vigorous enforcement of laws and business codes advised.

The appeal was directed primarily at sympathizers in metropolitan France, but also tried to enlist the support of Frenchmen resident in West Africa. This brought few concrete results because the competition was nowhere as acute as in Senegal. It had a larger French and Lebanese population than any other colony in the area, and was the only one in which their interests came into such obvious and direct conflict.[2] An attempt was made to enlist the support of the Africans by

[1] See, for example, October 1935, pp. 53, 57.
[2] Most of the protest against the Lebanese in this period in other colonies in West Africa originated with African merchants and consumers. See R. B. Winder, 'The Lebanese in West Africa', *Comparative Studies in Society and History*, Vol. IV, No. 3, April 1962.

demonstrating the evils of Lebanese employment policy and business practices.[1] Despite these attempts, the audience of the campaign remained confined to the French in small and middle-level commerce and independent trade, inside Senegal.

URBAN DEVELOPMENT AND SOCIAL STRUCTURE

Dakar, which rapidly became the centre of colonial society in the twentieth century, required a great deal of construction and public works to make living conditions suitable for Europeans. Two improvements were undertaken from 1900 to 1910 and an effort was made to combat the not unwarranted reputation of Dakar as one of the most cursed and unhealthy overseas stations in the French empire.[2] From a small group of 125 European merchants and company employees in 1900, the European population of Dakar rose to 2,500 by 1910,[3] most of whom were employees in the newly created Government-General of French West Africa. There was a growing distinction between European and African neighbourhoods which before the decade of construction and improvement had been entirely mixed.

Official geographical segregation was finally introduced because of the expediency of public hygiene and health. Separation of the European 'Plateau' from the African 'Medina' in Dakar was a reflection of common colonial practice in West Africa in the period.[4] This physical division of facilities gave reality to the idea and sentiment of racial separation which was not previously possible in the nineteenth-century settlements. It added a new dimension to the relationship of ruler and ruled and to the framework of colonial domination.

[1] The Lebanese work traditionally in a family unit and have often been criticized by Africans for their non-employment of an African labour-force.
[2] G. Ribot and R. Lafon, *Dakar, Ses Origines, Son Avenir*, Bordeaux, G. Delmas, 1908, p. 7.
[3] *Dakar—A.O.F.*, Editions Françaises de L'Afrique Noire, Dakar, No. 2, May 1951, p. 168, and Afrique Occidentale Française, Haut Commissariat, *Annuaire Statistique de l'A.O.F.*, Edition, 1949, Tome I, Tabl. XLI, p. 82.
[4] See Jean Dresch, 'Villes d'A.O.F.', *Les Cahiers d'Outre-Mer*, Vol. 3, No. II.

Urban Development and Social Structure

Life style, employment patterns and leisure activities tended to reinforce this separation. In 1934, it was noted that 'a visitor who spends a few hours in Dakar might reasonably wonder whether he is in Africa at all; except for the dockers and taxi drivers, there are not so many Negroes as are to be seen in Marseilles'.[1] By this time, commercial development in the urban environment had superimposed a functional division on the city and its existing residential quarters. European business and the administrative headquarters were found in the 'Plateau' with its adjoining market area, 'Kermel'. African petty trade was almost exclusively confined to the 'Medina'. The Lebanese worked and lived in the sector which emerged between the two. These three distinct yet interacting circles of activity were maintained, as the urban area grew larger and became more densely populated.

The new inhabitants of the Plateau were primarily civil servants in the federal administration. The élite of the colonial services was now largely recruited from the ranks of urban middle-class France. Of the 259 students who passed through the *Ecole Nationale de la France Outre-Mer* in Paris between 1930 and 1935, 10 per cent only came from the rural land-owning class, 35·5 per cent were from backgrounds in commerce and industry, and 53·7 per cent from the army, the administration and liberal professions.[2] Colonization had, according to an eminent colonial historian, become a technique rather than an adventure, and the days of the '*gentilhommes de fortune*' were numbered.[3]

The geographical origins of the recruits to the colonial service were widely varied, while participants in trade continued to come mainly from the south and southwest. There are several explanations for this concentration in origin among the latter. To begin with are Senegal's traditional maritime links with Bordeaux and Marseilles, which made the colony well known in these cities and their hinterlands. In addition there is the proximity of this area to the coast of Africa and the

---

[1] G. Gorer, *Africa Dances*, London, Faber and Faber, 1935, p. 63.
[2] R. Delavignette, *Service Africain*, Paris, Galimard, 1946, p. 49.
[3] G. Hardy, *Histoire de la Colonisation Française*, Paris, Larose, 1931, pp. 434–5.

Colonial Society, 1900–1945

relative similarity in climatic conditions between them. The most immediate reason, however, lay perhaps in the poverty of the southern villages whose peasants could not be absorbed into the urban labour force because of retarded industrialization in the area. If one were not in line to inherit the land, or out of a job, the option to go to the colonies came readily to mind. Once an initial pattern of immigration was established, knowledge of Senegal spread further among the townsmen and villagers of the southern region, reinforcing this connection.

The Ariège, a rugged rural province in the southwest, had a rather special relationship with Senegal, the reputation of which endured far beyond the numerical impact of the *Ariègeois* in the colony. They were encouraged to go to Senegal by 'one of their own', who was the Governor of Senegal in 1900. Called *les mange-mils* (the millet-eaters) because the way they descended on Senegal was thought akin to the way the birds of this name covered a field of millet, they were sentimentally considered the true *colons* of Senegal. The villagers of the Ariège, and neighbouring Lot, Tarn and Tarn-et-Garonne, were found throughout the colony, although mainly in the interior—a life for which, it is said, their native villages had well prepared them. Their colonial experience had an impact even in their native villages. The meetings of the town council of Prades, in the Ariège, were said to have sometimes been conducted in Wolof, the principal native language of Senegal, so that the retired '*Sénégalais*' (as they called themselves) could keep their adopted language alive. Another version has it that the town crier of Prades gave the news in Wolof to amuse them and any others who might be on leave. This might be considered a kind of reverse assimilation, perhaps, but these practices seem to have reflected only a sentimental attachment for the colony in which the *Ariègeois* spent their working years.

The death of the patriarch of a well-known Ariègeois family in the colony in 1935 permitted a eulogist to combine romanticism about the *Ariègeois* in Senegal with that of the model colonial type:

> I went to see him at his home in the Ariège, at Prades, where he spent his last leave.... For him as for all of them, home

Urban Development and Social Structure

leave was neither the gambling house, nor the dancing hall. It was, with biblical wisdom, the return to the native soil where one renews one's health in tranquillity, close to one's own. A formula which, though certain may smile, permitted the *Ariègeois* to colonize Senegal in a prosperity which had no equivalent in Black Africa.[1]

This is part of a set of oft-quoted *Ariègeois* stories which are bound to a region in metropolitan France. Unlike the settlers of Algeria, who formed a distinct sub-culture, the French in Senegal remained only for their working years—they were born and died in France. They never ceased to be Frenchmen, and the idiom of their stories reflects this.

The growing presence of European women in the colony, nearly 1,500 by 1926,[2] had a marked effect on the character of the white society. It is reflected in the colonial literature in which the solitary and celibate aspects of the nineteenth century give way to a much more domestic scene, with a conscious attempt to bring life in the colonies closer to family life in France. Although the presence of women was encouraged, they remained an acknowledged problem, their inactivity, boredom and depressions, always a potential disturbance to their husbands' work. Suggestions for women's activities and diversions were found in a series of colonial handbooks dedicated to the problem. To complement the colonial hero of the nineteenth century, several ladies noted for their good works in the colonies were held up as models of behaviour for the women about to join their husbands overseas. They were reminded that such women were not only found among the rich and well-born, but also among the simple and virtuous who made their small contribution to colonial society. Suggestions for women's activities included social work, care of African children, and studies of flora and fauna.[3] Occupations for the colonial housewife were easier to find in the town than in the isolated stations of the interior.

Documentation on white society at Dakar and St. Louis was

[1] *France-Afrique Noire*, November 1935, back cover.
[2] L. Cross, *L'Afrique Française pour Tous*, Paris, Albin Michel, 1928, n.p.
[3] See Chevas Baron, *La Femme Française aux Colonies*, Paris, Larose, 1929, pp. 184–7, and J. L. Faure, *La Vie aux Colonies: Preparation de la Femme à la Vie Coloniale*, Paris, Larose, 1938, pp. 192–221.

provided in several social gossip sheets which recorded activities and events. During the dry season, when the climate was good, there were balls at the Governor-General's palace, Sunday band concerts, travelling theatre and operetta groups from France and comedians who mocked the colonial life to the amusement of the audience. Social occasions were extremely formal—often only evening dress was accepted, and people were turned away if not properly attired. The provincial town of the tropics had a cultural and intellectual aridity which shocked the uninitiated,[1] and which lent itself easily to social pettiness and a taste for exaggerated formality.

The social élite was dominated by a series of social and professional groups or 'clans', as they were called, which divided the top military, administrative and commercial personnel. In St. Louis, social life was still dominated by the old *métisse* families who maintained a kind of courtly society together with military officers stationed in the colonial capital. The newer European elements were somewhat scorned by those in the social élite, for their 'base materialist attitudes' and their brief stints in the colonies to make money. The night life of Dakar, which included transvestites, strippers, epileptic dancers and exhibitionists was regarded as a reflection of their 'poor moral qualities'.[2]

As white society became larger and more stable, it became further insulated from the African majority. Contact with Africans was limited to work, and usually only politics drew them together in other circumstances. 'Europeans who got too close to Africans were suspected of demagoguery, or of using them for their own political careers.'[3] The non-white élite of the colony remained extremely small owing to the still very limited number either of educational facilities locally or of opportunities to go to France. While France still continued to cultivate its small minority of black Frenchmen, much more concern was devoted to administering the vast African empire than to expanding the élite of *assimilés*. Opposition to the policy of assimilation in all quarters continued well into the first

[1] *Le Journal de Dakar*, Nos. 1 and 2, 1–8 January 1931, p. 1.
[2] 'Les Folles Nuits de Dakar', in *L'Indépendant Colonial*, I, May 1932.
[3] Interview with a longtime resident of St. Louis.

decades of the twentieth century,[1] and the official non-racial policy of the Senegalese communes seemed still to have little effect on local social relations. The continued separation of Africans and whites cannot, however, be simply explained with reference to colonial policy. The development of the African urban social structure according to new economic or occupational categories, and the increasing differentiation of the class structure of local Frenchmen did not have a positive effect on contacts between the two groups—in fact, just the opposite. There was at this time a gradual enlargement of a sector of the French population which had insecure or even marginal positions in the economic life of the colony. Such people had everything to gain by demanding that superior status be awarded primarily on the basis of colour, and by raising barriers against those few non-whites who were in higher or equivalent socio-economic positions in the colony. To add to this, the presence of women in the colony in substantial numbers for the first time gradually reduced liaisons between Frenchmen and their black mistresses, and eliminated the dependence of celibate white society on a host of black clients and confidants of all kinds. Whether one can explain the growing insulation of the white minority in terms of the changing social structure, the increased domesticity of European life or of the more racist attitudes of European women remains open to question. It may have been a combination of all three.

Whatever the configuration of influences on the attitudes and behaviour of Frenchmen, it was obvious that some local whites chose to ignore the status of the African élite by defining their relationships to all non-whites on a purely racial basis. Owing particularly to the political heritage of the communes, this élite had always been separated from the African masses, and had indeed consciously separated itself by identifying with the French nation and remaining loyal to it. But educated Africans now began to react to the situation in the colony and take up their demands for respect in racial terms. In so doing, their recognition of the differentiation among Frenchmen now resident in the colony became explicit, and the criticism of certain unworthy representatives of French civilization and

[1] R. L. Buell, *op. cit.*, Vol. II, pp. 86–92.

culture became a most relevant theme. The grievances against the 'bad European' were threefold. First was their racial discrimination—'We protest, we the primitives, against the Europeans who scorn us for the colour of our skin'.[1] Second was their destruction of 'France's mission'—'The bad French vomited from metropolitan France ... far from continuing the mission initiated by the schoolmasters seem only to exist to undermine it'.[2] And third, was a plea against job competition— We demand 'the replacement of the wives of civil servants and soldiers in the administration by unemployed natives'.[3]

This resentment, which appeared in newspapers and petitions to the Governor, rarely took concrete organizational form. Although there were occasional anti-white undertones in politics, which were carefully noted by the administration, they seem only to have represented somewhat insincere demagoguery in this period. The African élite with secure positions in the economic structure did not define political differences in racial terms.

POLITICS

Politics after 1900 initially followed the pattern of activity already established in the nineteenth century; that is to say that the powerful trading houses sponsored candidates who divided the spoils of power among their followers, leaving the African majority in the communes and the rest of the white minority either to identify themselves with already established political leaders or to protest through extra-political means. Frenchmen living outside the four *communes de plein exercice* protested against the system of voting privileges whereby Africans by birthright alone were French citizens, and (without other qualifications) made up the majority of the electorate, while the franchise was denied to themselves. Although

[1] *Le Rumeur*, No. 7, 15 September 1932. This was a charge against the Europeans who supported B. Diagne in 1932, see below.
[2] Archives du Sénégal, Dakar, 17/13G/27.
[3] *Ibid*. This was a statement of '*Doléances*' of the 'unemployed intellectuals' of St. Louis, presented to the Minister of Colonies on a visit to Senegal in 1936.

these Frenchmen were allowed to participate in the election of Senegal's deputy from 1910, this had little effect on the established political machines in the communes or on the outcome of elections.

From 1900 to 1914, politics in Senegal was largely a struggle between rival *métisse* families, whose patriarchs had become company owners and powerful local businessmen. In addition to white merchants, traders or professional people, French candidates were sent to Senegal expressly for elections by the trading houses, but these were becoming increasingly difficult to put over on the electorate. The rotten borough aspects of Senegalese elections were coming into question.

In the election of 1914, Blaise Diagne became the first African deputy after an extraordinarily heated campaign. His success was built on an unusually effective organization and an appeal to the mass of African voters, but can also be attributed to the failure of the commercial houses and powerful *métisse* families to come to an agreement on a candidate.[1] He was accused of being anti-white for saying (allegedly) that 'the time had come for the black mice to eat the white mice'.[2] The companies then tried unsuccessfully to have the election annulled. Diagne was to be of great assistance to the colonial administration in recruiting African troops during the Great War, and, for this, he was awarded a high symbolic status. While on a recruiting tour for the war effort in 1917, the wife of a European administrator wiped his shoes—a fact which was commented on for many years. By the time of the next electoral contest, 1919, Diagne had thus proved his loyalty to France, and had also developed links with French business interests, in particular, the Bordeaux trading houses.

One of the most important things that Diagne achieved on the local political scene was to establish that a European could no longer hope to be elected deputy or lead a successful political faction. The African majority wanted one of its own, and the companies, the administration and local European interests

---

[1] See the excellent article by G. Wesley Johnson, 'The Ascendancy of Blaise Diagne and the Beginning of African Politics in Senegal', *Africa*, Vol. XXXVI, No. 3, July 1966.
[2] Archives du Sénégal, Dakar, 13G/17.

had to adapt accordingly. The pattern of his success was followed closely by the next African deputy, Galandou Diouf: use radical or inflammatory slogans to gain African majority support in the first campaign, and once in office accept a handsome retainer from the French companies and demonstrate your loyalty to the administration.

Europeans who participated in politics usually fell into two categories: those who were active in parties in France, a small minority of whom hoped to further their political careers in the colony, and those local businessmen or professional people who looked upon politics as a means of improving their business or financial situation through the rewards of political activity. They were a very small minority, however, for most Europeans remained outside politics, and were generally apathetic to exercising even their right to vote.

One of the rising political factions in Dakar in the nineteen-thirties was the Socialist Party (*S.F.I.O.*), which was later to become of considerable importance, as its leaders—Paul Bonifay, a French lawyer, and Lamine Guèye, an African lawyer—played a significant part in post-war politics. In its early days in 1936, the party chiefly consisted of a small group of Frenchmen who came together to discuss the meaning and future of socialism: according to Bonifay, it was 'a rather "academic" movement which had few African members until it began to contest elections'. As he saw it, the major obstacle to building a successful party at this time was that 'there was no working class in Africa, nothing on which to base a militant socialist movement. Although Europeans were earning miserable wages and living quite poorly, they were small independent shopkeepers and not a labour force organized into unions.'[1] The party had to adapt its posture to the local situation and thus the socialist ideology—which was of little interest either to African militants or French shopkeepers and traders—was retained only as a formality. The organizational link with the metropolitan party remained strong, however, for the national office was interested in the Senegalese deputyship and the possibility of establishing a political base overseas.

[1] Interview with Bonifay, 1st Sec.-Gen. of the *S.F.I.O.* Federation in French West Africa, Dec. 1966, Dakar.

Politics

Like the political clans of the nineteenth century, the successful parties of the nineteen-thirties were local political machines organized around a leading boss, rather than around a set of principles or a party programme. The fact that they were nominally tied to metropolitan movements made very little difference to their structure and appeal.

The General Council,[1] which had been established in Senegal in 1879, remained the only territorial representative body in any of the West African colonies under French rule which was elected on the basis of a single-college system. Its French members, many of whose names reflected a continued influence of Bordeaux families, were often absent and occasionally boycotted the meetings, causing a certain amount of local scandal. R. L. Buell, one of the few close observers of Senegalese politics in this period, expressed surprise at the multi-racial character of the council:

> That eight Europeans should have exactly the same status as thirty-two blacks in a situation which would strike the Anglo-Saxon as anomalous to say the least. The visitor to the Council will frequently witness a black President calling a European to order for rowdyness.[2]

That black citizens were not usually awarded the same status outside representative institutions in this period is reflected in the comment that they 'showed great pleasure at any indications of acceptance as equals by Europeans'.[3] The attitude of the local whites to these citizens was described by a contemporary observer as one of 'hostility and mockery'.[4] The fact remained that although the Senegalese were eligible for French citizenship by virtue of birth in the four *communes*, they were only juridically or constitutionally an élite. Their citizenship remained an unusual remnant of a former era in colonial thinking. Although there was some contact between black and white militants in political movements, this hardly stretched into

[1] For a discussion of its functions and historical role, see L. G. Cowan, *Local Government in West Africa*, New York, Columbia University Press, 1958, p. 49, and Buell, *op. cit.*, Vol. I, p. 968.
[2] R. L. Buell, *op. cit.*, p. 980.
[3] Ruth Schachter Morgenthau, *Political Parties in French-Speaking West Africa*, Oxford, The Clarendon Press, 1964, p. 129.
[4] Jacques Weuleresse, *Noirs et Blancs*, Paris, 1931, p. 6.

social life. Politics was an activity apart, wherein distinct patterns of behaviour, involving only a small group of activists, were acceptable.

THE WAR

From 1940 until the end of 1942, Dakar and the administration of French West Africa were controlled from Vichy. The majority of the European population remained calm throughout an attempt by General de Gaulle and the Free French Forces to invade in 1940. The local population 'would', according to administrative assessment, 'have followed either the British or Germans if they had occupied Dakar'.[1]

The Vichy experience in Senegal had several immediate effects on the administration. One highly placed Jewish civil servant was forced to resign his post as Secretary of the Government General, which was said to have had an adverse effect on morale in the administration.[2] About thirty or forty Freemasons met the same fate. Those in the administration who protested against these measures or who were known for their radical or socialist sentiments were removed from Dakar to remote stations. Only one German ever visited Dakar, however, and for a very brief time. Decisions were left in the hands of local administrators who interpreted policy and propaganda as they saw fit.[3]

The Vichy regime ignored the privileges of Africans who had French citizenship because of their residence in the communes or had achieved the status of *evolué* or *assimilé* through educational achievement in the French tradition. Official policy at this time made no distinction between Africans of the élite and all others: rationing was conducted on a strictly colour basis, as were the allocation of quarters in the army and compartments in trains.

---

[1] Archives du Sénégal, Dakar, 17/13G/56, 'From General Security to the Director of Political Affairs'.

[2] No formal protest was, however, made. See treatment of the incident by his successor Armand Annet in *Aux Heures Troublées de l'Afrique Française, 1939–1943*, Paris, Eds. du Conquistador, 1952, pp. 50–1.

[3] *Interview* with M. Gereudel, Chef du Cabinet (of the Governor-General) for the Circonscription de Dakar, 1940–42, Paris, April 1966.

The War

The Senegalese élite was humiliated by these measures, but it would be misleading to assert that Vichy introduced a type of policy which scarred race relations in the colony.

Vichy was too brief an interlude to have had a lasting effect on attitudes towards blacks among the white minority, who seem to have accepted whatever happened with a certain degree of apathy. That Africans were made to use separate entrances or queues during the two-year Vichy domination would have been appreciated by the majority of Europeans, but their fundamental attitudes, which were shaped in the pre-war colonial environment, remained much the same. Above all, what is interesting is not that they would succumb to a short-lived overtly racist policy, but that the official non-racial policy of the communes had made so little impact on daily life over such a long period of time.

The total experience of the war and the isolation from France had a significant effect on the European minority. The wartime tour of duty in the administration lasted far beyond its usual length, and few changes or few new appointments could be made for several years after liberation. In addition to this, the European population was abnormally inflated by the presence of troops in Dakar.[1] Because it was difficult to return to France owing to the shortage of ships and planes both during and immediately after the war, several new types of services had to be provided locally. The need to simulate Paris or Nice for the temporarily exiled expatriates was far more pressing than even before. In 1948 in Dakar, it was observed that 'Europeans appeared far more settled than seemed possible in any overseas station before the war'.[2] This wartime isolation and inflated European population provided the background which Senegal's towns, and in particular, Dakar, needed to sustain a much larger European resident community in the immediate post-war years and the Fifties.

---

[1] *1940-6*, 513, *1941-18*, 233. Afrique Occidentale Française, Haut Commissariat de l'A.O.F., *Annuaire Statistique* ... 1949, *op. cit.*, Tabl. XLIV, p. 90.

[2] D. Whittlesey, 'Dakar Revisited', *Geographical Review*, New York, 1948, p. 632.

3. *The* Petit Blanc, *Changing Economic and Social Structure, 1945-1960*

EUROPEAN MIGRATION

The disruption of personal and family life during the war in France, together with the limited possibilities for employment in the immediate post-war period, made a 'promised land' of her overseas colonies. In Dakar there was in particular a wide variety of opportunities for those with little educational background or training: even a primary school certificate was sufficient to command quite a good salary. The proportion of European workers and artisans in the total working population of the city rose steadily from 1946, reaching a high point about 1955 and then beginning to decline; a reflection of post-war economic expansion and contraction.[1]

Economic change also brought about an increased diversification within the total European group, through which the differentiation of socio-economic sub-groups became much more marked. The growth in expatriate personnel in the colonial services as well as in the private sector attenuated the traditional divisions to be found in European society before the war, which began to give way to objective class distinctions for the first time. The newest element in the European group was the *petit blanc* (roughly, 'lower-class white'), who brought with him to Africa a minimum of relevant skills, and whose success epitomized the potential for upward mobility in the colonies at

[1] From 1946 to 1951, this proportion increased from 5 per cent to 11 per cent. Paul Mercier, 'Le Groupement Européen de Dakar', *Cahiers Internationaux de Sociologie*, Vol. 19, 1955, p. 36. Mercier adds in a note that this increase was checked after 1953 in Dakar by the business situation, although the census for Dakar in 1955 (République du Sénégal, Ministère du Plan, *Recensement Démographique de Dakar*, 1955, 2ème Fascicule, 1962), which was not of course available to him when his article was published, puts the percentage of European workers and artisans at 16·5 for 1955, falling to 12 per cent in 1959 (estimate of the *Inspection Regionale de Travail* of that year), p. 23.

this time. The long-term effect of this influx was felt in later years when company directors and executives in local branches of the trading companies had a much lower educational background and training than their subordinates, recruited to overseas posts during a period of greater stability than that just following the war.

Ex-servicemen were a prominent group among the recruits for overseas employment from 1946. Young men who had travelled to Africa and Asia during the war developed a taste for expatriate living and remained dissatisfied when they returned to the circle of their families and friends in France. Several hundred soldiers and sailors who were serving in Dakar requested to be demobilized there and remained to seek employment, an option made easy for them because the French government offered to repatriate them at official expense at any time within a ten year period. The economic impetus behind the influx of Frenchmen both from the metropole and from the overseas armed services was a postwar boom in commerce, building and industry in Senegal, focused on Dakar, the thriving commercial capital of the Federation.

The political background to these developments lies in the constitutional legislation following the Brazzaville conference of 1944, which affirmed the continuity of France's influence over her 1940 empire in Africa. It did so while making nominal concessions to the demands of African leaders for greater territorial autonomy and greater participation in the political system.[1] At the same time the colonies of French West Africa and particularly Senegal remained an integral part of the French economy and the French Union. There was to be free circulation of peoples to all parts of the Union, which notably meant white immigration to Africa, and, given the importance of trade and marketing centres, especially to the coastal cities.

Large-scale metropolitan immigration to Africa was suggested as a means of actually, and not merely legally, integrating the

[1] R. Viard, *La Fin de l'Empire Coloniale Français*, Paris, Maisonneuve et Larose, 1963, pp. 1–33, gives a summary of the points under discussion, the outcome and the roads opened by the conference.

The Petit Blanc

overseas territories into the Union structure. This scheme had its proponents and opponents. On the positive side, the arguments were that white immigration would encourage a local consumer market, and contribute human resources to the development of these countries, while also raising exportable production and the standard of living of the local inhabitants.[1] Those on the other side of the debate contested the ideal of integration through large-scale immigration within the Union by looking critically at the kind of Frenchmen who were attracted to Africa, and finding that although trained cadres were needed, unskilled labourers in large numbers were more difficult to justify.[2]

While the general discussion about the merits and demerits of this policy were going on in Europe, the influx of whites into Senegal was having some quite specific effects on urban arrangements and the social structure. Between 1947 and 1951, 2,560 Frenchmen joined the private sector in Senegal, and some 4,000 more filled posts in the administration and the army.[3] By 1955, slightly more than half of all those Europeans working in Senegal were employed in the private sector, and the rest by the administration or the army.[4] This was an alteration from the pre-war period when administrative and military personnel were numerically predominant.

From 1946 to 1956, the total number of Europeans resident in Dakar more than trebled,[5] outpacing quite substantially the rate of growth in the African population of the town, even when allowance is made for the large rural exodus of Africans in search of jobs. By the end of the decade following the war, Dakar no

---

[1] See Xavier Lannes, 'Les Problemes de Main-d'Oeuvre dans l'Eurafrique', in *La Nouvelle Revue Française d'Outre-Mer*, No. 6, June 1953, pp. 151–3.
[2] Henry Didier, 'L'Immigration Européenne en Afrique', *La Nouvelle Revue Française d'Outre-Mer*, No. 6, June 1953.
[3] Haut Commissariat de l'Afrique Occidentale Française, Service de la Statistique Générale, *Recensement de la Population Non-Autochtome de L'Afrique Occidentale Française en Juin 1951*, p. 46.
[4] République du Sénégal, Ministère du Plan, *Recensement Démographique de Dakar*, 1955, 2ème Fascicule, Paris, 1962, 'Repartition de la Population Active Selon le Secteur d'Activité', Table B.3, p. 17 annex.
[5] Haut-Commissariat de la République en A.O.F., *A.O.F. 1957, Tableaux Economiques*, p. 101: in *1946*, it was 11,200; in *1951*, 21,787; *1956*, 34,013.

longer looked like a small colonial town: it was the only really European-type city along the coast, providing shops, services and leisure activities demanded by the growing white resident population. Lodgings, dress and daily life became less and less colonial in character, although the new Mediterranean-style city was not immediately a comfort to all Frenchmen. The rapid increase in this group put a tremendous pressure on housing and urban facilities, creating many social and public health problems. The housing shortage was so intense that families were forced to take poor lodgings, including converted garages, which they rented at very inflated prices. Local newspapers reported this as they scorned the idea of the European 'paradise in the tropics' (see Cartoons pp. 70–1). But salaries were very high and the prosperity was still attractive despite temporary discomfort. Dakar had acquired a certain 'boom town' quality.

The male predominance in the demographic structure of the European population initially reflected the unusual employment opportunities, although an equilibrium was reached by 1955. The arrival of women before the war had begun to cut down the imbalance between the sexes, but the large inflow of labourers just after the war reintroduced male predominance, especially in the age group between twenty and twenty-nine. In 1946 the ratio among the French-born was 168 men for 100 women, and it remained steady until the end of 1951, but then made a dramatic adjustment to a more stable situation of 108 to 100 by 1955.[1] Family groups remained small (3·2 persons on average), although there was a significant rise in the total number of children compared with the pre-war situation, from 10 per cent to 35 per cent of the total white population.[2] Despite housing problems, there were sufficient medical and educational facilities available to alleviate most of the pre-war dangers to expatriate family life.

---

[1] République du Sénégal, Ministère du Plan, *Recensement Démographique de Dakar*, 1955, 2ème Fascicule, 1962, Table A.3, p. 3 annex.

[2] Assane Seck, *Dakar*, Université de Dakar, Faculté des Lettres et Sciences Humaines, Travaux du Département de Geographie, No. 9, 1963, p. 15.

Cartoons depicting certain aspects of European life, as well as certain attitudes of the time, from 'Les Echos d'Afrique Noire', April 1952

Comment pas de logement? Mais on m'a dit que c'était le paradis l'A.O.F.

How come no housing? But they told me it was paradise in French West Africa.

Fainéantise et boisson fraiche sont trop souvent les deux besoins du noir evolué et du blanc nouvellement débarqué...

Laziness and cool drinks are too often the two needs of the *evolué* black and the newly arrived white...

—*Tas vu? . . . c'est un Commandant de Cercle qui porte nos valises.*

—You see? . . . it's a *Commandant de Cercle* (local administrator) who carries our cases.

—*Bonjour mon vieux! Comment ça va. La famille se porte-t-elle bien? Et ta femme? Est-ce que ça va toujours? Et depuis quand fais-tu ce métier-là? Es-tu bien payé? Eh dis donc! qu'est-ce qu'on joue au cinéma ce soir? . . .*

—Good day old chap! how are you . . . Is the family well? And your wife? Is all going well? And how long have you been doing this job? Are you well paid? And tell me, what's on at the cinema tonight? . . .

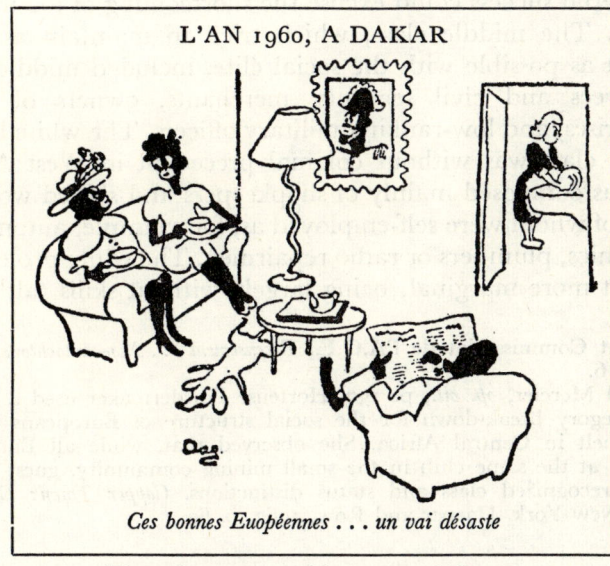

Ces bonnes Euopéennes . . . un vai désaste

These European maids are a real disaster.

The Petit Blanc

CHANGING SOCIAL STRUCTURE

The European minority was now also more mobile, both because of an introduction of shorter contracts by private firms and frequent transfers in the administration and the army. The 'career colonial' was beginning to disappear. The expatriates remained a working population, only 1 to 2 per cent of the total group remaining beyond retiring age.[1] Yet the growing mobility of overseas services as well as the introduction of new socio-economic categories reduced the cohesiveness of the white community, with some serious implications for group identity. Class differences were considerably less rigid than in France, but it remained possible to identify four distinct socio-economic groups within Dakar white society: an upper class or social élite, a middle class, a lower-middle class, and an unstable proletariat. Social interaction and clubs tended to be concentrated within each of these four segments.[2]

The first group, the élite, included the directors of trading houses, industrialists, banking executives, senior civil servants and military officers. Acceptance in 'Dakar society' did not necessarily depend on pre-colonial background: a certain degree of material success could excuse the shortcoming of too modest origins. The middle class, which tried to maintain as close contact as possible with the social élite, included middle-level employees and civil servants, merchants, owners of small enterprises, and low-ranking military officers. The white lower-middle class was without colonial precedent in West Africa, and was composed mainly of shopkeepers and skilled workers, many of whom were self-employed as, for example, automobile mechanics, plumbers or radio repairmen. The white proletariat was yet more marginal, being largely without skills (although

---

[1] Haut Commissariat de l'A.O.F., *Recensement . . . Non-Autochtone*, 1951, *ibid.*, p. 6.
[2] Paul Mercier, *op. cit.*, p. 137. Hortense Powdermaker used a similar four-category break-down for the social structure of Europeans on the Copperbelt in Central Africa. She observed that, while all Europeans mingled at the same club in the small mining community, guest lists at parties recognized class and status distinctions. *Copper Town: Changing Africa*, New York, Harper and Row, 1962, p. 69.

rarely so classified for official purposes). It included waiters, sales clerks, truck drivers, for example, who were usually employed on annual local contract and whose good fortune lasted as long as the economy was expanding. The only exceptions to the class differentiation of leisure activities were found in the few ethnic or regional associations, the *amicales* (friendly societies) such as those of the Corsicans and the Bretons. The Italians were a relatively important minority and had a very active *amicale*.[1] Recruited as labourers, most of those who remained after the first period of rapid economic expansion assimilated easily into the French majority.

New arrivals, especially those of the lower-middle class and working class, tried to minimize the differences between the various socio-economic groups of whites to be found in the colony.[2] By trying to ignore the objective distinctions in material conditions and social position they attempted to identify with a homogeneous white community (which of course no longer existed). The purpose of seeking anonymity lay in the expectation that status would be awarded automatically on the basis of skin colour. Newcomers felt strongly the need to maintain white unanimity in the face of the black majority. It was therefore also in their interests to ignore the relative promotion in class and status of certain African groups, and, where possible, to revive the racially based superior-inferior distinction which had been built into the colonial relationship. The remainder of the European group, at the same time, not only recognized the apparent divisions within their own ranks, but were intent on conserving their status, and were concerned that the new arrivals were lowering the general prestige of whites. The more established residents lamented this 'invasion', and the destruction of colonial society as it had been, with its leisurely pace, formality and closely-knit social cliques. The *petit blanc* thus became the inheritor of the qualities of the much criticized 'bad Frenchman' of the nineteen-thirties, who was not

---

[1] Before the war, they had a weekly newspaper, *La Voce di Dakar*, published from 1932–36. Mario Gozzini, 'Gli Italiani in A.O.F. Ante 1940', *Affrica*, Revista Mensile di Interessi Affricani, Vol. VII, Nos. 7–8, July and August 1953, p. 198.
[2] P. Mercier, *op. cit.*, p. 146.

The Petit Blanc

only accused of being devoid of colonial purpose and civic-mindedness, but who also set no example for the majority of blacks.

The term *petit blanc* was used pejoratively not only by local whites, but also by Africans who competed with them for jobs and accused them of overt racist sentiment. As a label, it provides difficulties for objective definition or for the precise location of a socio-economic category to which it may be applied. Mercier's informants felt that it involved a lack of job specialization and a very low salary.[1] An informant of mine (the Secretary-General of the Dakar Chamber of Commerce) believed that it excluded all employees who were under contract because, for him, the crucial feature was the instability of future employment. Yet *petit blanc* has been variously used to include the *petite bourgeoisie* of small shopkeepers and independent artisans, low-level public employees, labourers brought to the colony under fixed contract for a stipulated period of time, as well as unskilled labourers under local contract whose employment situation was unstable. When used as a term of contempt by other groups in the society, no distinction was made between labourers, artisans and shopkeepers, although the functional differentiation between them, and therefore their reaction to the colonial environment, is extremely important.

One reaction of this kind is provided by the appearance and popularity in Dakar at this time of *Les Echos de l'Afrique Noire*, a weekly newspaper calling itself 'the defender of Franco-African fraternity and *la présence française*', with an average circulation varying between eight and twelve thousand. Often called 'the authentic voice of the *petit blanc*', it was considered a Dakar version of the French satirical *Canard Enchaîné* (see Cartoons 1, pp. 70–1), and was widely read and discussed, particularly for its local gossip. Its main interest was the protection of French presence in the colonies, which led it to be anti-Lebanese, anti-administration, and anti-large companies. It was self-consciously *not* anti-African *per se*, but took many strong positions against those local leaders, politicians or intellectuals whom it considered to be anti-French. It proclaimed itself to be 'protecting' the African masses from being

[1] *Ibid.*, p. 139.

Anti-Lebanese weekly strip cartoon, 'Les Echos d'Afrique Noire', 1954

'The Adventures of Faycal Kombhine and Djemal-al-Haratt'

(1) *Natif du Djebel Druze (Syrie), le petit Fayçal Kombhine se rendit, tout jeune, à Damas pour y faire son chemin et gagner son méchoui, à la sueur de son front.*

(2) *Ce n'est qu'à sa majorité qu'il put enfin trouver sa voie et, exercer un métier dur, mais lucratif. La chance surgit, un jour, au coin d'une rue et . . .*

(1) Native of Djebel Druze (Syria), little Faycal Kombhine went as a young man to Damascus to make his way and earn his keep by the sweat of his brow.
(2) Only when he reached full manhood did he finally discover his vocation in a hard but lucrative profession. His chance came one day at the corner of a street, and . . .

(3) *. . . Fayçal ne l'ayant pas manquée, se trouva soudain, transporté dans la plus grands et . . .*

(4) *. . . la plus belle des aventures. Il s'agissait d'un billet de quatrième classe pour l'Afrique!*

(3) Faycal didn't miss his chance but found himself suddenly carried into a great and . . .
(4) Glorious adventure. A fourth-class ticket to Africa!

The Petit Blanc

misled by certain members of their race, or influenced by anti-white propaganda. *Les Echos* was the new equivalent of *France-Afrique Noire* of the nineteen-thirties: the appeal and the language were much the same, the rootless journalists who edited each of them and who arrived to 'save the colony from destruction' were similar personalities. The crises which provoked their appearance were different: the depression for the first, the fear and then the reality of decolonization for the second. The depression, being much more generally felt, gave a certain legitimacy to the appeal of the nineteen-thirties, in which, for example, the Chamber of Commerce had been involved. Although *Les Echos* had a much wider circulation, its editor, Maurice Voisin, and the various organizations for the protection of French interests which were founded by him were regarded as much more marginal. He was frequently in jail and his paper confiscated for its highly personal and vociferous attacks on members of the administration.

White shopkeepers and other small businessmen created a series of organizations to defend their interests in this period, including the *Union Syndicale des Commerçants Indépendants*, founded in October 1951, and the Federation of Taxpayers in 1952. Their aims were similar: to agitate for lower taxes and import duties, and for retention of the best part of taxes earned in French West Africa towards the maintenance of local services, such as those inadequately provided by the municipal administration of Dakar. These groups had limited objectives and were devoid of continuous activity. Maurice Voisin was responsible for the foundation and leadership of most of them, and the columns of his newspaper awarded them free publicity. He was also instrumental in founding a local branch of the Poujadist movement in Dakar, the advent of which was given much coverage in *Les Echos*.

Anti-Lebanese agitation was revived again in this period among the expanding group of French shopkeepers. Several short-lived anti-Lebanese organizations were formed on a supposedly multi-racial basis, which occasionally suggested the use of violence against the Levantine minority. Africans were recruited to protest against the Lebanese contribution to unemployment, exorbitant profits and usury. Although the

Anti-Lebanese cartoons from 'Les Echos d'Afrique Noire', April 1952 and April 1954

*Rien de changé depuis BECHARD . . .
Ça débarque toujours . . .*

Nothing has changed since (Governer-General) BECHARD . . .
They're still coming . . .

Tiens Farid . . . J'ai fait rechauffer ton bain du mois dernier.
Here Farid. I reheated your bath from last month.

administration took a strong position against the mass-hate meetings, it could do nothing effective to stop the barrage of derogatory outbursts in *Les Echos* (Cartoons, pp. 75, 77) which continued for more than twelve years, the life-span of the paper.

Les Echos had its most loyal audience among *petits blancs*, whose marginal position in the colony and fear of decolonization led them to follow avidly its wide-ranging attacks. Small shopkeepers and artisans who identified with the causes of *Les Echos* presumably regarded themselves as the last of the 'creative colonials', on whose sacrifice, hard work and dedication the colony was built.[1] It seemed to have revived the colonial romanticism of a former era, in becoming the spokesman for creative colonialism, warning of the impending ruin of France's mission by the influx of worthless people to the colony. The administration was, however, no longer concerned with maintaining the colonial romanticism found in the official handbooks of 1900, which ironically now fell to the use of anti-administration critics. The columns of *Les Echos* often added a new dimension to the appraisal of colonial life—the alienation and depersonalization of the colonial process by the administration and big companies. In an article entitled 'The *Colon* is at the Edge of a Precipice', came the familiar warning that French officialdom in West Africa was 'nothing more than the representative of big capitalism, and that the colonial process had been depersonalized'.[2]

Ultimately the rapid alterations in the European socio-economic structure which occurred in this period did not create serious cleavages among the white minority, as some might have expected. All expatriates were benefiting from the flourishing economic situation, universally referred to now as 'the good old days'. The French were living and earning in conditions of inflation in the nineteen-fifties. It is not the first

---

[1] For a colourful expression of this from a slightly earlier period, see the 'model life' of a French businessman in Dakar as expressed in a letter to the Governor of Senegal in 1941, a grateful acknowledgement for receipt of public office, reprinted on p. 88.

[2] *Les Echos*, 8–14 May 1952, p. 1. Big companies like *C.F.A.O.* and *S.C.O.A.* had their base in France and took little part in local affairs which did not directly affect the companies' local interest, since the most important matters were decided at the Ministry in Paris.

Employment

period in which expatriate society in Senegal was described as being dominated by the desire for making money[1]—nor would it be the last.

ECONOMIC EXPANSION, EMPLOYMENT AND LABOUR RELATIONS

The growth and diversification of the economic infrastructure of Senegal effected significant alterations not only in European social structure, but in the whole pattern of employment and labour relations in this period. In the immediate post-war years, the controversy between the administration and the European traders remained focused on the *Sociétés de Prevoyance* and wartime controls. This resentment dissolved almost entirely during the prosperity which followed. In 1949, the Federation of French West Africa returned to free trade, and the removal of controls ushered in a euphoric period for business at Dakar. Contrary to the practice in British West African territories, the administration purchased goods from local suppliers. This actually meant that the biggest trading companies, *C.F.A.O.* and *S.C.O.A.*, because of their influential metropolitan contacts and their extensive organizational framework throughout West Africa, received the biggest contracts. It was chiefly because of their metropolitan links with banks and investment firms that they had weathered the depression and wartime restrictions relatively well, and now they were given renewed impetus by government contracts.

Assembly plants and light-manufacturing industries were built very rapidly after the war in Senegal, because France could not meet the demand for consumer goods from French West Africa and because there was a chronic difficulty in ensuring the transport of merchandise. The economic boom in Senegal which began in the late Forties was partially fostered by the substantial investment of the *Fonds d'Investissement pour*

[1] P. H. Siriex, *Une Nouvelle Afrique: A.O.F. 1957*, Paris, Plon, 1957, p. 62. He described Dakar as a 'white and dirty town', where one finds elegant and well stocked shops and small shopkeepers dominated by the *'mentalité* CFA' (referring to the franc CFA or French West African currency).

The Petit Blanc

le Développement Economique et Social (F.I.D.E.S.) which provided the colony with an improved transportation and communications infrastructure, as part of a ten-year development scheme for France's overseas dependencies. In addition, new private investment was given special tax and fiscal benefits as well as easy loan arrangements.[1]

The prosperity brought with it certain negative features, however, including a dangerous inflationary spiral which continued throughout the decade. Despite the attempts of the French government to protect her overseas dependencies from the post-war metropolitan inflation by creating the C.F.A. *franc* in 1945 at a double parity of 1·70 to the *franc metro* and raising it in 1948 to 2 to 1,[2] it failed in this aim in French West Africa and especially Dakar because, among other things, of the speculative activities of local merchants who did not adjust their prices in recognition of the new exchange rates. Several attempts were made by the government to control the inflation of prices, but these were relatively unsuccessful, except for such drastic measures as the closure of shops and arrest of a number of European shopkeepers. Prices were stabilized finally only by competition with large metropolitan retail chains such as *Galéries Lafayette*, *Monoprix* and *Printania*, which opened branches in Dakar at this time.

In 1954, after the defeat of the French at Dien Bien Phu, there was a temporary and unfounded fear that many French traders, shopkeepers and settlers fleeing from Indo-China would invade Dakar and the other cities of the Federation. Most of the post-colonial transfer from Indo-China to West Africa after 1954 was in fact of capital and not of people. It meant mainly that large commercial houses like OPTORG redirected their interests towards the West African market. Those Frenchmen from Indo-China who did come to benefit from the expanding markets of West Africa went mainly to

---

[1] Institut de Science Economique Appliquée, *Les Industries du Cap Vert: Analyse d'un Ensemble des Industries Legères de l'Afrique Occidentale*, Dakar, 1964, pp. 10–15, and André Hauser, *Facteurs Humains Affectant la Productivité des Travailleurs Industriels du Cap Vert* (also distributed by I.S.E.A.), Dakar, 1963, pp. 68–9.
[2] V. Thompson and R. Adloff, *French West Africa*, Stanford, Stanford University Press, 1958, p. 248.

Employment

Abidjan, the capital of the Ivory Coast, where there were better long-range economic possibilities at this time than in Dakar.

The alteration in the European employment structure in Senegal after 1945 was not only a reflection of local economic prosperity—it contributed substantially to it. European labour was readily available in the decade following the war and essential to contractors and businessmen in Senegal because of the absence of local skills and facilities for training. The chief advantage of overseas employment for the French labourer was that wages were as high as four times the rate for equivalent work in Europe. In order to give a return to the employer on the payment of such high wages, skilled labourers were chosen in fields they already knew well, given rapid training for the tropics, and often organized into work camps where they remained for about twenty months. Not unlike the recruitment of expatriate mining staff in central Africa or that of labourers for timber companies in French Equatorial Africa, this pattern of recruitment was entirely new to West Africa, and was retained only for the limited prosperity of this period. Many of the labourers were Italian in origin and had been recruited after seeking work permits in France. Despite the high cost of European labour, employers claimed that they were well worth the price, as they were 'ten to twelve times superior in time and cost' to local labour.[1]

The slow pace of Africanization in the civil service seemed at times even more dramatic. Difficulty of entry had long remained a source of grievance for the educated élite, who turned to other professions. And while the lower echelons of the civil service in the neighbouring British territories (including such posts as clerk, typist and book-keeper) were being rapidly Africanized, the opposite was true in French West Africa. Mercier summed it up as follows: 'rather than a progressive Africanization of the upper echelons, there had been (sic.) a Europeanization of the lower echelons'.[2]

Trade unions were organized on separate racial lines, for

[1] Paul Humbolt, 'L'Immigration Européenne en Afrique Tropicale', *L'Afrique Française*, April 1952, p. 6.
[2] Paul Mercier, *op. cit.*, p. 136.

The Petit Blanc

the interests, grievances and demands of Frenchmen and Africans were entirely different. Only one major European union which was active in Dakar had African members, the *Conféderation Générale des Travailleurs (Parti Communiste)*, and those Europeans who were members in France therefore often switched their allegiance on arrival to the white-dominated *Force Ouvrière* (S.F.I.O.).[1] A combined union of European employees from all branches of the private sector existed at least nominally since 1884, and was revived in 1952, although it was decidedly a company union whose role in defending employee interests was insignificant. There were a few local union organizers who had been active in France and were interested in initiating serious union activity in Senegal, but these efforts were often forestalled by employers who could send troublesome employees to a company branch in some other part of the Federation, a technique also used by the administration for potential political agitators. European union activities remained of very minor importance and had very little impact on labour relations. Europeans in Senegal were not much interested in union membership, protests or strikes, for they had far greater earning power than their colleagues in France and were aware that they could be fairly readily replaced from the reservoir of available labour in Europe. In addition to this, most expatriates were under very lucrative contracts which were negotiated and signed in France and therefore not subject to review. Those who were not under contract were intimidated by the availability of local European job-hunters.

The advantages for Europeans in the colonies included not only high salaries, but assured upward employment mobility. A labourer from France almost automatically became a works overseer or a foreman, and those with even the most limited technical qualifications were sometimes absorbed into management. A European regardless of his type of employment would have some African aides or apprentices, which for many provided their first post of command in the organization. The

[1] André Hauser, 'Quelques Relations des Travailleurs de l'Industrie à leur Travail en A.O.F. (Senegal, Soudan, Guinee),' *Bulletin de L'Institut Français d'Afrique Noire*, XVII, Series B, 1955, pp. 138-9.

Employment

resentment of articulate Africans was aroused by this assured employment mobility: 'Europeans who in Europe only belong to the middle class constitute a privileged group here, whether they are in the administration or the private sector.'[1] A certain rate of upward job mobility could be directly attributed to skin colour.

That Europeans in Senegal had a privileged employment position relative not only to the African majority, but to the equivalent metropolitan population, is indicated by their educational qualifications. At the level of technical and university education, expatriate achievement was much higher than the overall average in metropolitan France, as one might expect. On the other hand, however, 55 per cent of the local European group were without any diploma at all or had only a primary school certificate in 1955, which for an expatriate population in a non-settler territory was a remarkably high proportion (see Table 1, p. 90).

Despite the extensive recruitment of European skilled labour, the basic outline of the occupational structure of Dakar remained a typically colonial one: Europeans monopolized all the managerial and most of the salaried posts, while unskilled employment was reserved entirely for Africans (see Table 2, p. 91). The rise in the number of European skilled labourers did not in any case go unchecked until the end of the decade. There seems to have been a high point about 1955 when 15·5 per cent of Europeans employed were classified as workers and artisans, after which the relative importance of the group dropped slightly.[2] The immediacy of the demand for skilled labour, especially in the building industry, did not give sufficient time for developing the local labour market through training. And employers wanted labour where they could be sure of the market and quality, which meant France, not Dakar.

---

[1] Assane Seck, 'La Formation d'une Class Moyenne en Afrique Occidentale Française', *Institut des Civilisations Différentes, Compte Rendu* de la XXIX Session, London, 1955, published at Brussels, 1956, p. 161. Above all the elite wanted equal pay for equal work, which was accorded at least officially for administrative posts by the *Loi Lamine Guèye* of 1950, although it was never entirely effective and never fully applied.

[2] Rép. du Sénégal, Ministère du Plan, *Recensement... Dakar*, 1955, 2ème Fasc., Table B.17, p. 23 annex.

The Petit Blanc

A caricature (symbolic of the period) would have been the African holding the ladder for the window washer, or the pail for the European mason. Employers found it useful to make it known to their clientele that they had European employees working for them: 'Service provided by Europeans', or 'Exclusively European Work' were openly advertised, and with obvious favourable response.

By the second half of the decade the construction boom which had initiated much of the prosperity had subsided. A few investors felt that the growing African political agitation was becoming disquieting and withdrew their capital and returned to France. Above all, however, the first dip in the business situation seemed to indicate to employers that it would soon be necessary for reason of economy to replace Europeans in many posts with Africans. In 1955, it was noted that the cost of the high standard of living required by Europeans, together with the added benefits of free lodgings, furnishings, and transportation could no longer be justified by the economics of the business situation.[1] Yet from 1955 to 1959 there was only a 1·4 per cent improvement in the ratio of Africans to the total working population, and most of these remained confined to the lowest grades of employment—unskilled labourer and apprentice.[2] The global employment figures for this period indicate only the extent of Europeanization; the more subtle and complex problems which this engendered are to be found in a differentiation of the employment structure. Working relationships had to be considered against a matrix of attitudes, which often inhibited the development of positive interaction on the basis of skill, capacity and competence alone. Thus there were two dimensions to consider in relations between white overseer and black labourer, white executive and black clerk, or less frequently, colleagues of each racial group. There was actually a slightly increased Europeanization in all echelons of work above unskilled labour from 1955 to 1959.

Unemployment among Europeans was virtually unknown during the decade, while unemployment of African men

[1] André Hauser, 'Quelques Relations...', *B.I.F.A.N.*, *op. cit.*, p. 138.
[2] See Rép. du Sénégal, Ministère du Plan, *Recensement Démographique de Dakar*, 1955, 2ème Fasc., p. 23 annex.

between the ages of twenty and sixty in Dakar remained at a steady average of 25 per cent.[1] Full-employment among Europeans extended to wives who managed and were employed in shops, or were employed by the big companies and the administration as typists, clerks and secretaries. There were 2,000 European women who filled such posts in 1955[2] in Dakar, and while this labour source was readily available, there was no incentive to provide training for Africans to replace them. Thus at the same time as Standard Seven boys in Nigeria and Ghana were absorbed into a skilled or semi-skilled employment structure as typists and clerks, these important posts remained the nearly exclusive reserve of European women in Senegal (and did so until well after independence).

The presence of Europeans in a wide range of jobs during the nineteen-fifties either prevented Africans from being hired, or restricted the number of skills which the African labour-force could acquire. It is difficult to assess the amount of African unemployment which could actually have been attributed to competition with Europeans, for other factors such as lack of skills, illiteracy, and an unusually inflated rural exodus to the cities kept the rate quite high. Competition was particularly evident at two distinct levels and phases: the skilled labourers and clerks, especially early in the decade, and executive and technical posts, especially in the years approaching independence.

The increase of the white population from 1945 to 1955 substantially increased at least the potential for competitive situations between white and African and raised the pitch of racial tension. The existence of this potentially competitive situation was not necessarily understood spontaneously by all those Africans who were disappointed with the employment opportunities. But it was brought to their attention through political movements or demonstrations based on anti-white sentiment which were organized for the first time in Senegal. African militants criticized the administration for not providing sufficient technical schools in Senegal, and for thus permitting

[1] *Ibid.*, Table B.2, p. 17 annex.
[2] *Ibid.*, p. 65.

The Petit Blanc

the wage benefits of the economic boom to go mainly to Europeans.

One could certainly not speak of a colour-bar in Dakar at this period, although the ambiguity of the situation only added fuel to the flames of African resentment. A colour-bar, as practised in Southern Africa, legally restricts and therefore abolishes racial competition at the level of employment. In Senegal multi-racialism and assimilation were still the prevailing basis of colonial policy at least in the communes. Yet, European employers were reluctant to place Africans in positions in which they would exercise the same responsibility alongside Europeans. Although there had been successive reforms of wage rates in French West Africa, in this period, equal pay for equal work did not in practice apply to Africans and Europeans alike. Expatriate contracts, which were not affected by this legislation, were still calculated at an inflated rate. And for those Frenchmen employed locally in the same type of job as an African, discriminatory wage rates were maintained for a time by simply calling the post by a different name. The situation in which an African was in a position of authority over a European was totally unacceptable. It was avoided equally in the administration and in the business sector, although the necessity of placing Africans with university degrees in positions of at least nominal responsibility was recognized.

The commercial sector showed the highest resistance to Africanization, including even the large trading companies, in which European predominance remained unchanged. In the building industry, on the other hand, of a total of 4,140 employees in 1955, 96·1 per cent were African, a similar ratio to that of the transport sector.[1] Here again, the global figures do not tell the entire story. The bulk of these African employees were, of course, unskilled or barely skilled. There was an attempt to redress this through the introduction of an apprenticeship system in a number of sectors of employment throughout French West Africa, but it remained very limited in scope because employers were unwilling to underwrite the

[1] République du Sénégal, Ministère du Plan, *Recensement*... *Dakar*, Table B.18, p. 23 annex.

cost of the system, and the small number of apprentices who were hired were paid so little that they often became discouraged and left the job before they were fully trained.[1]

Outside the official apprenticeship system, the training of African employees was done most un-systematically. Apprentices were often taken on as 'servants' to skilled labourers and were never given a chance to learn the trade. There was a large amount of underemployment through redundancy of African labourers. What could not be achieved by a single sufficiently trained person, was left to a quantity of poorly paid individuals who were often employed by the day or job or only during peak periods. While the administration had lent some official support to Africanization in the private sector, its efforts made only marginal impact.

One of the chief obstacles to promoting a competent African labour force was that the European overseer himself usually consciously resisted directing (or simply did not know how to direct or train) his working team. As already mentioned, for many, this was their first post of authority or command. Resistance to adquate training on the job can be explained not only by the fear of African advancement and the desire of the Frenchman to retain his job, but by the difficulty of communication across racial, cultural and linguistic lines.[2] Thus the absence of skilled Africans owing to the available supply of European labour was compounded by the difficulty of training Africans on the job, leaving Senegal at the time of independence and afterwards with a critical shortage of trained or well-trained African personnel, and the consequent need for continued dependence on expatriate direction.

---

[1] V. Thompson and R. Adloff, *op. cit.*, p. 496.

[2] André Hauser comments: 'A major inconvenience of using European personnel is that they have adapted insufficiently to ambivalent conditions. The European supervisor is not prepared to play the role of educator. Certain of them just hold on to their positions without even very much aptitude for their vocation.' 'Quelques Relations...', *B.I.F.A.N.*, *op. cit.*, p. 139.

Appendix to Chapter Three

Letter from an 'Old Colonial' in Dakar to the Governor-General in thanks for the award of political office, 1941, from Archives du Sénégal, Dakar.

L'AUTO GARNITURE
Manufacture Générale de Sellerie et Garniture d'Automobile

LOUIS CONTIVAL
6, Rue Bérenger-Feraud, Dakar (Sénégal)
Inventeur de 'l'Universelle Chappe'
Fournisseur des Administrations civiles et militaires Diplomé des Hautes Récompenses aux Concours Professionels
2 Médailles d'argent grand module—Diplôme d'honneur
Dakar, 24 October 1941

The Governor-General of French West Africa
High Commission of French Africa-Dakar

High Commissioner:
I take pleasure in thanking you for having designated me to take part in the Municipal Council of our great and beautiful town of Dakar.

The confidence which you have just accorded to me permits me to assure you that, as in the past, I shall endeavour to merit it, and you can trust in my Patriotism to be worthy of the honour with which you have just, once again provided me.

I SWEAR TO YOU HERE that with me you do not have to deal with a doubtful Frenchman: But indeed with a pure Frenchman, a stubborn Potevin (his region of origin) and proud to be French 100%.

I am the eldest son of a family of poor farmers of which the father died a victim of duty, having perished in a fire as a volunteer fireman, when I was only 9 years old, I was able, after receiving my primary school certificate, to leave an

Letter from an 'Old Colonial'

apprenticeship and to make a beautiful tour of France, which I did in part on foot by working at TOURS, ANGERS, NANTES, LA ROCHELLE, BORDEAUX, TOULOUSE, MONTPELIER, and MARSEILLE, which I left in November 1897 for TUNISIA, and after that I became and remained AFRICAN, and it was in March 1916 that I arrived at Dakar as a soldier, and I remained to create the industry which I profess since and without taking any leave.

I have until today taken only 10 MONTHS of leave in 45 YEARS of the COLONIES of North Africa and West Africa, IN WHICH 4 months were in Tunisia and six months were here.

Which proves to you, that in leading a reasonable life, it is possible for a European to persist, while working in this country which is supposed to be depressing.

It is not the climate that is depressing, it is alcohol and its various companions of other voluntary imprudences.

To resist, one must avoid the abuses which empty the pocket, the health. Go to bed early, get up early, don't drink or smoke and do as I, never go to the Cinema. In my case, I have never been to the talking Cinema, even though there was one installed just near my home.

My own distractions are my animals and birds in the midst of which I live, since my wife and I sleep on camp beds, installed each evening in our court.

Here you have our life of real colonials which it is very easy to copy, in such a way that savings and benefits follow.

My wife is Bressane and is aged 65, and I am Poitevin and aged 63 years, we have neither a cook nor a 'boy' and do everything ourselves. We were married in 1904 in front of the Consul of France at Bizerte where we lost two sons who died in Tunisia.

Here I live secluded, doing my duty as a man, a colonial, a merchant, a worker, a citizen and a FRENCHMAN.

Would you please forgive M. Governor-General my long expose and allow me to assure you of my most respectful sentiments.

(signed) M. Louis Contival

TABLE I

Education of the Non-African Population of Dakar, 1955*
(compared with the total in Metropolitan France)

Standard of Education	Total	ORIGIN		
		Other Eurs. French	Lebanese	Met. France
Primary School certificate	28·0	30·1	13·6	43
Secondary School-elementary level	14·3	15·9	3·2	3·7
Secondary School-*Baccalauréat*	12·3	13·7	2·2	2·5
University degree	5·7	6·5	0·4	1·6
Technical College diploma	5·3	6·2	0·3	5·2
Other diplomas	2·7	3·0	0·4	0· not known
No formal education	31·7	24·6	79·9	49
	100	100	100	100

* Based on a percentage of the groups in question adapted from a table in *Recensement Démographique de Dakar* (1955), Résultats Définitifs: 1er Fascicule, 1958, pp. 60, 62.

TABLE 2

Categories of Employment, by Origin (Men only)

DAKAR, 1955

Category	ORIGIN						DISTRIBUTION, per 100 PEOPLE				
	Africans		Non-Africans		Total		Of same origin, acc. to category		Of same category, acc. origin.		
	No.	%	No.	%	No.	%	Af.	Non Af.	Af.	Non Af.	Total
Employers, Directors, Managers, Senior Civil Servants	1,169	1·5	4,678	6·0	5,847	7·5	2·0	40·0	20·0	80·0	100·0
Small Entrepreneurs, Foremen, Overseers, Clerks, Secretaries, Accountants	16,764	21·5	3,508	4·5	20,272	26·0	25·0	30·0	82·5	17·5	100·0
Skilled Workers, Artisans, Soldiers, Domestic Servants	30,408	39·0	2,339	3·0	32,747	42·0	46·0	20·0	93·0	7·0	100·0
Unskilled Workers, Apprentices	17,933	23·0	1,169	1·5	19,102	24·5	27·0	10·0	94·0	6·0	100·0
TOTAL	66,274	85·0	11,694	15·0	77,968	100·0	100·0	100·0	85·0	15·0	100·0

* Adapted from Table B.24, *Recensement Démographique de Dakar*, 1955, Résultats Définitifs, 2ème Fascicule, Paris, 1962, p. 26 annex.

4. Race Relations, Politics and Decolonization, 1945-1960

Following the separation of European and African residential areas in Dakar at the beginning of this century, neighbourhoods tended to remain racially defined: the Plateau was more than 80 per cent white, while the Medina remained an African ghetto. Some mixed quarters of African, Lebanese and European residents grew up between these areas owing to the rapid rise in the urban population during and after the war (map p. 94). But even at the peak of the housing shortage in this period, a newly arrived European family preferred to live in a garage on the Plateau rather than a stone house on the edge of the Medina. In addition to the health and sanitary concerns of an earlier period, there was at this time an additional reason why newly arrived European residents felt compelled to separate themselves from the black majority—because they felt a greater need, consciously or unconsciously, to reinforce white solidarity and status.

The only exceptions to the prevailing situation of racial separation in the social sphere were certain political associations, religious groups and clubs. Their participants usually included middle-class students and intellectuals, a small element of the total population. Because they were in such a minority among their own race, African university students returning from France often sought the company of Europeans of similar intellectual background and interests, although owing to the political preoccupations of the period they usually restricted their choice to those few Europeans who were sympathetic to African nationalism. The older generation of the black and *métis* élite, the lawyers and politicians of the colony, maintained contact with a select group of European friends in France and Senegal throughout this period; their own high status would have kept them from seeking contact with most local Europeans.

Integrated social activities did, however, remain marginal to the dominant pattern of separation.

Personal inter-dependence, of the type achieved between black and white when the European minority was very small, had been considerably affected by the domestication of French life in the nineteen-thirties. Liaisons between white men and black women became important again during the war and during the period of heavy labour recruitment from 1945 to 1955, but such relationships tended to be casual and never acquired the legitimacy and status which were awarded to them during the period of the *métissage* and assimilation in the early days of the colony. One unhappy result of these liaisons was the frequent abandonment of the mulatto children by those who fathered them. The support of these children became a significant social problem, as they were sometimes also abandoned by the mother or turned out by the mother's family. (While childbirth out of wedlock is not usually a cause of rejection from African society, a half-caste child was quite often not given the same consideration.)[1] In the nineteenth century, a white man's responsibility for his bastard children was a part of the colonial ethos. Continuing this tradition in the first decades of the twentieth century, those mulatto children who had been fathered by high-ranking army or colonial officers were supported and educated in a privately endowed orphanage in Dakar. After the Second World War, the responsibility for black mistresses or bastard children was no longer considered important. This can perhaps be explained by significant changes in the composition of the European minority itself: the rapid increase of its male population, recruitment among people of generally lower socio-economic status, and the brevity of overseas employment. Liaisons with African mistresses were no longer regarded as socially acceptable by local Europeans, and the accidental offspring of such liaisons were kept in well-guarded secrecy.

Alterations in the relationship between white and black in this period could be attributed not only to the increased size and domestication of white society, but also to the progressive

[1] Interview with a doctor at the psychiatric research institute at Fann (Dakar) who did some work with an orphanage in Dakar, March 1967.

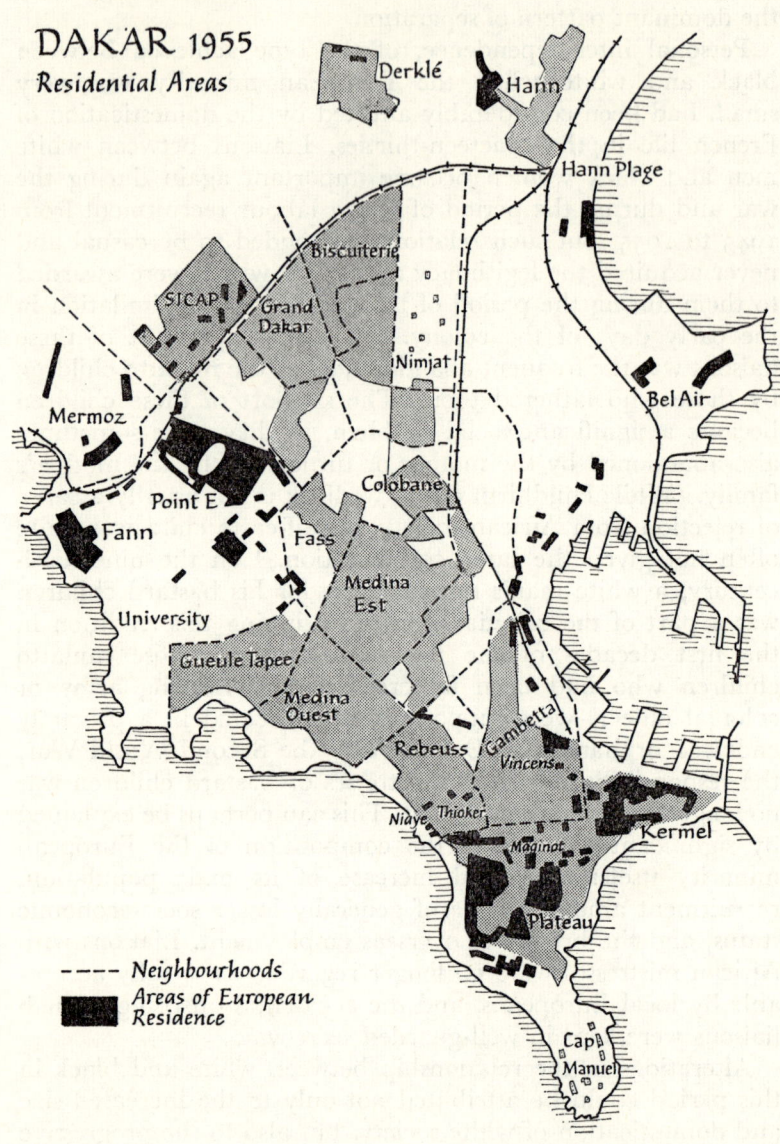

disintegration of a well-defined structure of interaction between them: the colonial relationship was changing. A certain type of relatively close personal interaction was perhaps possible within a strictly prescribed social framework such as that found in Senegal in an earlier period, particularly in the relations between peasant and trading agent, employee and company executive, and master and faithful servant. Although within a paternalistic framework, such relationships could be the basis of mutual understanding and a certain measure of personal intimacy. From the close of the war, however, tension began to be generated by the gradual breakdown of the previously accepted framework of interaction between the races. The colonial relationship was brought into question by the fact that the assumption of African inferiority and European superiority could hardly any longer be made with assurance chiefly because the growing European minority included a significant sub-group of people of low class and status at a time when the number of educated or skilled Africans was increasing. Hence, earlier racial stereotypes were no longer appropriate.

The European of relatively low class and status, however, the newcomer, the *petit blanc*, the economically marginal

---

European Residential Areas of Dakar, 1955

The *Plateau* area is composed mainly of large multiple dwellings, built chiefly during the post-war building boom. *Kermel* which is the oldest European residential area in Dakar is dominated by old style sprawling colonial houses with verandas and courtyards, which by 1955 were in a fairly poor state of repair. The areas of scattered European dwellings along the east coast of Dakar (*Bel Air* and *Hann*) are choice sea-front properties. Both *Fann* and *Point E* are post-war developments which are exclusively European and dominated by luxurious single dwellings. It is in this area that most of the company directors and executives and high-ranking civil servants live. S.I.C.A.P. (*Société Immobilière du Cap Vert*) is a semi-private construction company with lucrative government licence for building and town planning. It was started in the early nineteen-fifties, and provides a range of moderately priced to cheap single dwellings and flats. In this period, only a few Europeans had begun to move into the housing estate, although more did after 1960.

Because of the housing shortage in 1955, Europeans spread into mixed areas just off the Plateau (*Maginot*, *Niaye*, *Thoiker* and *Vincens*) which had chiefly Lebanese and African residents. These sectors had multiple and private dwellings, with nearly all street level space taken up by shops.

employee felt the most pressing need to cling to the former stereotype of African inferiority, as if to reassure himself that his status was measured on an entirely different scale.[1] Newcomers expressed their need to win the approval and respect of fellow-Europeans by demonstrating their willingness to conform to the prescribed limits of racial antipathy they thought expected by the established order.[2] This included an attempt to deny the distinction between the African élite and non-élite by asserting that all blacks were the same. Disapproving of those 'who tried to imitate whites', newcomers and *petits blancs* preferred the *bons nègres* who knew their place.[3] For those Europeans who needed, for whatever social or psychological reason, to cling to the former stereotypes of the African, a trip from the centres of rapid social change and racial tension in the cities to the rural areas could still in this period provide a comforting experience: the unquestioned superiority of the white man and the deference of the peasant could reassure him of the remaining viability of his point of view. The opportunities for contact

[1] In a study conducted in the United States which sought to examine critically the thesis that social mobility and prejudice were directly related, the authors demonstrated that it was not necessarily mobility which predicted prejudice: 'Status-seeking groups tend to be more prejudiced, regardless of mobility history; and the greatest prejudice is found among those who are status-minded. . . .' F. Silberstein and H. Seeman, 'Social Mobility and Prejudice', *American Journal of Sociology*, 65, 3 Nov. 1959, p. 261.

[2] What is particularly interesting about this is that while the separation of the races had been expected by the established order, antipathy had not been expected until the changing structure and attitudes of Europeans had made it a prevailing sentiment. New arrivals might have no *a priori* negative feelings about Africans, but antipathetic attitudes among colleagues ('getting to know the colonies') might demand this, or at least provide a reserve explanation if things went wrong, as they often did for those with too high expectations for their future in Africa. This was also true in the Copperbelt towns of Northern Rhodesia in the early nineteen-fifties. Newcomers to the mining companies were chastised for their initial friendliness to Africans. Because of their disappointment in not being accepted, they went to the other extreme. Thus while a white clerk in his first week of work offered an African fellow-worker a cigarette, two weeks later he was calling Africans 'dumb monkeys'. Hortense Powdermaker, *Copper Town: Changing Africa*, New York, Harper and Row, 1962, p. 72.

[3] In addition to those respondents who characterized '*bons nègres*' as traditionalists, and those who were 'friends of France', and *mauvais nègres* as those *évolués* who were anti-French, a number of Mercier's respondents felt that all blacks had the deficiencies, faults and incapacities which merited them in the classic image of the 'big child'. P. Mercier, *op. cit.*, p. 115.

beyond the cities were limited, however, since the sources of white employment were almost entirely urban-based.

How did the European, faced with the breakdown of colonial stereotype, come to terms with the changing social structure? Some adapted grudgingly to the new state of affairs, avoiding, where possible, confrontation with the problem. Others, whose hostility was more deeply rooted, tried to cling even more desperately to the negative stereotype or partly to transfer hostility to the Lebanese.[1] One should not, of course, look only to psycho-social factors for an explanation of antipathy to Africans—there were also concrete economic and political factors which contributed to it. African political demands were being given favourable attention by the administration, while many local Frenchmen who were trying to assure their future in Africa felt that they were not getting a fair hearing,[2] and were going to be abandoned by France.

Those Europeans in more secure business or professional positions were less susceptible to the anxieties of the newcomers about their future, and did not feel so readily the need to ignore the differences between categories of Africans. While the changes in status and attitudes of the African urban élite may have occasionally given rise to alarm among local whites, the most secure among them could afford to accept these alterations in colonial society with a minimum of difficulty.[3]

The older African élite who had secure status and position could also afford to ignore the racial tension generated by the changing social structure and attitudes of Europeans—except where useful for political purposes. They would have had little contact, in any case, with low-status whites who tried to deny

[1] 'The refusal to adapt or at least make an effort towards rudimentary adaptation to the new situation prevailed—which gave rise to aggressive compensatory reactions.' P. Mercier, *ibid.*, p. 146.

[2] In particular, the juridical transformations in this period made some Europeans feel that they were being discriminated against. *Les Echos* repeatedly carried reports of 'injustices' to whites at the labour exchange (13 February 1952) and the courts (3 March 1963).

[3] The crucial factor may have been that the secure middle-class whites did not necessarily owe their status to residence in the colony, coming from a roughly similar class background in France. Certainly their distaste for the behaviour of the more marginal white elements in Dakar towards blacks is apparent in the vigorous outbursts concerning the solidarity of whites among their lower class compatriots.

their position and importance in the social structure. It was the younger generation who felt more directly the hostility and racial tension which contributed in large measure to these anti-French feelings.

The alterations in class and status among the French population brought into question the superiority of the white man. Africans now saw whites in jobs, sometimes rather menial, which had never before been filled by a white man. And white superiority came further into doubt over the real or imagined competition with Frenchmen for jobs. Although actual competition only affected a very small proportion of the African unemployed, this became a very useful political issue for those in the independence movement.

> The importance of Africanization is obvious. The whole of the Administration and of Industry are in the hands of foreign elements to this country, who are indifferent to its needs and its future.[1]

Although most anti-French protests were made in terms of the local situation and the local political and labour structure, they were also perhaps influenced by broader world movements, especially independence in the Third World, and general ideological trends making all Africans less willing to accept the assignment to an inferior role.

An attempt has been made (in the context of Madagascar) to explain the rejection by the blacks of notions of white superiority in psychological terms.[2] The first stage of this argument rests on the assumption of innate dependence of the African personality, which is held to be generated in traditional society and transferred to the European colonizer. As a participant in an industrial society, the European is supposed to misunderstand the African demand for personal dependence, which generates resentment, and hence nationalism. Although this may be a suggestive thesis, it has few explanatory powers in the context of Senegal. The drive to nationalism in this

[1] Article signed by K. Sall, *La Lutte*, 26 October 1957.
[2] O. Mannoni, *Prospero and Caliban: The Psychology of Colonialism*, London, Methuen, 1956. His position could be described as psychological reductionism, since he explains the colonial relationship (which involves economic, social and political referents) in psychological terms only.

context was generated in the urban areas, wherein real economic or political grievances were translated into organizational terms. Anti-white feeling which was sometimes concomitant with nationalism was found among those who, having once absorbed the idea that they were entitled to equality of respect, and finding reinforcement for this idea in the changes in the relative positions of blacks and whites in the occupational hierarchy, began actually to demand that equality of respect.

Certain cafés, restaurants, bars and nightclubs directly or indirectly tried to ensure an exclusively European clientele. But greater effort was now required to maintain the physical separation of races than before the war, when Africans 'knew their place'. The majority of the urban African population was still either prohibited by standard of living or uninterested in any case in patronizing these places. A few young Senegalese did, however, try to invade these exclusive European reserves. It was soon made implicitly clear by the behaviour of the white owner, employees and clients that they had crossed an accepted barrier and were unwanted.[1]

The columns of *Les Echos* during this period reflected the potentially tense racial situation and recorded a series of incidents which exemplified it. At the same time as it was trying to cultivate an African audience, by giving large coverage to Muslim observances, and running African beauty contests, it rejected complaints concerning the derogatory use of the word '*nègre*' in its columns.[2] It admonished white shopkeepers for racist attitudes and for addressing African clients with the disrespectful '*tu*', and young 'lay-abouts' (*zazous*) for stealing from African street-sellers (*bana-banas*). Yet at the same time it viewed with alarm and recorded in detail insults to whites and anti-white occurrences. It complained about the 'unreasonable' protection given to African 'boys' (stewards) who did not do their work properly. It commented on racial hatred among young Africans, who wrote anti-white slogans on the

[1] Paul Mercier in Hauser, Massé, Mercier, eds., *L'Agglomération Dakaroise*, I.F.A.N., Etudes Sénégalaises No. 5, St. Louis du Sénégal, 1954, p. 19. An official protest to the government was made by a left-wing political party in Dakar, which presented a list of restaurants and cafés where properly dressed Africans were refused service, *Le Réveil*, No. 2, 1947, p. 1.
[2] 3–9 February 1951 and 1 January 1952.

walls, attributing their incitement to the new generation of political activists. It frequently recorded anti-white proclamations made at party meetings and anti-white petitions which circulated in the Medina.[1] And although it continually requested that the administration 'do something' about this, officialdom preferred to remain silent on such matters, not wishing to provoke a response from the African majority in the potentially volatile political atmosphere of the time.

The younger members of the political parties, especially students returning from France provided the most vigorous attack on the resident French minority in the context of more general demands for jobs, equality and power:

> The class struggle manifests itself not between the middle class and the African masses, but between all Africans and all Europeans. The social problems double here for racial problems, in spite of the infiltration of a few Blacks—very few in number—into the privileged reserve of Europeans.[2]

These younger members of the élite were willing to use racialism as a political tool not because they were 'incompletely assimilated', as in the image of Shakespeare's Caliban:

> You taught me language and my profit on't
> Is, I know how to curse....

but because they wanted jobs and a stake in the political order. In 1954 Senghor, who was then Deputy for Senegal in the French National Assembly, warned that 'one must not forget the aspirations of the rising generation, who express themselves with the utmost clarity on their return from studies in France. If a programme is not proposed to them as voters, one must fear the presentation of a group of demands which will be much more radical'.[3] The new generation were willing to use racism as a

---

[1] 24–30 October 1955. Some of these were probably fictional, as they were attributed to such unlikely racists as Lamine Guèye.

[2] Assane Seck, 'Face aux Problèmes Sociaux de l'A.O.F.', *Réalités Africaines*, No. 18, 17 August 1956, pp. 1–2.

[3] From a commentator who also added that Senghor felt that education could no longer prevent nationalism from growing and that this younger group might be less inclined than he towards Franco-African harmony. K. E. Robinson, 'Senegal: the Elections to the Territorial Assembly, March 1957', in W. J. M. Mackenzie and K. E. Robinson (Eds.), *Five Elections in Africa*, Oxford, The Clarendon Press, 1964, p. 323.

political tool unlike the older Senegalese political leaders who remained largely silent on the matter. The latter group owed their exclusive élite positions to the success of assimilation, and had been able to rise above racial obloquy. They had a stake in the existing order and the denial of racial conflict. If change were necessary, they favoured a very gradual variety, although they found themselves eventually lagging behind prevailing political ideas in the rest of French West Africa.[1]

The European reaction to the nationalist appeal which engendered anti-white feeling was varied. Certain independent businessmen withdrew their investments, fearing a forced exodus. The upper echelons of the business community and those in the administration were much more confident, however, that the trusted leadership of Senghor and Lamine Guèye would bring Senegal to a 'moderate' independence followed by continued co-operation with France. This racial tension, they felt, only punctuated (rather unfortunately) the gradual path to independence. Their assessment of the situation was correct.

Frenchmen in Senegal did not express their dissatisfaction with local events by exercising their political rights. Throughout this time, and although counselled from all quarters to participate in elections, the majority of the Europeans remained apathetic to politics as they had for decades before. Only a few hundred participated in territorial elections, and about 5 per cent of the total in the election for deputy.[2] *Les Echos* maintained its anti-socialist campaign and somewhat reluctantly urged Europeans to vote for Senghor in order to prevent 'the Arab League, dangerous to the stability of North Africa, from establishing itself here.'[3] A more active European Senghor supporter, André Peytavin, wrote on the eve of the elections in March 1957:

[1] As late as 1958, in Cotonou, Dahomey, both Senghor and Guèye voted against a resolution supporting the independence of French West Africa, although it passed the conference. R. Schacter Morgenthau, *Political Parties in French-Speaking West Africa*, Oxford, The Clarendon Press, 1964, p. 162.

[2] Estimated by Paul Bonifay, who kept the records of European voting registration for the Municipality of Dakar when he was Deputy-Mayor. Communicated personally in December 1966.

[3] Cited in *Les Echos*, 'Au Bon Blanc qui ne fait pas de Politique', 2 March 1952, pp. 1–2.

> We Europeans have to try to create a spirit of Eur-african co-operation—promote economic co-operation. This promotion cannot exist except in a new political climate. We cannot remain deaf to the frequent call of African leaders for us to participate in the political life of their countries ... In our interests, those of *métropolitain* and African, we must show our solidarity.[1]

It was only a small group of political activists, however, who adhered to the idea of a multi-racial union in Senegal.

Solidarity with a colonized people seeking independence would of course have been unthinkable to most of the white minority. Even recruitment among registered communist voters was impossible, partly because their participation in the colonial system had altered their political views. A European party militant of the P.C.F. in Senegal summarized it as follows:

> In France they lived in modest surroundings and voted Communist. In the colonies they were most anti-communist in their behaviour. The conditions of life placed them in a relatively superior position—and this changed their mentality entirely. They had 'boys' to do domestic work. A butcher's boy from France became the head of a workshop in the Public Works department.
>
> Thrust for the first time into positions of authority, they quickly developed a *petit bourgeois* mentality. They returned to France as *petits bourgeois* and remained so in their political expression. They never voted Communist again.[2]

Although such a proposition has never been tested empirically, nor indeed have any of the French returning from the colonies been asked about their change in political attitudes, the tendency for upward mobility to correlate with more conservative voting behaviour is familiar to political sociologists.[3]

Europeans served in Senegalese municipal and territorial assemblies both before and after independence, not necessarily

---

[1] 'Les Européens Doivent Voter', *Afrique Nouvelle* (liberal Catholic newspaper in Dakar), March 1957, p. 1.

[2] Interview with Guy Etcheverry, an active participant in left-wing movements in French West Africa, Dakar, April 1967.

[3] See for example the work of R. Centers, *The Psychology of Social Classes*, Princeton University Press, 1949, pp. 56–64.

because of their skills or even of pressure from France, but in order to include those with real economic power in these local bodies.¹ The political groups open to Europeans at this time took varied account of specifically European interests or included the demands of local businessmen in their programme. The Socialist Party (S.F.I.O.) had not been dominated by European interests since its early years, although Paul Bonifay remained a party leader and Lamine Guèye's chief lieutenant. The national office of the S.F.I.O. in Paris tried to retain a vaguely multi-racial outlook. It warned Africans, for example, that they 'must learn to live with the *petits blancs* they criticize, for they were overseas in support of the French Union'.² The *Parti Socialiste Sénégalais* was a breakaway from the S.F.I.O. which accused the latter of 'racism' because it did not support a separate European candidate for local business interests.³ Under the leadership of Charles Graziani, it was regarded locally as a *toubab* (white man's) party, a not unjustified label. It was composed of a few local Frenchmen, who formed curious alliances with any African minority faction, in the hope, perhaps, of better defending their investments and thus promoting a secure future in Senegal.

There were a few European members of the Marxist *Rassemblement Démocratique Africain* (R.D.A.). These included Guy Etcheverry, their newspaper editor, the historian Jean Suret-Canale, and a small group of lycee and university teachers in Dakar who had been active in left-wing politics in France, and whose attitudes and activities cut them off entirely from contact with the local European minority.

The *Bloc Démocratique Sénégalais*, Senghor's party, was built on mass support from the countryside, yet included a number of European businessmen whose presence reflected Senghor's idea of multi-racial co-operation—*le dialogue*. These men had the foresight to finance party activities and to remain personally loyal to him up through the move towards independence. They were appropriately rewarded by office or other favours after 1959. One rather unusual example was André Peytavin,

¹ See P. Guillemin, 'La Structure des Premiers Gouvernements Locaux en Afrique Noire', *Revue Française de Science Politique*, Vol. IX, No. 3, September 1959, pp. 682–3.
² *Bulletin Interieur du Parti Socialiste*, June 1955, No. 56, p. 8.
³ *Clarté*, No. 73, November 1965.

who became the first Minister of Finance in the Senegalese Republic. He was recruited to the B.D.S. by Senghor in 1957 because, among other things, he controlled a group of votes which were crucial to an election in the *Grand Conseil* of French West Africa and, in consequence, to Senghor's political career. Another was Robert Delmas, director of the well-established Delmas family enterprises who was taken into the B.D.S. as a symbol of Senghor's willingness to co-operate with local business interests. Although Delmas had not been active in politics locally, he was respected by Senghor for his activities with the French during the war.

The Poujadist movement had a short-lived existence in Senegal. A branch of the metropolitan party was founded for the 1956 metropolitan elections, just after the establishment in Dakar of local branches of French retail chain stores, like Printania and Monoprix, which offered severe competition to independent local shopkeepers. It obviously drew on this latter group for membership.[1] Other local Europeans with less specific grievances yet general rightist tendencies remained apathetic throughout this period, while deploring 'opportunism' in the administration which gave in too easily to African demands. This tendency was supposed to have been particularly apparent among colonial administrators 'who were more interested in maintaining their positions after independence than in disciplining Africans, as was necessary'.[2]

There were a number of dramatic steps leading to the disintegration of France's overseas empire in the nineteen-fifties: withdrawal from Indo-China, the beginning of the Algerian war, and the independence of Morocco and Tunisia. The *Loi cadre* in 1956 in French West Africa, which decentralized and democratized territorial affairs, was in retrospect the most important milestone on the road to territorial independence. There were several significant events throughout Africa and the rest of the Empire, as well as in Senegal, which

[1] *Les Echos*, 15–21 February 1956, p. 2.
[2] Interview with a long-time resident of St. Louis in April 1967, who had married into one of the old *métisse* families of that town. He had become very disillusioned with politics in the nineteen-fifties, and especially with independence which he felt was awarded prematurely.

were obvious steps in this irreversible process. The impact of these events on European attitudes was summarized by several community leaders I interviewed in the spring of 1967, all of whom had been in Dakar through the Fifties, including prominent members of the Chamber of Commerce, political activists, journalists, scholars,[1] who were asked to respond to a standard list of questions. Their retrospective summation of the reactions of local Europeans to these events provided a political guideline to this period.

The situation in Algeria had been given wide coverage in Dakar as in all French newspapers. The majority of local Europeans were for *l'Algérie Française*, as the issue was seen in the wider context of the preservation of the Empire. On the whole, however, it seemed that Frenchmen in Senegal were perhaps marginally less concerned than metropolitan Frenchmen, and they never feared a *pied noir* invasion in the event of a rupture. There seemed to have been no real sense of solidarity with the settlers of Algeria. The *pied noir* was disparaged by the local expatriates as something of a lower-class element, and was certainly not felt to be equivalent in status to whites in Senegal. When Algeria was mentioned, certain of those interviewed were quick to emphasize the manifold differences between Senegal and Algeria and their respective white minorities, although they were not specifically questioned on this point. The general reaction to the defeat of the French at Dien Bien Phu in 1954 and the aftermath of French withdrawal from Indo-China provoked much less immediate interest, probably because it was so distant geographically and considered therefore remote from their own situation. They seemed on the whole to have had the same scale of reactions to this as did most metropolitans.

The abrupt independence of Guinea in 1958, after a referendum in which a majority voted against joining the French Community, provoked a most vigorous reaction. Frenchmen

[1] They included: M. Mariani, Secretary-General of the Chamber of Commerce; Paul Bonifay, lawyer and former Secretary of the S.F.I.O. in French West Africa; Guy Etcheverry, Presidential Press Attaché, former political activist; Yves Mersadier, Sociologist, *Institut Fondamental d'Afrique Noire*; Ernest Milcent, former correspondent of *Le Monde* in Senegal; Charles Graziani, businessman and former political activist.

in Senegal appear to have been somewhat divided in their feeling. Many agreed with General De Gaulle that it was necessary 'to make an example' of Guinea to neighbouring countries by punitive reprisals. A significant group of French businessmen in Dakar, particularly manufacturers and exporters, felt, however, that De Gaulle had made an excessively 'political decision', based on personal pride, partly because they resented the loss of the market in Guinea and of the possibility of future investment under favoured conditions. They also saw the rupture, however, as a disquieting factor in the general stability of the countries and markets of West Africa which they wished to preserve.

The most critical period of political tension in Senegal was in 1957 and 1958. During this time, the attitudes of local Europeans fluctuated through phases of relative complacency and generalized anxiety, the latter resulting usually from political demonstrations and anti-white incidents such as the stoning of cars. The obvious presence of the French army, which carried out manœuvres in Dakar at various times to try to forestall any political trouble, was both reassuring and disquieting. This period culminated in De Gaulle's visit to Dakar in June 1958 when he was campaigning for the Constitutional Referendum of September in that year. The local French reflected with surprise and uneasiness on the fact that neither Senghor nor his associate, the designated head of government, Mamadou Dia, were in Senegal at the time to greet him. Was this to be viewed as a warning that one of France's most loyal colonies was considering a 'no' vote in the referendum? On the actual day of the visit, Europeans were warned by the administration that it would be best to stay indoors, and very few of them therefore witnessed the anti-French demonstration organized chiefly by the local Marxist-Leninist party, the *Parti Africain de l'Indépendance*. The extent and effectiveness of this outburst, however, frightened some Europeans into thinking of 'packing their bags'. The more studied view represented that of the Chamber of Commerce and the leading businessmen who realized that the demonstration had been organized chiefly by young political activists, and that the older more moderate leaders could be relied upon.

Europeans in French West Africa were naturally relieved and gratified by the sizeable 'yes' vote to the referendum, not only in Senegal but in the rest of the Federation, excluding Guinea. Most of them were not only relieved because continued French influence was assured but also because they were Gaullist in sentiment, as were most French expatriates throughout the Empire. Those who did not fit into this category or who had any reservations about the 1958 constitution were in a strange position, for disagreement with any part of the proposed referendum meant automatically a vote for separation from France. Those who criticized De Gaulle from the right were disappointed for they felt that independence was being awarded too easily, and that it should have been a much more gradual movement to autonomy, spread perhaps over a decade or more.

Senegal became independent in January 1959 as part of the Mali Federation with neighbouring Soudan. Although Senegalese political leaders were careful to consult the French government about the matter of federation, local Europeans had no apparent influence on their decision to join with Soudan. French businessmen had no reason however to fear the Federation. Dakar manufacturers, in fact, wanted to maintain close relations with Soudan in order to extend their markets under favourable conditions.[1] Since all commerce and industry for the Federation of French West Africa had been based at Dakar, the local company directors had always favoured political movements which were interested in maintaining a federation or reconstructing one. Mali was seen by local French businessmen as the first step towards the reconstruction of the West African Federation. Once established, however, the militant ideology of the Soudanese leaders, together with the fear of nationalization under a combined governmental structure, spread disquiet among local businessmen. Above all, the company directors and other leaders in the business community had established a working relationship with the Senegalese political leaders, and they were unfamiliar with the Soudanese. The latter had been much less influenced by

[1] William J. Foltz, *From French West Africa to the Mali Federation*, New Haven, Yale University Press, 1965, pp. 117 and 157.

French assimilation, and were regarded by the French as much less francophile than their Senegalese counterparts. By the time the Federation had broken up and the Soudanese had returned to their own side of the border (August 1960), the Dakar business community was openly relieved.

When Senegal finally attained her separate independence, the realization of autonomy and its political implications had been muted by the clear decision of President Senghor to retain close ties with France. It was comfortably acknowledged by the local Europeans that independence only meant a change in political leadership. The Africanization of posts was not regarded as a crucial policy issue, or even a very important one by Senghor and the leaders of his party. It was not to be supported 'to the detriment of the efficiency and the stability of the administration and the private sector'.[1] Above all, the progression to actual political or economic independence was to be slow and cautious. Senghor's brand of African socialism was reassuring to local Frenchmen, for his intellectual constructions were never exclusivist. His proposals for the future of Senegal not only allowed for, but were contingent upon, co-operation with France.

There was, however, a certain amount of concern among European groups over a new law on Senegalese nationality. There had been several French deputies in the National Assembly of Senegal and in other elective offices at the time of independence. But Senghor was under pressure from some of his colleagues who felt that this was carrying his policy of co-operation with local businessmen too far. As a result, a law was passed requiring that all elected officials be of Senegalese nationality. At the same time, those who maintained French citizenship and wished to remain in Senegal were to be regarded as 'privileged foreigners' by the government.[2]

Only five or six Europeans opted for Senegalese nationality, including Robert Delmas, who remained the single deputy of French origin in the Senegalese National Assembly; André

[1] L. S. Senghor, speech to the *Jeunesse du Parti de la Féderation Africaine* (party of the Mali Federation), May 1960.
[2] Keba Mbaye, 'L'Attribution de la Nationalité *"Jure Soli"* et l'Option de Nationalité dans la Loi Sénégalaise du 7 Mars 1961', *Penant: Revue de Droit des Pays Africains*, 71 (687), June–July 1961, pp. 347–53.

Peytavin, who was then the Minister of Finance; and Pierre Crémieux, who owned a large cement factory in Rufisque. Paul Bonifay and others resigned their seats in the Assembly and retained French citizenship, because of their uncertainty about the future of Senegal and their role in it. Several of those Frenchmen who so chose, were, however, given another chance to participate in the formation and discussion of policy in Senegal when the Economic and Social Council was created shortly thereafter. This body has much the same legal functions as its namesake in the Fifth French Republic, although it was principally designed in the Senegalese context to bring European community and business leaders together with prominent Senegalese (see Chapter Eight).

The trust and confidence of local Europeans was placed above all in President Senghor. They have begun to realize even more in the eleven years since independence just how important is their reliance on him personally. They know him well and can speak to him on their own terms, for he is considered 'nearly a Frenchman'. They became gradually less certain of some of the other political leaders and considered several to be 'dishonest and useless'.[1] Already in 1960, for example, they were showing a certain wariness about Mamadou Dia, Senghor's Prime Minister, and his radical ideas for planning and economic development in Senegal.

An article written by a local Frenchman at the time of independence recounted that in 'the perfect cohesion of the two communities' (French and Senegalese), there was only one note of uncertainty: 'We must ask M. Dia what he means by African socialism.'[2] Local businessmen and company directors were to find out soon afterwards, for the marketing of groundnuts was nationalized under his direction in 1961, at great loss to European influence and financial interest.

---

[1] Such observations were drawn from questionnaire responses on my survey, and will be discussed in later chapters.
[2] C. Duchemin, 'Les Français à Dakar', *Europe-France Outre Mer*, No. 376, March 1961, p. 49.

5. Changing Patterns in Commerce and Industry

The present Senegalese economy remains largely dependent on France for its monetary stability and balance of trade equilibrium. As a participant in the franc-zone preferential system, Senegal is assured a free circulation of her goods throughout the zone exempt from customs duties (except for certain new industries protected with France's consent) and a guaranteed quota and price for export products. The latter is extremely important to groundnut production, in particular, which continues to provide the largest part of Senegalese exports, and which has until very recently required a French subsidy to make it competitive at world market prices. All economic and monetary arrangements between France and her former colonies were designed to fit within the requirements of membership in the European Economic Community but this has however only marginally diversified aid and capital investment to other European countries.

The Senegalese government has adopted a very favourable view towards the encouragement of French private investment, as is perhaps inevitable with the present ties to France and the franc zone. Despite an initial inclination towards African socialism, which culminated in the nationalization of groundnut marketing, subsequent government policy has maintained the rhetoric of socialism along with renewed co-operation with French private enterprise. As a local French magazine with considerable interest in the business situation has put it:

> African socialism hasn't a doctrinaire basis.... In several speeches, President Senghor has expanded on this point and declared in a very clear manner and without any trace of ambiguity that Senegal intended to leave industry and commerce in complete liberty.[1]

[1] *Echos de France*, leader, p. 4, May 1964. See also Chapter 9.

Changing Patterns in Commerce and Industry

While Senghor tried to encourage industrial investment in particular, with guarantees against nationalization and a flexible policy on the necessary rate of Africanization of company personnel, the market and development prospects in Senegal just after independence were hardly promising. As the Secretary-General of the Chamber of Commerce put it in 1967: 'Africans are slaves of their vocabulary, but it is not the ideas and theories which worry us, rather the instability of the economy.'

The decline of Dakar as the centre of commerce and industry for French West Africa began when the Federation disintegrated and independence was awarded on an individual basis to each of the former colonies. While Dakar had benefited somewhat artificially as the market and industrial centre for all the eight colonies of French West Africa, which had formerly purchased Senegalese manufactured goods, each of these newly independent countries started their own small factories and erected tariff barriers to protect them. This left Dakar industries over-equipped for the small market of Senegal. The development of several new ports in former French West Africa, especially that of Abidjan, together with bi-lateral shipping agreements between these franc-zone countries and France led to the decline in importance of the port of Dakar. In addition, the role of Dakar as a *relais* or port-of-call became much less important than that of the Canary Islands, better placed for the European-South American trade routes.

The sudden departure from Senegal of much of the French personnel in the colonial and federal administration, together with a significant reduction in the number of Frenchmen privately employed, was a severe blow to local shops and services. The gradual reduction of French troops intensified this situation, although the brunt of this was not entirely felt until the massive military cutback in 1965. There was no longer a market for luxury products, as the spending patterns of those Europeans who remained changed considerably. This was only partially counter-balanced by increased purchasing power among Africans, for a number of reasons, including the fact that limited Africanization of managerial posts in the private sector did not promote many new consumers who, unlike expatriates, would spend in the local market.

Repatriation of those Europeans with little means became a serious problem in the years just following independence. The French Ministry of Repatriation, created to deal with the Algerian problem in 1961, while extending its services to all overseas territories, restricted the interpretation of its jurisdiction to include only those Europeans who were actually expelled from the countries in which they were resident.[1] Thus, for Frenchmen with failed or bankrupt businesses in Dakar or any other ex-colonial city, there was little recourse. While the 'little man' had his assets threatened by the upheaval of independence, a general decline in the market situation throughout Senegal affected all investors. Private investment which remained viable under these conditions, however, was felt to be reasonably safe from government interference, which elsewhere in Africa at this time was of considerable importance.

The initial confidence of the French business community was shattered, however, in 1961, by the creation of the *Office de Commercialisation Agricole* (O.C.A.), a government marketing structure for groundnuts which meant effective nationalization of this sector. The O.C.A. was designed and put into operation by Prime Minister Dia, representing the left-wing of the ruling party, together with a well-known socialist economist, Father Lebret, and his technical advisory organization, *Economie et Humanisme* (which helped draw up the first economic plan in the same year). They were joined in their efforts by other French technocratic organizations of liberal or Christian socialist orientation,[2] which together were labelled 'a pernicious cabal' by local businessmen, who dubbed Lebret and his clerical colleagues in particular 'the red priests'. Dia retained many of this group in the capacity of technical assistants, who acted as a kind of inner cabinet, and were to be responsible for organizing the rural sector of the economy.

---

[1] 'Accueil et Reinstallation des Français d'Outre-Mer', *Journal Officiel de la République Française*, No. 1215, 1964.
[2] CINAM (*Compagnie d'Etudes Industrielles et d'Aménagement de Territoire*) and SERESA (*Société d'Etudes et de Réalisations Economiques et Sociales dans l'Agriculture*).

Changing Patterns in Commerce and Industry

Co-operatives were established in the towns and villages of the interior, meaning that nearly all Europeans and a majority of the Lebanese who had acted as local agents in the groundnut trade were deprived of their jobs in the buying centres, and were compelled by necessity to move to Dakar.[1] This caused serious pressure on the few existing jobs in the capital, and most of the French trading company employees were eventually repatriated. The nationalization of groundnut marketing created among other local directors a generalized fear that perhaps no enterprise was any longer safe from nationalization. European businessmen had considered themselves a counter-lobby to Dia and the left-wing of the party, but now felt that they had lost their influence.

At the end of 1962, however, Dia was imprisoned after an alleged *coup d'état* attempted by him and his supporters.[2] While there is not conclusive evidence that local European business had a direct influence on these events, which were basically a clash between various factions and personalities within the party, they made no secret of their sentiments concerning Dia and his intentions for economic planning. After his political demise a business journal in Dakar carried the headline: 'Confidence is Restored!'

With Senghor once again firmly at the head of the party and state, under a presidential constitution, a new period of liberalism began for European business, and although the co-operative system remained intact, a favourable situation for investment remained largely unchanged by subsequent events. The second economic plan (1965–68) discarded any consideration of extending nationalization. President Senghor in an address to the National Council of the *Union Progressiste Sénégalaise* (U.P.S.) in May 1967 reiterated his personal

---

[1] This movement was reflected in the demographic statistics, which put the European population outside Dakar in 1960 at approximately 8,000 (most of whom were in the region of Thiès and Kaolack). After its initial decline in 1960, the European population of Dakar rose slightly at the end of 1961 to 45,000 (just after the creation of the O.C.A.). L. Verrière, *La Population du Sénégal*, Thèse pour le Doctorat des Sciences Economiques, Université de Dakar, 1965, pp. 31, 33.

[2] See P. Thibaud, 'Dia, Senghor et le Socialisme Africain', *Esprit*, Paris, No. 9, September 1963.

position on this, for the benefit both of the left-wing of his party and the European businessmen:

> In order to nationalize, one must have abundant national capital and abundant qualified national cadres. This is not yet our case.... Our code of investment guarantees foreign capital against nationalization and assures them a reasonable profit. We would be particularly ill-advised to refuse a frank and loyal co-operation with the holders of capital who have agreed to participate in our task of development. That they also get their own advantage is only natural![1]

The task of European commerce in particular from 1961 was to adapt existing investments to wholesale and retail trade in manufactured goods and foodstuffs. Around the new economic framework of groundnut marketing run by the O.C.A., the civil servants in charge of economic development, in co-operation with local expatriate investors, set about to try to initiate a departure from the strictly colonial monocrop economy. The attempt can be considered in a series of stages. First, the reconstruction of markets by the O.C.A. which led to the formation of government-run co-operatives and consortia, which were privately financed but directed in part by government officials. Second, the diversification of private investment, particularly towards industrial enterprise, and the support (through politico-economic favour) of all those private firms which seemed to be adaptable to the national market. Third, the diversification of external markets and investment, aid and other sources of revenue from abroad, to try to break the heavy economic dependence on France, a problematic and to date largely unsuccessful undertaking. Fourth, preparation for a gradual increase in Africanization of commerce and industry, a process which was also beset by problems, many of which were inherited from the pre-independence period.

There were several factors which favoured French suppliers to the local market. In addition to the preferential system of the franc-zone, the Senegalese government inherited a comprehensive system of price controls for imported goods from its colonial predecessor; discriminating against 'cheap labour'

[1] *Dakar-Matin*, 16 May 1967, reprint of speech delivered on 13 May, p. 3.

exporters such as Japan, Hong Kong and India,[1] although a great many such goods come in by contraband through Gambia. While this system of price controls was of some assistance to local French commercial firms, Lebanese merchants, who are their chief competitors, also bought goods on the French market, and a number of them had ways of getting around the local price controls.

Adaptations to the local market which were required by trading companies after the loss of activity in groundnuts were achieved with varying degrees of success. Certain traditional houses and other individual investors joined together into a number of consortia at the suggestion of the government. Many of the trading companies did not, however, have the financial latitude or desire to participate in them, considering it a somewhat risky undertaking. The larger companies, backed by French or international investment firms, had the most latitude of all, and were able to make a choice between two alternatives. The first of these was to create a new marketing framework in partial financial co-operation with the government, a choice taken by S.C.O.A. The second was to branch out from the strictly commercial sector into services and industry. The latter option was chosen by the traditional trading house of Peyrissac, which had been bought by a large investment firm from the Far East in 1955.

The intention behind the government policy to sponsor the formation of commercial consortia was in part an attempt to Africanize the commercial sector. Capital was to be supplied by European firms, and while there were only a few Senegalese civil servants on the boards of Directors, all the local retail agents were African. This was felt to be an alternative to the creation of actual consumer co-operatives, a suggestion to which European business remained vigorously opposed. After their formation the consortia were beset with a series of problems: the French investors looked for guarantees from the government on investment and supply which were not forthcoming; and there was no effective control of the accounts of local agents, while

[1] *Syndicat des Commerçants Importateurs et Exportateurs de la Rép. du Sénégal*, (SCIMPEX), 'Regime des Importations dans la République du Sénégal', Dakar, roneo, 1964, communicated by the Administrative Secretary.

theft of the day's receipts was quite common. Nearly all the consortia ended in failure or bankruptcy. One exception to this is SONADIS, a successful mixed enterprise (S.C.O.A. and the Senegalese Development Bank) which is today the largest distributor of manufactured goods and foodstuffs in the rural area with eighty local agents in 1967.[1]

The director of SONADIS is a Frenchman, although the Board of Directors is entirely composed of Senegalese cabinet ministers and selected merchants; 108 of their total 115 employees in 1967 were Senegalese. The company has a training programme through which all prospective retail agents have to pass. Its object is to try to instil in them a commercial vocation, after which they are closely surveyed at their work for a period of probation. 'Commercial receipts have not been fantastic', according to the director, however, 'as one cannot reform the commercial circuits and habits of people in such a few years.'[2] SONADIS has, however, made a considerable impact already on local consumer spending in the smallest hamlets.

The traditional commercial houses which have not been willing or able to adapt their investment and organizational structure to the new economic situation have been in considerable financial trouble. Chauvenel, an old family-run firm, preferred to close their hundred shops throughout the country, rather than be compelled to Africanize their central administration. Maurel et Prom, Vézia and Petersen chose not to join SONADIS, as a result of which they face discriminatory supply from government organizations, especially on the staple consumer commodity of rice. Bulk distribution of rice is conducted by the O.C.A. in favour of African merchants, certain Lebanese traders and SONADIS.

Both the consortia and the older trading houses are faced with serious competition from the Lebanese merchants, who can usually undersell them because they are willing to accept a much lower margin of profit. The Lebanese are considered by Europeans in the commercial sector to be responsible in large

[1] 'Création de la SONADIS', *Le Moniteur Africain*, February 1964.
[2] Interview with M. Dupont, SONADIS executive offices in Dakar April 1967.

measure for the stagnation in business. They are specifically accused of selling goods below the import price by securing merchandise through fraud or contraband and thus avoiding the payment of import duties. In addition to this they are condemned for not having any system of accounting through which receipts and expenditure could be verified, and for evading social service charges by not declaring their hired labour.[1] In their responses to direct questions concerning the Lebanese, the French interviewed in the private sector[2] were on the whole much more negative about Lebanese activities than were the technical assistants, many of whom were customers of Lebanese retailers, and tended to see more positive aspects to their role in Senegal. Teachers in particular, who are regular Lebanese customers, were very favourable to them.[3] Among those most hostile to the Lebanese were small businessmen or shopkeepers and their employees, for whom the Lebanese provided the most direct threat. Directors and managers in commercial houses were somewhat less hostile to Lebanese activities in Senegal, and those employed in industry even less so, certainly far less than employees in commercial houses and independent businessmen (see Table 3, p. 131).

Unfavourable attitudes to the Lebanese, which were obtained from interviews with Frenchmen, fall into some of the following categories:

(1) 'They don't fight with the same "arms" as legitimate commerce; their business practices include cheating "bak-

[1] The former accusations are impossible to prove, although they are regarded as 'common knowledge' among both Senegalese and French in Dakar. Little can be done about the latter situation, because the reservoir of unskilled Africans seeking jobs at almost any price and any conditions maintains it.

[2] Specific data on the attitudes of the French expatriates currently in Senegal are naturally drawn from my survey and will be used in this and the succeeding chapters without specific citation or reference. On aggregate responses attention will be drawn to the relevant table or appendix. Unless otherwise specified, aggregates will be based on the total group of (250) respondents or, if indicated, on all those employed in the private sector (175), or those employed as technical assistants or teachers (60).

[3] Seventy-three per cent of the teachers interviewed felt that the Lebanese fulfilled a useful economic function in Senegal in contrast with only 36 per cent of all respondents.

sheesh", excessive credit rates and the evasion of taxes and import duties.'
(2) 'They are pernicious because they allow the Senegalese to buy on credit and teach them bad habits. They corrupt the Senegalese politicians and civil servants.'
(3) 'They are economically parasitic because they repatriate capital earned in Senegal back to Lebanon.'
(4) 'There are too many of them: they are redundant.'
(5) 'They don't hire Africans.'[1]

Among those respondents who found fault with their business practices specifically (38 per cent), a minority blamed this on particular 'Levantine' racial or cultural characteristics:

'They have an Arab mentality; they are always bankrupt.'
'They work like typical Orientals—they thieve and cheat.'
'They are the plague of Africa, a kind of "yellow peril". In business, they're like Jews.'

Only 15 per cent of all expatriates interviewed proposed that the Lebanese should be judged individually. They acknowledged that some were upright, having made productive investment in Senegal and re-invested their profits, while they considered that others were dishonest and did not respect the existing tax and import regulations. The former group was meant to include the financial leaders of the Lebanese minority, generally in Senegal for several generations, and with substantial investments in real estate, industry, supermarkets or transport. This financial élite centred on only about a dozen families of a total population of some 15,000 people of Lebanese origin.[2]

Despite the long-standing hostility between the French and the Lebanese in business in Senegal, 35 per cent of the total group interviewed agreed at least that they provided a useful economic function in Senegal, chiefly by maintaining a circulation of money and goods throughout the country and having a

---

[1] Where direct quotes are used which are not given specific attribution, they will indicate responses drawn from the questionnaire survey. Where it is interesting to know the identity of the respondent(s) in question, it will be mentioned either in the text or in a note.

[2] The precise number of those who are culturally defined as Lebanese is very difficult to estimate since many have French or Senegalese nationality.

Changing Patterns in Commerce and Industry

good sense of commerce, which was lacking in the Senegalese.[1] Their role as middle-men, perhaps inevitable in an underdeveloped country without an indigenous capitalist class, was felt to be an asset to European importers and manufacturers. According to most respondents in this group, the Lebanese merchant provided a function which could not be fulfilled either by the Senegalese, because of inexperience or incompetence, or the French, whose unwillingness to accept the small profit margin and meagre returns kept prices high, and usually quite beyond the reach of most Senegalese consumers outside the cities. For some respondents this was a way of sneering at the standard of living or way of life of the Lebanese 'for not being like us'.

Certain trading houses in Senegal were untouched by either Lebanese competition or the restricted market. They took an entirely new investment objective which was outside the import-export sector. The Delmas enterprises, for example, which remained very much a family concern, had long since left the groundnut trade and invested in shipping, insurance, transport, and the repair and supply of automobiles and farm equipment.[2]

Another successful multiple enterprise, the largest single private investor in the economy between 1964 and 1967, is Peyrissac.[3] It was one of the older companies in Senegal and West Africa (founded in 1862), and was taken over in 1955 by

[1] Some used the opportunity to turn it into an explicit criticism of the Senegalese. For example, 'The Lebanese are different from the Africans, they're more like the Chinese; they work very hard. They are also much harder than we are on the Africans, which is how it should be—"the rule of the stick". We Europeans haven't understood how to handle them. We wear kid gloves and are too kind, and they do not work.'

[2] A part of the Delmas family remains in Bordeaux where Pierre Delmas is a member of the Chamber of Commerce. Since Robert Delmas has taken on public office, he has turned his investments over to his sons. Robert Delmas, *Notes et Documents Recueillis pour Servir à l'Histoire du Sénégal jusqu'à l'Indépendance*, Dakar, 1964 (privately printed), Vol. II, p. 278.

[3] Peyrissac was founded by Charles Peyrissac who came to Africa from the Haut-Vienne. In 1872, he installed his first independent enterprise at St. Louis after working as a trading company employee for ten years. From 1872–1902, he extended his activities throughout the interior of Senegal, and after 1908, throughout French West Africa. Before the Second World War, the firm specialized in cloth, while after 1945, it began in the rather lucrative market of retail hardware, automobiles, motorcycles and bicycles.

Changing Patterns in Commerce and Industry

OPTORG, a large Far Eastern trading firm which withdrew its investment from the Orient after the defeat of the French forces in Indo-China. Thus, at exactly the most opportune moment, when most companies in West Africa were wondering in which direction to move in the event of independence and market instability, Peyrissac had the flexibility to explore the most lucrative possibilities, with the capital and backing of one of the largest overseas investment firms in France.

OPTORG's directors assured themselves that 'the political independence of these countries (in West Africa) was only formal', and that 'their leaders had generally manifested a desire to retain something of the pre-existing economic system',[1] and thus, initiated some long-term investments in stock, capital installations and a small amount of land. After 1960, OPTORG joined in association with *Monoprix*, a major French retailer and distributor of clothing and other goods, and *Quincaillerie Centrale*, the largest French hardware supplier, at which time it centralized its buying and selling procedures in France and abroad. Its policy for overseas investment included the distribution of financial risks through the diversification of investments to various countries, a contribution to industrialization and Africanization in the countries chosen for an investment base, and the creation of commercial circuits between West Africa and the Orient. In Senegal, Peyrissac's most important capital installations remain at Dakar with six wholesale and retail outlets in the major provincial towns of the interior. Since 1958 they have doubled their profits,[2] owing partly to the maintenance of favourable relations with the government.

As for the firms in the commercial sector, the market and financial situation for Dakar industries at the time of independence was not very hopeful. Having been established to supply the whole of French West Africa, they had to undergo some major reorganization and restriction when faced with the need to confine their activities to the Senegalese market alone. In the first economic plan there were several objectives for existing industry, and target plans for the creation of new light industry

---

[1] OPTORG, *Entreprise*, Extrait du No. 443, 7 March 1964, 'La Compagnie Optorg, Un Moteur des Echanges Internationaux', p. 2.
[2] Interview with the local director of Peyrissac, spring 1967.

for exporting consumer goods, which would contribute in the short term to the external balance of payments and absorb the unemployed. Many of these new proposals never came to fruition, a failure which was attributed in part by local businessmen to the lack of civic spirit among the Senegalese. While the government, like that of most new countries, wished to enlarge its industrial sector in order to diversify from its predominantly agricultural base, and thus raise national prestige, Senegal seemed to provide little scope for new industrial investment in the first decade after independence.

There are two main types of industries in Senegal: those catering to the export market, which are now confined principally to groundnut oil refineries; and those manufacturing light consumer goods for the domestic market. The majority of industrial firms are French-owned and directed. A few have mixed financial backing from French investors and Senegalese public funds, like SONADIS in the commercial sector, and an even smaller number are owned by non-French investors (within the E.E.C. preferential system) from Italy and Germany. Many firms are not working to capacity, because of the limited size of the Senegalese market, and the continued difficulties of external expansion owing to import restrictions in nearly all other former British and French colonies in West Africa. For similar reasons, the Senegalese domestic market is exposed to little competition, which has created monopolies in certain sectors, and ensured for at least some industrial investors a high rate of profit and fast amortization of capital.

Protection of the domestic market has been of enormous assistance to investors who have had to reorganize their interests in structural and financial terms to cope with restriction of activities to the national market. In these difficult circumstances, the larger units have survived best: while some firms may have started as individually-owned small enterprises, almost all are now linked for supply, distribution or finance to metropolitan firms.[1] The soap manufacturing company, H.S.O.A., started by Petersen in 1930, and making use of a groundnut oil by-product, is now, for example, linked to a

[1] From an inventory of industries in Senegal, 'L'Industrie Sénégalaise', a special supplement of *Le Moniteur Africain*, 16 February 1966, pp. 11–14.

Changing Patterns in Commerce and Industry

Marseilles group of oil refineries. Similarly in the commercial sphere, the largest French cloth manufacturer, Boussac-France, has opened retail and wholesale outlets throughout Senegal, under the name CITEC, and small suppliers find it difficult to compete with its volume and efficiency.

The mainstay of Senegalese industry remains its groundnut oil refineries, which employ 3,500 people, and process over 60 per cent of the Senegalese groundnut crop annually.[1] Its directors' association is quite naturally one of the most powerful influences on national economic policy. Three of the refineries are in provincial towns (Kaolack, Diourbel and Rufisque) and because of their location have the benefit of government favour, owing to official interest in the devolution of industrial and commercial power from the capital city. One of these, the *Société Electrique et Industrielle de Baol*, in Diourbel, is a multipurpose industrial installation, which employs about 420 people and in addition to groundnut oil, produces electricity, soda-pop, pharmaceutical products, perfume, vinegar and ice-cream. It is considered by the Senegalese government to be a very hopeful model for further industrial investment.

The boards of directors of many of the expatriate-owned companies in Senegal have a number of the same members.[2] While this might appear to provide evidence of an overlapping industrial-commercial élite, it is really nothing more than a kind of old boy network among Dakar businessmen. The Dakar headquarters of all of these companies, except those few which are solely under local ownership, has very little independence in making policy for the company on any significant matter (in local usage, Dakar is a *siège fictif* for most French companies). Policy is made by stockholders or directors in France and only executed by the local managers.[3] Dakar

---

[1] About five hundred to five hundred and fifty-five thousand tons. Interview with the Secretary-General of the *Syndicat des Huiliers*, December 1966.

[2] Guide Economique, NORIA, *Sociétés et Fournisseurs d'Afrique Noire et de Madagascar*, Paris, La Documentation Africaine, 1966, pp. 433–97. Charles-Henri Gallenca, the former President of the Chamber of Commerce, for example, was on seven boards of directors, and the members of the Delmas family each belong to several.

[3] Some must even request permission from Paris to purchase an advertisement in the local business newspaper. Interview with the editor of *Le Moniteur Africain*, Spring 1967.

directors have no power over major issues of company policy and retain influence only on matters of employment.[1] Apart from this, local company directors make only short-term administrative decisions of relatively little importance.

French company directors in Dakar are naturally very considerably influenced in their views by the sector of business or industry in which they find themselves, the general prosperity of their particular firm, and the length of their colonial experience. On the basis of views or attitudes, one may distinguish at least two distinctive types of company directors: an older type with colonial experience, who are attached to the pomp and ceremony of colonial society; and young university-educated technocrats with a non-colonial background who are only interested in investments and profits. The former, characterized best by Robert Delmas and the past-President of the Chamber of Commerce, Charles-Henri Gallenca, are mollified by decorations, visits with the President of the Republic, and a place of honour at national parades. To extend the definition of this 'old guard', one might also include some less noted local figures, like the directors of traditional trading houses who are in the unfortunate position of presiding over the demise of a type of business which served a former era. They are considerably embittered by this situation, which naturally affects their attitudes towards Senegal, its future and the Senegalese. The younger group of executives and technocrats tend to view the limitations of the Senegalese market and economic situation in purely technical or economic terms and are less concerned with the use of racial or cultural stereotypes to explain these limitations. They have tried, though to little effect, to make contact with Senegalese civil servants and other Africans through organizations like the Junior Chamber of Commerce, Lions and Rotary Clubs, and are regarded as being a bit naïve by some of their older colleagues.

[1] The author of a recent study on industrial labour in Senegal found that more than half of the twenty-six industrial directors he interviewed said they had complete independence on matters of wages and employment, and another quarter on local African labour only. G. Pfeffermann, *Industrial Labour in the Republic of Senegal*, New York, Praeger, 1968, p. 58. The effect of this local autonomy on hiring policies will be discussed in the context of labour relations in Chapter 6.

Changing Patterns in Commerce and Industry

The attitudes of French company directors towards the business situation in Senegal and its prospects are not only influenced by these individual views and other factors specific to their own firms. There are certain problems which are general to the economic situation and thus affect all companies, some of which have remained chronic since the breakup of the Federation and its market system in 1958. Profits in Senegal have been considerably reduced in nearly all spheres, in comparison with the fortunes made during the colonial period, owing among other things to the rise in the cost of labour. It is fair to assume that most companies are still clearing gross revenues at a higher level than metropolitan firms, however, in order to absorb the additional cost of expatriate personnel and transport, for they would have otherwise withdrawn to France. Only in special circumstances have Europeans been compelled to remain in Senegal when this margin fell below what is locally considered to be a reasonable profit level—when, for example, they had sunk all their capital into the small enterprise and had no opportunity of moving elsewhere.

The greatest single setback for small European commerce was the massive departure of French troops from Senegal early in 1965.[1] Many specialty shops and services were forced out of existence, and with them a major part of the European shop-owners, at least a few of whom were the wives of military personnel long in the colonies who would probably have returned to France in any case. The setback was aggravated by the growing tendency of Europeans to stock up on annual needs for clothing and other consumer durables in France, where they are considerably less expensive. (Shopkeepers believe that some even buy annual stocks of foodstuffs). This change is part of a general pattern of the changing life style from colonial to expatriate society. Even the upper social echelons in Dakar seem to have lost the taste for entertaining and spending on a lavish scale as before. It is no longer so needed as when it was a compensation for being isolated from metropolitan society. With improved communications bringing France

---

[1] In just over a year they were reduced from 27,800 to 6,600, the reason given being the enlargement of African armies, and thus reduced need for them. Information from the French Consul in Dakar, November 1966.

nearer, expatriates live and spend like metropolitans abroad for a fixed period of time, wherein inflated salaries and exchange rates provide lucrative possibilities for accumulating savings for life back home.

In order to compensate for some of this loss, certain enterprises have made attempts to cultivate the urban African consumer. New branches of retail trade have been directed at the African middle class, especially in ready-made clothes, household appliances, cars or jewellery. A firm manufacturing soda-pop has tried to replace some of its West African market by increasing consumption within Senegal, achieved to date rather successfully by widespread advertising. Other firms, such as those manufacturing and selling cloth, have been hurt by changing buying patterns among Africans who used to spend a disproportionate amount of their income on clothing,[1] but are more interested now in home-furnishings, electrical appliances and radios. The changes in the character of the Senegalese market are not, however, entirely without difficulty for suppliers and retailers, or entirely open to further expansion. Once the commercial techniques required to appeal to the taste of the new consumer had been mastered, it became apparent that the increased earnings of the African middle class continued to be absorbed by increased family responsibilities, and did not necessarily lead to the purchase of consumer goods.

In a series of questions (see Appendix 3, questions 49–53), expatriates were asked to give their assessment of the state of the market and its future. When questioned about the place of private investment in Senegalese economic policy, only slightly more than half of those working in the private sector considered that they were compatible.[2] The obvious uncertainty rests in part on a lingering discontent over the O.C.A., and the lingering potentiality of nationalization in other sectors,

---

[1] This is partly a function of the diversification of buying patterns as incomes rise, bringing them closer to European buying patterns. Thus, whereas cloth used to be the first item in the Senegalese family budget, it is now sixth or tenth. Information from the director of CITEC, the largest cloth retailers in Senegal, Spring 1967.

[2] 'Do you think that Senegalese economic policy is compatible with private investment?' (175 respondents employed in the private sector) 'YES'—42%, 'NO'—35%, 'DON'T KNOW'—17% (mainly women).

although the more astute observers comment that 'perhaps because the Senegalese have learned their lesson, the current attitude is distinctly liberal'. When asked further if private investment and Senegalese economic policy were a fruitful basis for economic expansion, a more positive response was forthcoming.[1] Potential doubts about Senegalese economic policy were diluted by the certainty of the need for French capital investment as the only source for development, to which several added that its past successes were manifest.

While a small minority of those interviewed in the private sector suggested that it was not only possible but fruitful to combine private investment with state capital, many felt that without an effective public administration, such a possibility was remote. More explicit dissatisfaction was expressed about the waste, mismanagement, laziness and corruption of the Senegalese civil service. But businessmen were, above all, discouraged by *la parole*, the palaver of Senegalese leaders and politicians, which they felt evaded concrete issues and made it difficult to know in which direction actual policy might go.

Among the difficulties of effecting a viable economic policy for independent Senegal are, first, that the government inherited a superfluous number of civil servants from the colonial period to which it has added new recruits every year, and second, that the country still has a monocrop economy, based on groundnuts, the world market for which is gradually declining (owing to the use of synthetic and other vegetable oils). Attempts at agricultural diversification and planning have produced elaborately prepared documents and few concrete results. The first two economic plans fell far short of their intended goals, particularly in agriculture, which remains the largest sector of the economy. There was wide criticism among my respondents about the failures of planning and production:

> I'm not sure if the Senegalese know what economic development is. They have a lot of money at their disposal—through investment and aid. They have spent millions of francs

[1] 'Do you think that the co-existence of Senegalese economic policy and private investment is a fruitful and effective base for economic expansion in Senegal?' (same 175 respondents)
'YES'—54%, 'NO'—26%, 'DON'T KNOW'—15%.

looking for petroleum deposits which do not exist, and not enough on the peasantry and the agricultural sector.

The government has grasped things a bit better now. Right after independence they thought that they'd arrived at a Golden Age economically, and thought only of industrialization. They still don't study their own problems closely enough. The essential one remains that of making investments technically effective.

Those interviewed in both the public and the private sector were critical of the general behaviour and effectiveness of Senegalese politicians and civil servants, and the limited extent to which they had grasped the problems of economic development: 48 per cent said they had not, 38 per cent that they had.[1] Those Frenchmen directly involved in commerce and industry were marginally more negative on average about this than technical assistants. But even those who felt that the Senegalese had grasped the problems of economic development were not without some reservation:

> Only Senghor and a few of his stature have understood what must be done, not the rest.

> They have understood the problems intellectually, but can do nothing because they are not well organized.

> They have good ideas but lack personnel and resources to achieve them, that is, they have grasped the importance of economic development, but actually producing it is another matter.

The altogether negative replies were composed of a range of criticisms from those concerning general economic policy and its execution, to an assessment of the capabilities of the Senegalese bureaucracy, to those concerning the capacity of 'all Senegalese' or 'all Africans'. To a certain extent the

[1] Respondents who gave a positive answer were asked to give a concrete example of how they thought this was best illustrated. These included: agricultural development in the Senegal River basin (especially the Richard Toll scheme); the attempt to rectify the mistakes of the O.C.A. and economic planning; the fishing industry; tourism; the moderate path of President Senghor; and Senegalese awareness that they must rely on the technical assistants.

attitudes they reflect are based on the professional status and educational achievement of the respondent in question (see Table 4, p. 132). One typical strongly negative response was as follows:

> The Senegalese is an overgrown child, who doesn't work hard enough because he has been spoiled by France. He is aware of what we have asked him to do, but its fulfilment is not certain.

Reference in such a reply to 'pampering or spoiling' recurred occasionally among responses which were usually fairly hostile to the Senegalese. It was intended to refer to the premature award of independence and what was considered lavish French aid and technical assistance since then. Such remarks also partly referred to the colonial history of Senegal—the 'favoured or spoiled' colony with the four communes and their special relationship to France, or with the *évolué* and his special status in French culture and society. These also became frequent themes in the attempt to explain the 'Senegalese personality'.

Explanations of Senegalese individual or collective incapacities were not of course the only elements entering into the expatriate's long-term assessment of business possibilities. While most respondents (72 per cent) gave pessimistic answers to a direct question on the future prospects of expatriate business and investment in Senegal, the reasons most often given were objective economic factors: limited resources, the small local market, or discouragement with government fiscal policy. To this was occasionally added the relative political uncertainty of the future of Senegal and, in particular, what was considered by local businessmen to be the government's indecision between 'liberalism and socialism', often contrasted with the Ivory Coast, 'where a much greater spirit of liberalism and open favour to private investment prevails'. Although some Frenchmen recognized that this indecision might be due in part to the nature of the Senegalese political system, which required President Senghor to maintain a balance between various factions in the governing party, they obviously could not always be certain that the outcome would be favourable to business interests. 'In the Ivory Coast', reflected the administrative secretary of a large employers' association, 'there was no such problem, for Frenchmen had a much more direct and constant influence on policy.'

The future of Franco-Senegalese relations was, according to a small number of respondents, dependent entirely on economic ties between the two countries. It was obvious to them that while Senegal remained in the franc zone, she must maintain close relations with France, although others recognized the need to pay at least lip-service to the necessity for diversification of sources of aid. This was the publicly asserted view of the directors of large business firms, and, for example, the director of the Chamber of Commerce, as reported in *Le Moniteur Africain*:

> Senegal must now sustain the closure of neighbouring markets, and open its own more widely to the industrial countries of the Common Market. It must be ready for an overall decline in French direct and indirect aid.[1]

The French director of the *Banque Centrale* gave some indication of the ideas of the financial and business élite in France, who had never been much moved by Gaullist sentiment about the need to sustain the connection with former overseas dependencies:

> We are losing interest in the amount of financial support required by Senegal, because she has an internal market of no importance, and a monocrop economy which we do not wish to keep subsidizing to our loss. Naturally there are a lot of sympathetic ties between Senghor and De Gaulle, and Senegal has an important role in francophone African politics. We want to keep her on our side, but must make a realistic appraisal of her economic potential and our economic commitment.[2]

The most natural direction for the diversification of Senegal's economic ties is towards the Common Market, of which she became an associate member in July 1963. (And this is at least acceptable to local businessmen who would, above all, like to preclude any arrangements between Senegal and the United

---

[1] *Le Moniteur Africain*, 9 January 1965, p. 1.
[2] Interview with M. Eude, who was seconded to Senegal from the French Central Bank on a three-year mission to ensure the co-operation of the West African countries in the franc zone.

Changing Patterns in Commerce and Industry

States, either for aid or investment, for they fear a general American takeover and the loss of French hegemony in business.) As a result of her associate status, all the European members of the Common Market have in principle the same investment advantages in Senegal as does France: this has not, however, been the case in reality. The Italian director in Senegal of the *Fonds Européen de Développement*, the aid programme of the Common Market, commented on this with a certain amount of bitterness after a few years at his post in Dakar:

> The French want to keep Senegal all for themselves and don't co-operate with anyone else. They jealously guard Senegal close to them. This relationship is damaged by the fact that all of the French in Senegal are entirely ridden with a colonial mentality; it is impossible for them to see the Senegalese in anything but this light. They have been here too long and cannot adapt to the idea that Senegal should become a reality as an independent country.[1]

French presence is deeply entrenched in the Senegalese economy. And after a century of exclusively French investments and company structures, as well as personal relationships between the French and the Senegalese which span decades, it seems perhaps easier to proceed along already well-trodden paths.

[1] Interview in Dakar, April 1967.

TABLE 3

Attitudes Towards the Lebanese

Do you think that the Lebanese in Dakar and in the rest of Senegal fulfil a useful economic function? (question 57)

i)

	Private Sector (172)	Total Respondents (250)
Yes	28%	36%
No	50%	43%
That Depends	16%	16%
Don't Know	4%	3%

ii)

	Tech. Assts. (63)	Expat. Contract Private Sector (126)	Local Contract (40)	Professional (6)
Yes	64%	36·5%	31%	0
No	22%	43%	50%	67%
That Depends	14%	16%	10%	33%
Don't Know	0	4%	8%	0

iii) COMMERCE

	Self-Emp. (12)	Sales Clerk (10)*	Management (25)	Employees (27)†
Yes	8·3%	10%	35%	39%
No	67%	70%	48%	44%
That Depends	8·3%	20%	16%	14%
Don't Know	16·6%	0	0	3%

iv) INDUSTRY

	Executives (30)‡	Technicians (26)	Off. Employees (14)	Foremen (9)
Yes	26%	32%	35%	11%
No	33%	57%	50%	44%
That Depends	37%	7%	7%	33%
Don't Know	3%	4%	7%	11%

* In small business (shops).
† In trading companies.
‡ Including employers, management and professional employees.

TABLE 4

The Senegalese and Economic Development

Do you think that the Senegalese leaders have grasped effectively the problems of economic development? (question 54)

i)

Employment	Yes	No	Don't Know
Technical Assistants (63)	45%	39%	10%
Private-Expat. Contract (126)	34%	52%	10%
Private-Local Contract (40)	17%	57%	20%
Professionals* (6)	50%	34%	17%

ii)

Education†	Yes	No	Don't Know
Primary School (24)	29%	58%	12%
Secondary School (59)	38%	45%	7%
Technical School (13)	37%	47%	16%
Baccalauréat (51)	41%	50%	9%
University (45)	45%	49%	6·6%
Post-Graduate including technical studies in *Gds. Ecoles.* (47)	47%	41%	12%

iii) *Total Sample* (250)

	Yes	No	Don't Know
	38%	48%	9·2%

* Doctors, lawyers, dentists (self-employed).
† Either attended or completed course, in each category.

6. Expatriate Employment and Africanization

EMPLOYMENT STRUCTURE AND UNIONS

The participation of expatriates in the private sector in Senegal does not at first seem dramatically different from that of expatriates in most neighbouring West African countries, except perhaps that there are rather more of them, and that they fill a wider range of posts. A closer analysis of the expatriate employment structure since independence and of its effect on labour matters in general requires an understanding of labour relations from the previous decade. For, while the total number of privately employed expatriates in Senegal has been considerably reduced since 1960, and while national planning for African manpower and technical training has been about the most advanced in West Africa,[1] certain problems inherent to expatriate employment and the relations between Frenchmen and Senegalese at work have proved continuing obstacles to both Africanization and the optimal use of local human resources.

Commercial firms, banks and insurance companies still have a higher absolute number of expatriate employees than any other sector of the economy, a total which continued to rise as late as the mid nineteen-sixties (see Table 5, p. 157). And while expatriate personnel in the industrial sector fell by 10 per cent from 1959 to 1963,[2] industries maintain European employees in a wider range of job than any other sector—from director to skilled worker.

The posts of Europeans in the lower echelons of industry, in particular, are defended by company directors because of their superior education and skill by comparison with their African

[1] Ken Post, *The New States of West Africa*, London, Penguin Books, 1964, pp. 147–8.
[2] G. Pfeffermann, *Industrial Labour in the Republic of Senegal*, New York, Praeger, 1968, p. 156.

counterparts. Frenchmen remain in supervisory posts (as foremen and shop stewards),[1] because continuing difficulties in the system of training and labour relations make their presence indispensable. There is a particularly high proportion of expatriate skilled labour in new industries, which have an immediate need for specialists who cannot be readily trained on the spot.[2] Where Europeans remain in the category *'ouvrier'*, they are usually classified as *'ouvriers professionels'*, or skilled workers, as distinct from *'ouvriers spécialisés'*, who are Senegalese trained on the job. There is in general a wide gulf in educational standard between Europeans and Africans in these grades,[3] as a large number of the African workers are entirely without formal education.

In both the highest and the lowest grades of employment in the private sector, the pattern is one typical of West African countries which rely on expatriate capital and senior personnel while supplying a largely unskilled or semi-skilled local labour force (see Table 6, p. 158). There are still many more European employers than African, for while there are thousands of Africans involved in petty trade and business throughout the country, few of them have any declared or regular employees. Europeans retain a near monopoly of executive and managerial posts, and remain predominant even among low-level white collar workers. The Senegalese pattern in middle-level employment is rather different from that in, for example, former British colonies, where Africanization has been much more rapid and effective. This includes technicians, foremen and supervisors (*agents de maîtrise*), office employees, clerks and secretaries (this last category almost exclusively reserved to

[1] Among the twenty-six industrial firms consulted by Pfeffermann in his study, he found that one-third of them had more than half expatriate foremen, and one-quarter had more than 75 per cent expatriates employed in this grade, *ibid.*, p. 67.
[2] André Hauser, 'L'Emergence de Cadres de Base Africains dans l'Industrie', in P. C. Lloyd, *The New Elites of Tropical Africa*, London, Oxford University Press, 1966, p. 231.
[3] This was generally true of all grades of employment below the managerial level, in which the educational qualifications of Africans and Europeans were about the same. André Hauser, *Les Problèmes du Travail*, roneo paper presented to a Dakar conference, communicated by the author, pp. 10–12. The study was based on 1964 labour statistics.

Employment Structure and Unions

locally recruited women).[1] Expatriate women are willing to work at salaries considerably lower than would be offered in France for the equivalent job, because of the advantage of accumulating savings in CFA francs at the highly favourable exchange rate and the amount of free time they are afforded by having low-cost African domestic employees in their homes. There are more than 2,000 European women currently employed in commerce and industry, chiefly in Dakar. The obvious poor quality of most Senegalese secretaries and typists[2] is partially explained by the lack of local training facilities in such skills until very recently, and the abundance of European women with typing and secretarial skills in the nineteen-fifties which obviated the need for local training. Unemployment among Europeans is almost unknown. Except for a few isolated cases, nearly all the expatriates registered as unemployed at the Labour Exchange are women.[3] Unemployment among Africans is by comparison, much higher but this can only in a limited way be still attributed to direct competition with Europeans. Several Senegalese whom I interviewed (see Introduction) felt, however, that because there were so many Frenchmen in the private sector one could attribute a certain amount of local unemployment to them as well as a retardation of Africanization. Whether or not it is objectively verifiable the fact that there exists a belief in the relationship between expatriate employment and Senegalese unemployment is an important consideration. Only one Senegalese informant (an employee in the electricity company) volunteered the information that he felt directly that he had been the victim of employment competition with Europeans. For most others, this contention was more vaguely formulated or wholly denied.

[1] For details of expatriate employment structure in 1964, see Table 7, p. 159, which was used as the framework of the stratified quota sample for the private sector.
[2] Most African secretaries with any position of responsibility are non-Senegalese and almost always French-trained. The new generation of Senegalese secretaries are mainly employed in the administration, where their inefficiency and poor training hinders administrative business.
[3] In 1967, for example, there were 903 French women inscribed as 'unemployed', 700 of whom declared that they had been previously employed in the commercial sector or in banks. André Hauser, *Les Problèmes du Travail*, op. cit., p. 13.

Expatriate Employment and Africanization

The participation of the French in the economy was considered beneficial by most Senegalese respondents employed in the private sector, who felt that French directors 'took an interest in, and aided the economic development of Senegal'. The provision of employment by the French firms was felt to be important:

> Companies battle against unemployment, which is disastrous for a country like ours; an underdeveloped country cannot grow if unemployment grows. Private enterprise helps to elevate the national income and the level of life.

Several thought that private companies also contributed to the country's national income, through the payment of taxes: 'There are certain companies which are large enough to bring prosperity to Senegal—they must be interested in the general economic situation of the country, for it is with this that they flourish.' One civil servant who worked on community development gave an alternative point of view:

> There are no benevolent capitalists. At the end of the first development plan, for example, there was a suggestion to expand retail trade in the rural areas, in order to help prevent further rural exodus. The directors of the private companies refused because it was not in their interests. They put money into that which turns out immediate profit, not necessarily what the country needs.

More general critical comments concerning French activities in the private sector were that the French were only interested in profit and that the capital they earned left the country. Some critical informants concluded that the only way in which French-owned industries would be of service to the economy was if they were nationalized. Several respondents seemed to consider eventual nationalization as inevitable, although it was long ago dropped from development plans in Senegal, where it only appeared earlier in the most vague terms in any case. Those informants who wished to reserve judgement on the value of French private business as a whole felt that there were certain companies, because of their magnitude and facility of reinvestment, which were beneficial to the country, while the value of others in this context was more questionable. Others felt that the only companies which showed an interest in the country were those which actively trained Senegalese cadres.

Since expatriates in the private sector fill a much wider range of posts than technical assistants, they naturally have a lower level of educational achievement. This level is kept low by female employees whose posts require very few educational qualifications. Among those interviewed in my survey, all those who had reached only *baccalauréat* (A level) status or below were privately employed. The global educational qualifications of expatriates, however, remained considerably higher than the average for metropolitan France and higher than it had been for Frenchmen in Dakar in the nineteen-fifties. The level is kept high principally by technical assistants, almost all of whom have university degrees. Higher education would not be required for any posts in the private sector, except those of a professional or advanced technical nature, although it appeared that a fairly high proportion of employees in executive or managerial positions had at least some university education. Most of these would be younger men recently recruited to overseas posts, who had not 'come up through the ranks' of the colonial company, but whose education may have made them open to the idea of overseas employment.

On the whole, the length of colonial experience or overseas service among respondents in the private sector differed little from that of technical assistants, except that more had been recruited to the public sector during the three years preceding the interview. Most of the executive personnel of private firms had more colonial experience than other employees, and no foremen or technicians in industry who were interviewed had been recruited to Senegal since 1957, a reflection of the declining business situation and of a deliberate attempt to Africanize at least this level. The 'new look' among some industrial directors and executives (described in Chapter 5) did not necessarily reflect their recent recruitment to overseas posts. Although there are now fewer and fewer 'career colonials' in any sphere of activity, most industrial directors had already been in Dakar for at least ten years.[1] Many of these had

[1] Of twenty-three industrial executives interviewed, over two-thirds had been in Senegal for more than eleven years.

adapted their views to the new economic and political situation.

There are certain obvious personal advantages to overseas employment in the former French colonies, and many employees, especially those in the first third of their careers, seek to take advantage of the opportunity. Young men look upon overseas employment chiefly as a means of advancement. Promotion was written in to some contracts as one of the rewards of service overseas. And for others, advancement which could be expected in overseas positions provided them with the experience which they could use to acquire a similar position with the firm on return to France. For these reasons young men often sought jobs with firms which required a certain amount of overseas service. The most important attraction in taking a job overseas remains, however, not so much future advancement as immediate earning power. Salaries are set at approximately 35 to 40 per cent above the basic metropolitan salary[1] for a given job, in order to compensate for the increased cost of living and expenses, defined as 'expatriate costs'. And, since most expatriates save this increase by purchasing only the bare necessities overseas, it can be deposited as savings in a bank account in France, where the CFA franc effectively doubles its original value. The average expatriate salary in the private sector is about £2,760 per annum,[2] excluding the costs of transportation and housing, which are provided by the employer for all on expatriate contract. Taxes are paid locally and are marginally lower than in France, and medical expenses are covered by health insurance included in the expatriate contract.

Among the general advantages of being in Africa mentioned

---

[1] The calculation is not exactly proportional at all levels of employment, and tends to favour office employees, foremen and technicians, rather than management.

[2] Precise estimates were not obtainable from any official or non-official source. This assessment was made by the editor of *Le Moniteur Africain*, the local business weekly, but was considered slightly too high by certain union officials and employers I consulted. They estimated the salaries of expatriate middle-grade employees (*agents de maîtrise*) at about only £1,560–£1,800 per annum and executives at £2,400 plus, per annum. The figure of £2,760 was, however, confirmed as the average salary for French technical assistance personnel. All estimates calculated on a pre-tax basis.

by my respondents, 102 cited the material benefits. Among those who cited the accumulation of savings as the most significant advantage, all except two were privately employed, while it is ironically the technical assistants who are traditionally accused by those in the private sector of living in deliberately austere circumstances in order to accumulate savings. Another major advantage which was mentioned, was the availability of domestic servants, employed by all Europeans, which would have been beyond the means of the majority of this group when resident in France.

These factors contribute to an explanation of why many Europeans consider working conditions to be superior in Senegal to those in France.[1] Among the advantages specifically related to working conditions were professional advancement, and more diversity and responsibility on the job. Some expanded on this by explaining that in France they felt compartmentalized into a small slot of work, whereas in Senegal they had much more varied tasks to perform and more freedom and individual initiative in performing them. They naturally therefore found overseas jobs to be much more interesting and more satisfying, and they also appreciated the lack of rigidity and strictness in working hours. Several also mentioned the relaxed working conditions and easy transportation to and from work as compared with the 'frantic' pace of work and travel in the major cities in France. Life in Senegal for them took on a naturally slow pace of its own—partly a function of the tropical climate and partly reinforced by the traditionally easy rhythm of expatriate life in such an environment. One of the most distinctive advantages of expatriate working conditions was considered to be the 'European club' atmosphere of the company, in which the relationship between French executives and employees was much closer and more amiable than would have been the case in France. Several mentioned how the case of personal contact and European solidarity provided a pleasant working atmosphere.

Because of such advantages, and, above all, lucrative

[1] Fifty-four per cent of those interviewed in the survey thought that they were better; 9 per cent the same; 27 per cent worse; and 4 per cent both better and worse for different reasons.

contracts, expatriate employees had little interest in trade unions in Senegal. Although precise figures were unavailable, it was estimated by the French Embassy that less than 3 per cent of the male European working force were under local contract and therefore in a fairly unstable position. Nearly all of those forty Europeans interviewed who were engaged under local contract were female secretaries, shop clerks and primary school teachers, most of whom felt that working conditions were worse than in France because the wages were so low (they were paid at local rates).

Nearly all expatriate trade union activities are confined to giving advice and making employees aware of their legal rights under their own contracts. In response to most complaints and queries, local union officials can only answer: 'You have a contract which was negotiated in France, nothing can be done.' Just after independence, a union of expatriate employees in the commercial sector was formed. It was later amalgamated as UNISCAMPTA, the one remaining exclusively expatriate union. It takes up the problems of those Frenchmen under local contract, although it has little power or authorization to do anything about their situation and usually simply introduces those in a particularly desperate situation to a mutual aid society or to the Embassy for repatriation. Apart from this, expatriate union activities are even less important now than they were in the nineteen-fifties. The union's central office consists of only one room, and a Secretary-General who comes in if someone contacts him for a discussion or appointment. His relations with the Senegalese union leaders are few: 'You can't take them seriously because they really don't know what the principles of unionism are all about.'[1] Like many long-time militants in such orthodox movements as French trade unionism, he does not understand why his orthodoxy concerning the appropriate structure and activities of a union is considered irrelevant by the Senegalese.

---

[1] He cited for example the founding meeting of a local union of journalists in which the entire session was taken up with a 'ridiculous' discussion in condemnation of President Salazar of Portugal. Interview with M. Josse, Secretary-General of UNISCAMPTA, spring 1967.

ASSESSMENT OF AFRICAN WORK PERFORMANCE

The disadvantages of working in Senegal which were mentioned by those expatriates interviewed were in particular the heavy responsibility and work load they had to assume because they felt they were not adequately supported by their African colleagues or subordinates. Certain of them felt that the Senegalese were generally 'difficult' to work with, others, that they did not work as hard as Frenchmen because they were 'not Cartesian', or were slow and lack initiative.

The actual performance of Senegalese workers has been analysed in a number of studies. On general aptitude, Senegalese workers showed identical scores to French workers, but on practical tests there was a net difference between outputs when the employee was permitted to organize his own work.[1] Thus, Senegalese labourers in routine jobs, or on assembly lines, have exactly the same output, given equal conditions, as their French counterparts, but in jobs demanding some amount of independent decision and organization the Senegalese labourer was less effective. It was also found that Africans trained to take over supervisory posts in industry from expatriates did not always possess all the 'non-technical qualities' required to make efficient foremen. The appropriate technical skill and aptitude for promotion were often found among workers who lacked more general education or the personal authority and adaptability to handle unforeseen and (for them) unprecedented difficulties arising in production.[2]

Part of the explanation for the differences in output and performance doubtless lies in the general problem of transforming a peasant or the son of a peasant into a factory worker. Thus, of 442 Senegalese industrial workers interviewed in 1959, only 27 per cent had fathers who had been in paid employment

---

[1] A study conducted by a French agency for the *Centre de Perfectionnement Professionel* in Dakar, and various studies on migrant African workers in French industry. Results discussed with the Director of the Centre and labour sociologist, André Hauser, Dakar, spring 1967.

[2] G. Pfeffermann, *op. cit.*, p. 71.

(and only 9·5 per cent of these were in industry).[1] And of 188 industrial workers interviewed in 1964, only 6·6 per cent had been born in Dakar, and less than half had had any industrial experience before starting on their present job: nearly 40 per cent had come straight from agriculture.[2]

Senegalese skilled workers were found to have what was termed 'little desire for advancement in the industrial context',[3] an attitude condemned by local Europeans as *'je m'en foutisme* (I don't care-ism)'* the precise words used to describe African behaviour at work by 11 per cent of the expatriate employees interviewed. Generalizations concerning the behaviour of Senegalese workers and officials were abundant throughout questionnaire responses: their lack of practical knowledge, their inability to plan ahead, their lack of professional conscientiousness, and their ineptitude in financial matters were felt to contribute to their generally low output. These were most often expressed in catch phrases like the following:

They are indolent by nature.
They have no courage.
They have no taste for work, nor work in their blood.
They don't look further than the work specifically demanded of them, or have the mentality to carry it to conclusion.
They lack initiative and a sense of responsibility.
They lack a sense of rigour or duty in their character.
They are nonchalant; the time of day has no significance for them.

Eighty-nine per cent of those interviewed in the private sector stated categorically that Africans did not have the same output as European employees. Some felt that they did in certain circumstances, adding that it depended on the profession or job of the employee in question. Others declared that 'Africans could not successfully go beyond a certain level of demand or work'. The point here to be examined is, however,

[1] André Hauser, *Les Ouvriers de Dakar*, Paris, Office de la Recherche Scientifique et Technique d'Outre-Mer, roneo publication, 1968, p. 151.
[2] G. Pfeffermann, *op. cit.*, p. 45.
[3] André Hauser, 'Quelques Relations des Travailleurs de l'Industrie à Leur Travail en A.O.F.', *Bulletin de l'Institut Français d'Afrique Noire*, Série B, Sections Humaines, No. 1-2, January 1955, pp. 129-41.

Assessment of African Work Performance

not the truth or otherwise of these assertions, but rather the nature of the explanation given for that which is believed to be true by expatriates.[1] One such explanation was based on the physical and climatic conditions of the working environment. A second relied on *a priori* sweeping judgements of the racial, national or cultural characteristics of *all* Senegalese, the corollary of which was to attribute observed behaviour to specific personality characteristics which were seen as biologically or culturally determined. A third was to associate observed behaviour with a certain stage of human or cultural evolution, which it was believed could be directly related to the stage of socio-economic development of the country itself. The fourth category of explanation, which accounted for approximately 5 per cent of those interviewed in the private sector, relied on economic or social factors present in the existing situation—that is, the inexperience of newly trained executives and employees, underemployment owing to redundancy, or the lack of appropriate education or training at all levels.

The tropical climate and poor nutrition are explanations for poor work output which have at least some basis for possible verification. While the Senegalese diet is considerably better than that of some other peoples in the underdeveloped world, it is certainly not as rich in vitamin or protein intake as an average European diet.[2] The tropical climate seems to have some influence on work output which affects Senegalese and Europeans alike: 'the output of all employed people or the pace of all work in Senegal is quite markedly inferior to that of France.'[3]

Those who felt that sub-standard work was culturally deter-

---

[1] For an explicit delineation of their explanations, see question 65 (for the private sector only), Appendix 3.
[2] Information provided by an economist working on nutrition and economic planning at the Institut de Science Economique Appliquée, Dakar. According to another study of African employees in the towns of Senegal, there has been a considerable influence of the European dietary and eating habits on Senegalese employees; and particularly in Dakar, among young people with some education. Pierre Fougeyrollas, *Modernisation des Hommes: l'Exemple du Sénégal*, Paris, Flammarion, 1966, pp. 67–70.
[3] Information provided by the representative of the Federation of French Industries in Dakar, March 1967.

mined attributed this to such factors as African family structure, child-rearing patterns and a fatalistic attitude believed to be instilled by Islam (the religion of over 90 per cent of the people of Senegal). The assumed relevance of religion to inferior work output in this context is that since practising Muslims are promised paradise whatever their activity in the temporal world, they therefore must feel free to relax rather than seek rewards through work in everyday life. The causal relationship of such beliefs to inferior work output is, however, quite difficult to verify. With regard to Muslim devotional practices specifically rather than beliefs, European employers and employees complained about the frequent daily prayers demanded by Islam, although these are seldom practised during working hours in urban businesses. Those respondents who showed most concern about local religious practices were those interviewed during the Muslim month of Ramadan, when the daylight fast is very generally observed by Senegalese Muslims. In this instance there does seem to be verifiable evidence concerning the physical weakness or sluggishness of employees, which results from this religious practice.

Other explanations for low African work output drawn from the social or cultural environment included the lack of discipline in African child-rearing. This led, it was felt, to the absence of socialization to a disciplined working environment, or of any 'cult of work'. With regard to the family structure, a respondent stated that 'life is easy here—the family structure assures that those who don't work are cared for'. Certain respondents favoured the notion of a hierarchy of cultures, with all African cultures consigned to a very low position. They regarded certain aspects of Senegalese behaviour as a manifestation of the inferior or 'uncivilized' nature of African society: in particular, the fact that baptisms, funerals, religious festivities and family matters in general were more important to most Senegalese than a day's work. These were considered to be a clear indication of cultural backwardness: 'All civilizations are not the same. Here (in Senegal) economic evolution is not very advanced. The Senegalese don't know how to plan ahead and they lack practical knowledge.'

Occasionally respondents attempted to explain inferiority in the working environment in terms of ethnic or tribal differences —that it was something inherent in Wolof society, for example. Paradoxically, however, expatriates interviewed in the Casamance (the southern region of Senegal) said that Diola or Manjack characteristics were inferior to those of the Wolof who, it was said, worked hard. Others tried to explain Senegalese behaviour on the basis of national characteristics: 'The Senegalese have more of an inferiority complex (*complexé*) than the Ivorians, who are not ashamed to admit that the French still run their country.' Certain expatriate managers felt there was an obvious difference in behaviour among employees of different generations: 'The older ones are better because they are more responsible and polite; they were trained on the job and are more devoted to their European overseer than the younger generation who have "theoretical" (technical) training, but lack experience and politeness.' The lack of respect which was felt to be naturally owed to Europeans was accounted for in part by the breakdown of the traditional social system, and especially by the disrupted family life in the cities. Greater deference towards Frenchmen seemed much more apparent among the older Senegalese employees interviewed on my brief questionnaire survey.

The type of peasant farming done in Senegal was also thought to be a basis for inferior work output by some Europeans. Groundnut cultivation takes considerably less effort than rice cultivation, for example, and it was felt therefore that Senegalese peasants were used to relatively less work. While rice must be continually tended during the growing season, groundnuts require relatively little care after the land is cleared and the sowing is done. Some thought that the government had a responsibility to improve matters in this sphere: 'The government doesn't force the peasants to grow enough groundnuts. They're lazy, not like the Chinese who work at least thirty-five times harder.' Or, 'life presents no difficulties: there is no famine or hard climatic conditions. With the smallest effort, everything just grows.' A few respondents felt that the Senegalese had deliberately chosen groundnut cultivation because they were 'naturally lazy', or that they preferred a job with less pay because it involved less work.

Expatriate Employment and Africanization

A final category of respondents rejected cultural inferiority as the basis of explanation for inferior labour performance, because they felt that Africans would never achieve the level of European civilization, no matter what their efforts, owing to their basic racial inferiority. Explanations for inferior work output based on what are believed to be stable inherited characteristics were not, as one might expect, confined to the poorly educated respondents: most had reached at least secondary school or the *baccalauréat*, and some even had attended university. In the commercial sector, one half of those who spoke of racial inferiority were office employees, who were mainly women and had reacted similarly to other questions. Women, I found, were much less sensitive than men to censoring their actual feelings or disguising them with a veil of explanation or euphemism. They showed a consistently low tolerance of African behaviour and often indeed exhibited open hostility to African ways. Half of those giving social inferiority as the explanation for inferior work output were executives and managerial staff. A comparison between the results on work output and the results of questions on the economic situation in general (which were posed to all respondents and were discussed in Chapter 5) reveals a similarity in theme of response and explanation. Often, however, in the same interview, the question on work output (which followed the other) provided an opportunity to personalize the more generally expressed feelings, which often revealed more deep-seated prejudices than were initially apparent.

Among the nine foremen interviewed, none mentioned African racial inferiority as an explanation for inferior work output. Having the most direct contact with African workers on the shop floor, they were perhaps in a better position than other Europeans to judge deficiencies, which they attributed to lack of training and preparation for the job. Their assessment is particularly interesting because it was their posts, above all, which continue to be threatened with Africanization: fear or sense of competition with African subordinates did not necessarily lead them to the prejudice-based stereotypes found among other groups in the sample (see below for a discussion of foremen's attitudes to Africanization).

LABOUR RELATIONS AND AFRICANIZATION

No official percentage has been established as an appropriate rate of Africanization, although at the time of independence Senegal signed an international convention prohibiting any single firm from hiring more than 40 per cent foreigners.[1] A certain group in the U.P.S. (usually the Diaists or left-wing elements) wanted to raise the percentage, although this was not supported by the President, and it was ignored by most firms. Certain banks which made an attempt to increase their rate of Africanization began to cut back in 1964, 'because their work routines were so upset'.[2]

In 1964, a Franco-Senegalese Convention made a work contract obligatory for all Frenchmen who wished to come to Senegal. Contract renewal in the private sector is almost always accorded to expatriates and only when a European is to be replaced does his post come under review by the *Inspection du Travail*. If there is a qualified Senegalese to fill the post, it is Africanized. A law in 1965 extending the effectiveness of the reciprocal agreement has, according to the director of the *Inspection du Travail* 'put European employers into a new frame of mind'. 'More goodwill is needed, on the part of European directors', he felt however, 'for they continue to recommend expatriate employees to us as if they were indispensable, whereas often the only difference between them and a qualified Senegalese is their skin colour.'[3] On account of a Presidential order, particular attention has been given to the placement of professionally trained Senegalese who are unemployed. But

---

[1] Director, *Inspection du Travail*, Dakar, 1967.
[2] M. Ducrot, Vice-President of expatriate trade union, UNISCAMPTA, and generally prominent in union activities in Dakar since the early nineteen-fifties. Interview, spring 1967.
[3] Interview, spring 1967. As late as 1967, however, European employers still complained about being 'forced' to Africanize: 'Our demands for employing expatriates are not numerous. We have difficulty in understanding the obstacles created by the administration. We think that there are some points which still must be cleared up.' SCIMPEX (Employers Association for Commerce), *Procès-Verbal de l'Assemblée Générale du 14 Mars 1967*, roneo, communicated by the Administrative secretary.

these regulations are often evaded by company directors where desired by making such specific demands that they are tailor-made to fit the European job-seeker in question.

There are independent factors which have increased the global rate of Africanization at a slow but steady pace. Expatriate personnel, even though considered more efficient and reliable by local French employers and managers, is much more expensive. The restriction of markets and the general economic situation have compelled many firms to cut down on this considerable expense. But there are still not enough well-trained Africans to replace all Europeans, especially those in managerial or professional posts. For posts in middle-management, the technical schools and *lycées* are providing more and more each year. But the shortage of qualified people is not the only factor involved. European attitudes towards Africanization and interracial relations on the job continue to affect the rate of Africanization. Most important among such attitudes are those based on the beliefs concerning the work output of Africans discussed previously. Some respondents concluded that Africans were naturally unsuited for all commercial and secretarial jobs. Others claimed that the Senegalese worker simply did not care about his job or the company which employed him in the way that a European did, though their opinions were coloured by a somewhat unreal vision of labour relations in France. It is an observation which contains within it, however, a certain element of truth. A Senegalese employee may feel more remote from the executive level of a French company than does the ordinary French worker, given that the management is all white and the administration and direction of the company seem to have little to do with him or his country.[1]

In response to the direct question (asked of those in the private sector only): 'Do you think an accelerated Africanization is advisable in your type of work?', 50 per cent answered 'yes', and 46 per cent 'no'. Nine out of ten respondents who had

---

[1] 'Although (European) employers have established a *modus vivendi* with the government, and the trade unions, a potential danger remains a confusion by the African labour force of industrial grievances and anti-French feelings.' G. Pfeffermann, *op. cit.*, p. 275.

Labour Relations and Africanization

been in Senegal under three years were favourable to Africanization, which might indicate that they were either more 'liberal', or that over a certain time period expatriates are 'corrupted' by the local milieu. Affirmative responses were, however, often highly qualified. There seemed to have been a conscious filter on the attitudes of certain respondents, who realized that one should not *a priori* be opposed to Africanization, as it was a sensitive public issue. While they were willing to answer that they were in favour of it, qualifications indicated their actual opposition. Of the total affirmative responses, only 23 per cent, or 12·5 per cent of the total, gave a clear 'yes'. The remainder modified affirmation with some of the following qualifications:

> Yes, but in posts restricted according to their ability.
> One must hope for it, but there aren't enough of them, therefore it's impossible.
> It saves money for the company, but there are still too many problems.
> Yes, so long as they are directed by Europeans.
> Yes, but for a few only.

Certain expatriate employees frankly admitted that Africanization was not in their own interests. In both commerce and industry those in executive posts of all grades appeared to be more receptive than lower level employees (except foremen in industry as noted above). They perhaps felt a greater responsibility to be at least publicly amenable, and were continually made aware by their own national offices or company budgets of the saving involved in increased Africanization. Among the foremen interviewed there was also a considerable receptivity to Africanization, which follows logically from their earlier indication that inferior work output could be attributed to absence of training on the whole. The explanation for their attitudes is not easy to assess, and may be attributed to a bias of selection, for only a very small number (nine in all) were interviewed. Their receptivity does provide a marked contrast to expatriate office employees, most of whom do not work directly with Africans but in relative isolation with other whites (see Table 8, p. 162).

Expatriate Employment and Africanization

The gradual increase in the rate of Africanization in the private sector does not necessarily mitigate some of the existing problems of labour relations; in particular, the transfer of skills from European to African and the training of new African personnel in general. Inter-racial labour problems and inadequacies in the structure of the work situation lead to a questioning of the value of Africanization in its present form. Certain practices on the job in the pre-independence period serve to explain present labour problems: rather than train an African employee thoroughly for the job at that time, a Frenchman could always have been brought in to finish work which had been improperly done by an African. This was described by a French white-collar worker who had spent eight years in the Gold Coast before arriving in Senegal.

> The English had a better method for training labourers. If an African was required to do a job, and it wasn't done properly the first or second or third time, he did it until it was. In Senegal, when the work was not done properly, the French overseer would lose his temper and send the African away. There was always a Frenchman available to do the work improperly done by an African. In the British colonies this group did not exist, so the Africans had to be trained.

The results of this which are borne in the present working context are a host of poorly or half-trained Africans.

Many of the Europeans interviewed felt, as indeed did the President of the Republic, that the ineptitude of the Senegalese for posts of responsibility or command had become a grave problem. The publicly stated Presidential view was often mentioned by expatriates in support of their opinions. Senegalese absence of responsibility was attributed by those interviewed in part to the deference of the younger for the older in the traditional family structure, Islam, or peasant society. It could be argued more persuasively, however, that the remaining need for a substantial amount of direct supervision in the working environment comes less from primordial cultural characteristics than from a lack of skills and poor training. Feelings of dependency on or deference towards Europeans may be apparent among the older generation of African workers accustomed to working under European supervision, but this is hardly a national or cultural characteristic as some Europeans sought to imply.

A prevalent view on this question was stated by a French company director: 'Africans prefer to work with a European over them; when an overseer's post is Africanized, the other employees behave as if they have lost a certain standing.' Such an observation was acknowledged to be valid by young Senegalese executives as well. The 'loss of standing' felt by older Senegalese workers in French firms is complicated by the fact that younger men with training often take Africanized posts, and that the older workers find it difficult to adjust to working under their direction. This is largely a generational problem.

My Senegalese informants were asked to comment on whether or not they felt that Frenchmen and Senegalese would be given equal consideration in the same type of post or with the same level of training. Seven respondents felt that labour relations remained unaffected by group differences, and that a person was considered according to merit. Those dissenting from this view had, in general, opinions which were markedly more critical of the French than those they had expressed in previous, more general questions. Respondents who were in an executive or high-ranking specialist role in a French firm felt that the problem of equal consideration was particularly acute at their level; that their authority might be questioned by either European superiors or African subordinates (particularly older employees used to working under French direction). Most of the respondents who did not have subordinates of their own felt that there might be a problem of equal consideration by subordinates of an African and a European superior. They did not, however, feel that this would create really serious problems in the authority structure of a firm. One added parenthetically that 'those Senegalese who could not make their subordinates respect them because they were not white men were not capable of being in the position at all'.

Concerning the preference for either a French or a Senegalese boss, there was a diversity of opinion among Senegalese respondents: twelve preferred a Senegalese, eight preferred a Frenchman and five were indifferent. Civil servants on the whole showed a greater preference for Senegalese direction than employees in the private sector. Those civil servants who were employed in services which had no Frenchmen (police, municipal courts and post office) were not only unanimously in favour of working for a Senegalese, they also exhibited a greater self-assurance and independence of the French in labour matters than other respondents, especially employees in French firms. On the whole, preferences of respondents could be interpreted as a reflection of satisfaction with their existing work situation.

The question about preference for an African or European boss was posed to an entirely different group of respondents in a survey conducted in 1959 on about 450 workers in the manufacturing industries of Dakar.[1] The findings seem to correspond in at least one respect with the responses of my own informants, that familiarity with an African boss correlated with a preference for the same. Africans seem to be preferred or at least judged on the basis of their personal characteristics, while Europeans appeared to be judged on professional characteristics alone. The reasons given by the respondents in my survey for their preference for an African boss included: better understanding, more freedom at work, and fewer demands than a Frenchman would make. The industrial workers said they preferred Africans because of shared customs and language, and were occasionally more specific:

> He comes to my baptisms and family occasions, and gives me a little time off for prayer. I prefer being directed by a Muslim.[2]

On the whole, most of my respondents agreed that one could

[1] André Hauser, *Les Ouvriers de Dakar*, Paris, Office de Recherche Scientifique et Technique d'Outre-Mer, 1968. The industries which he studied included a cement factory, a groundnut oil refinery, and a textile company (p. 32). The sample included 35 per cent unskilled labourers, 31 per cent qualified workers, 28 per cent skilled workers or artisans, and 6 per cent foremen (p. 48). It was found that among the total group interviewed 62 per cent preferred an African, 11 per cent a European and 26 per cent had no preference (p. 158).
[2] *Ibid.*, p. 89.

expect more liberty from a Senegalese boss, but others felt that with a French boss the work had a tendency to go more smoothly, because he was in better command of the situation: 'The French are more competent at giving instructions because they have greater professional assurance and greater aptitude for leadership.' The industrial workers favouring a European boss placed some emphasis on the moral superiority of Europeans, a suggestion which was conspicuously absent among the employees and civil servants in my survey.

Problems of authority in French enterprises usually begin at the time of in-service training and integration of Africans into command posts. At the executive level, the in-service training of an African employee is usually carried out personally by the departing European whose place he is supposed to take. This is an unfortunate but inevitable means of achieving this specialized preparation. Feeling a certain amount of resentment over impending departure, the European may find it actually rather difficult to prepare his subordinate to effectively replace him. The following description of such a situation was given by a young Senegalese executive with a large commercial house in Dakar:

> My superior had six weeks to prepare me to do his work, but he did nothing. On the last day he handed me an enormous dossier, and said 'Here it is!' The actual know-how of executive or managerial positions is kept a well-guarded secret between Europeans themselves.

This happens at many levels of employment and training. Africans are frequently poorly prepared for the tasks they are supposed to perform, and they learn at best on an *ad hoc* basis. In a recent study of Senegalese industry the author noted that there was no incentive for expatriate foremen to raise the technical abilities of their African teams; indeed the very authority of a French foreman (often of mediocre ability) rested on the incapacity of his African subordinates.[1] Although this description hardly tallies with the impression given by the few foremen interviewed in my sample, it was corroborated by similar evidence from labour sociologists and technical

[1] See G. Pfeffermann, *op. cit.*, p. 73.

assistants working on training programmes for the industrial sector. Having little professional or technical training, many expatriates in supervisory posts advanced in the company at a time when these positions were reserved for whites. What to do with those who remain in such posts is an on-going problem for company management. They cannot be integrated under an African superior because of the potential racial tension, and have refused to be trained alongside other Africans. For the time being, therefore, they remain an obstacle to restructuring labour in the private sector.

There have been several attempts in national planning to meet the middle-management African manpower shortage, by the improvement of professional and technical training facilities throughout the country. While some employees are sent to apprenticeship centres to improve their skills, most firms prefer in-service training schemes, which cost them less. Their drawback is that they provide only limited training for specific tasks in the production process, and that they seem to have had, in any case, only the half-hearted support of most company directors. An obvious area for professional training is the upgrading of Senegalese employees to management or workers to foremen. A training institute was established in Dakar in 1964 with precisely this aim, that is, to raise the standard of African work by improving the professional skills which an employee already had.[1] Yet although the programme has already turned out several hundred qualified students, the results have been disappointing. While the employees are proposed for the course by their company directors, they are not always promoted upon completion of it. The newly trained employee is often complimented by his director or given a small bonus and then returned to his former post for several more years, creating a potentially difficult problem, in his relations with his European superior whose place he was given to believe he would occupy.

---

[1] *Centre de la Formation Fonctionelle et Professionelle* (formerly the *Centre de Perfectionnement Professionel*). It was initiated as a project of the Federation of French Industries in Dakar, and was paid for by them until 1967. It then became a Senegalese public institution under the Ministry of Technical Education.

Labour Relations and Africanization

The receptivity of various French companies to Africanization depends on several factors among which are whether they are a local firm or a branch of an international company; and above all, whether their prospects are favourable or unfavourable in terms of current economic expansion. In a stagnating market situation, a locally-based company which is unable to redeploy expatriate staff will usually bring out young European technicians on limited contracts to train Africans, while retiring older less skilled employees. At times, however, non-economic factors are equally strong in affecting company policy on Africanization. In an international company, for example, the decision to increase Africanization may be taken in Paris, but its implementation blocked by local management. Many of these company directors have had long colonial experience, having come up through the ranks of the company, with all the prejudices frequently associated with rapid upward mobility in a colonial environment,[1] the most common of which is to underestimate the capacity of African employees. They also feel a sense of solidarity with white employees and an obligation to defend their interest against Africanization. Mixed with prejudice may be an element of fear. As one company director openly admitted: 'How can I Africanize all these posts? One day I'll find myself alone in this corridor with nothing but blacks in the adjoining offices. That would be impossible!'

Apart from matters of employment, it appears that local directors have very little executive authority in making company policy, as has been previously mentioned. They therefore have no real sense of responsibility for the long-term interests of the company in Africa, and prefer to defend the position of other expatriate colleagues. Their oft stated view that Africans can never be prepared to do the work performed by a European is regarded with increased scepticism by executives in the head office. Those who work with these local directors on matters of professional training have come to regard their attitudes as similar to those of company directors of thirty years ago:

---

[1] See Chapter 10 for a discussion of this hypothesis, its relevance in the context of French attitudes in Senegal, and its analysis in American sociological literature.

Expatriate Employment and Africanization

'Nothing has been decolonized in their attitude or mentality.'[1]

It may be argued therefore that the possibilities of restructuring labour in the private sector so that it might contribute to an optimum use of local human resources is therefore inhibited by attitudes prevailing among the older generation of French executives and their long-term African employees. Even the ideas of the new generation of young French technocrats and their Senegalese counterparts seemed submerged in the overpowering beliefs (and resultant behaviour) of the majority, which has not freed itself from the past.

---

[1] Interview with M. Philippe, Director of the *Centre de la Formation Fonctionelle et Professionnelle*, April 1967. An interesting historical companion piece to many of the attitudes discussed in this chapter concerning African work aptitude and Africanization, is this account of thirty years ago, illustrating a surprising similarity and persistence in thinking:

> The explanation for (Senegalese) incapacity for good work is the mediocrity of the population. The native workers don't have the predisposition of finishing, one must be satisfied with only a rough approximation with them. The principle inconvenience is a native communal system which favours indolence and laziness which can be explained only in part by the climate.

From Pierre Faucheux, 'Premier Voyage à Dakar', *Lyon Colonial*, Bulletin de Reseignements Economiques et Coloniaux, publié par l'Association des Anciens Elèves de l'Enseignement Colonial et de l'Ecole Coloniale de la Chambre de Commerce de Lyon, No. 80, November–December 1930, pp. 161, 164.

TABLE 5

Distribution of the Total Labour Force in Senegal by Origin, Sex and Sector of Employment,* 1964 and 1965

SECTOR		FRENCH		TOTAL	
		men	women	men	women
Agriculture, Fishing	64	30	5	4,083	18
(registered employees)	65	24	13	4,049	41
Extractive Industries	64	261	83	2,540	—
	65	151	45	2,556	—
Manufactur. Industries	64	1,061	325	15,996	1,166
	65	938	292	14,598	1,174
Building, Public	64	484	122	14,665	240
Works	65	495	130	14,539	240
Utilities,	64	177	49	2,907	59
Sanitation	65	199	54	2,944	68
Commerce, Insurance,	64	1,543	984	14,835	1,630
Banks	65	1,626	1,094	14,973	1,892
Transport and	64	581	190	15,450	410
Communication	65	590	194	15,668	310
Services	64	508	706	10,249	1,764
	65	402	485	10,824	1,804
TOTAL	64	4,555	2,464	80,685	5,287
	65	4,425	2,307[1]	77,641[2]	5,863

* From Ministère du Travail et de la Fonction Publique, Service des Statistiques du Travail, *Rapport sur les Statistiques de l'Emploi*, Dakar, 1968, Tableau No. 4.

[1] The French labour force for 1963 was 4,509 men and 2,672 women.

[2] A breakdown of the total number of non-French males by nationality is for 1965 as follows:

Senegalese	'Other Africans'	'Other Foreigners' (mainly Lebanese)
71,973	3,628	1,613

157

TABLE 6

Distribution of the Labour Force in Senegal by Origin, Sex and Grade of Employment,* 1962

	FRENCH		SENEGALESE	
Category of Employment	men	women	men	women
Employers	410	130	374	21
Unpaid Family Employees	27	70	68	11
Executives, Engineers	1,383	110	326	24
Middle-grade Employees and Technicians†	2,215	399	2,112	26
Clerks, Secretaries, Accountants	332	1,846	12,996	715
Skilled Workers	105	108	20,889	523
Unskilled or Specialized Workers	4	—	21,808	223
Apprentices	33	9	1,528	24
TOTAL	4,509	2,672	60,111	1,567

* Includes entire private sector plus civilians who work for the army and non-technical assistants in the administration. It excludes only civil servants (strictly defined). Typescript summary of study communicated by André Hauser, labour sociologist, *Institut Fondamental d'Afrique Noire*, Dakar, 1967.

† This rather general category, *agents de maîtrise*, includes low level white-collar workers as well as foremen and works-overseers from the shop floor.

TABLE 7

*Distribution of the Total Labour Force in Dakar in 1964 by Origin, Sex, Sector, and Grade of Employment**

Sector, Category of Employment	NON-AFRICANS[1] men	NON-AFRICANS[1] women	AFRICANS[2] men	AFRICANS[2] women
Agriculture, Fishing				
Employers	4	3		
Management, Executives	4			
Middle-grade Employees, Tech.	3			
Clerks, Secretaries, Accountants	4	1	8	
		sub-T		
TOTAL	15	4	8	
Extractive Industries[3]				
Director	1			
Management, Executives	23	1	3	
Middle-grade Employees, Tech.	18	9	35	
Clerks, Secretaries, Accountants		13	72	5
		sub-T[4]		
TOTAL	42	23	110	5

* From *Les Problèmes du Travail*, roneo paper delivered to conference on Dakar in Senegal, Spring 1965, by André Hauser, personally communicated by the author.

[1] French and Lebanese. Some of the Lebanese, as will be evident from the figures, are employed in French industries, others own or work in Lebanese-owned industries. While most of the Lebanese are in the commercial sector (several thousand alone in Dakar), their numbers were obviously underestimated in the above table. The inclusion of Lebanese in the category 'Non-African' explains the discrepancy between this total and that for 'French' in Senegal in Table 5.

[2] Senegalese and others, usually from French-speaking West Africa.

[3] The large discrepancy between this total and that of 'French' in Table 5 is that the largest extractive installation in Senegal is outside Dakar in the region of Thiès: the Phosphates of Taïba.

[4] In this sector, the categories of skilled worker, manual worker and apprentice were omitted because they did not include any 'Non-Africans'. Thus, the total of Africans employed for the sector is naturally larger than the sub-total.

TABLE 7 (*continued*)

Sector, Category of Employment	NON-AFRICANS		AFRICANS	
	men	women	men	women
Manufacturing Industries				
Employers or Directors	77	18	27	1
Management, Executives	272	15	14	
Middle-grade Employees, Tech.	534	35	481	
Clerks, Secretaries, Accountants	69	231	1,023	27
Skilled Workers	46	6	6,345	693
Unskilled Manual Workers	1		2,777	95
Apprentices	3		111	
TOTAL	1,002	305	10,778	816
Building, Public Works				
Employers or Directors	41	2	22	
Management, Executives	146	6	8	2
Middle-grade Employees, Tech.	231	20	142	
Clerks, Secretaries, Accountants	10	87	372	20
Skilled Workers	103	2	3,595	1
Manual Workers	7		3,265	1
Apprentices			26	
TOTAL	538	117	7,430	24
Gas, Water, Electricity, Sanitary Services				
Management, Executive	8		8	
Middle-grade Employees, Tech.	117	34	149	
Clerks, Secretaries, Accountants	1	3	246	4
Skilled Workers	4		591	
Manual Workers			814	
Apprentices			12	
TOTAL	130	37	1,820	4

TABLE 7 (*continued*)

Sector, Category of Employment	NON-AFRICANS		AFRICANS	
	men	women	men	women
Commerce, Banks, Insurance Cos.				
Employers, Directors	223	32	69	4
Family Employees (mainly Lebanese—numerically under-represented)	33	18	7	2
Management, Executives	518	41	68	5
Middle-grade Employees, Tech.	533	108	380	4
Clerks, Secretaries, Accountants	218	707	2,783	206
Skilled Workers	54	19	1,391	114
Manual Workers	2	1	1,529	36
Apprentices			23	1
TOTAL	1,581	926	6,250	372
Transport, Communication				
Employers, Directors	26	4	30	4
Family Employees	1	2	3	1
Management, Executives	235	5	77	1
Middle-grade Employees, Tech.	201	56	529	14
Clerks, Secretaries, Accountants	29	104	1,750	49
Skilled Workers	27		1,565	
Manual Workers			4,540	3
TOTAL	519	171	8,504	72
Services[1]				
Employers, Directors	93	29	26	3
Family Employees	6	13	1	
Management, Executives	156	33	83	9
Middle-grade Employees, Tech.	95	51	160	12
Clerks, Secretaries, Accountants	74	483	1,942	403
Skilled Workers	23	12	1,069	53
Manual Workers	3	1	505	16
Apprentices	4		4	
TOTAL	454	622	3,790	496

[1] 'Services' includes hotels, restaurants, hairdressing salons, laundries, dry-cleaning shops and health centres. In this category of employment are primary school teachers under contract to the Senegalese government (most of the 403 'non-African' women), the army, the police and government social services. It also includes religious orders, those employed in recreational or sporting activities, artists and certain professionals.

TABLE 8

Africanization

Do you think that an accelerated Africanization is advisable in your type of work? (question 66 for members of the private sector only).

i) *Commerce*	Yes	No	
Self-Employed (12)	50%	50%	
Sales Clerks* (10)	60	40	
Management† (25)	66	31	
Employees (27)	41	59	

ii) *Industry*	Yes	No	That Depends
Executives‡ (30)	56%	40%	3%
Technicians (26)	42	40	8
Office Employees (14)	21	79	0
Foremen (9)	66	33	0

iii) *Education of Respondent*	Yes	No	That Depends
Primary School (24)	48%	52%	0%
Secondary School (27)	39	54	7
Technical School (13)	42	51	9
Baccalauréat (51)	56	44	0
University Studies (13)	57	43	0
University Graduate (32)	66	33	0
ost-Graduate Work and Advanced Technical Studies (47)	50	50	0

* In small business (shops).
† In trading companies.
‡ Including employers, management and professional employees.

7. Technical Assistance

ORIGINS AND STRUCTURE OF THE PROGRAMME

It is the purpose of technical assistance programming to indicate where the needs for foreign skills and training are most pressing, and to design a strategy for aid to ensure that the scarce resources are used where their yield will be greatest.[1]

Neither an assessment of the output of technical assistance nor the calculation of its effectiveness can be derived from such a simplistic formula. The 'architects' of such programmes often do, however, treat the export of knowledge or skill as if it were a tangible commodity which could have a reasonably calculable output. The disappointment with which the ineffectiveness of certain programmes is reviewed can perhaps be explained in terms of a dual misunderstanding. First is the lack of appreciation of the cultural and behavioural environment into which these skills are introduced, either by technical assistance programmers or those sent out to serve on the programme. Second is perhaps the absence of explicitly stated objectives for the general programme, apart from the training of local cadres and the provision of certain skills and knowledge until local civil servants are fully prepared to take responsibility, which gives no indication of the scope and purpose of the activities of the individual technical assistants. To have simply been designated in an advisory capacity leaves open to interpretation the limits of discretion and authority contained in the role of technical assistant. In consequence, this role may vary widely from post to post depending on the nature of the work and the personalities involved, or differing expectations

[1] Angus Maddison, *Foreign Skills and Technical Assistance in Economic Development*, Paris, Development Centre of the Organization for Economic Co-operation and Development, 1965, p. 164.

Technical Assistance

surrounding it may even provide a source of tension between the technical assistant and the local civil servants with whom he works. These problems are perhaps particularly evident where there is a massive personnel export to a particular country, as is the case of the French programme in Senegal.

There were 1,200 French technical assistants in Senegal in 1971,[1] whose services were provided by a programme administered through the Secretariat of State for Co-operation.[2] Three-quarters of these are in teaching posts and the remaining 318 are in the administration where their influence, although varying widely according to personal, political or policy factors, is disproportionate to their total numbers. The impact of the present programme lies less in the numbers of personnel than in the continuation of structures and attitudes derived from the colonial period which permeate the public service. Since the technical assistant himself often fulfils an ambiguous role, there is a natural tendency on the part of both Frenchmen and Senegalese to return to the more obvious patterns of behaviour established in the past; the ultimate effect of which is that a French network within the administration retains considerable influence on policy.

The continuity of the Franco-Senegalese connection is in part

---

[1] Information communicated by the Secretariat of State for Cooperation, Paris, 1971, figures as of January 1971.

[2] Its full designation is the Secretariat of State for Foreign Affairs in Charge of Co-operation. Previous to 1966, it was the Ministry of Co-operation. The administrative change made it part of an enlarged Ministry of Foreign Affairs to ensure that technical, economic, financial and cultural aid would be better coordinated. There are a number of technical assistance projects and schemes which are either financed by French funds or staffed by Frenchmen, but which do not fall under the rubric of the official programme. The University of Dakar, for example, is directed by the French Ministry of Education, and other ministries and departments can provide personnel on special contractual arrangement. Non-governmental programmes directed by several development agencies (including the *Compagnie d'Etudes Industrielles et d'Aménagement de Territoire* (C.I.N.A.M.) and the *Institut de Recherches et d'Application des Méthodes de Développement* (I.R.A.M.)) provide assistance on urban and rural planning, community development and rural animation. While the official French programme is predominant, there are also several United Nations projects and a fairly large contribution from Common Market technical assistance funds to agricultural development. Apart from university personnel, however, all of these other projects accounted for only about 100 technical assistants.

Origins and Structure of the Programme

explained by the extent to which Senegal's administrative and economic infrastructure was integrated into the French system in the years following the Second World War. Such French projects as F.I.D.E.S. (*Fonds d'Investissement pour le Développement Economique et Social*) provided African states with very complex administrative structures which were based entirely on metropolitan forms and methods.[1] The annual running costs of the system, and particularly of European personnel to direct it, became a considerable part of the colonial budget. In 1956, for example, the wages of the public sector in Senegal were 9·6 per cent of the Gross National Product, of which 3·2 per cent were for Europeans, while in the Gold Coast in the same year, the equivalent was 6·7 per cent and 0·7 per cent respectively.[2] This had a certain effect on the present structure and finance of the Senegalese public service. Independent Senegal has retained most of the French administrative structures inherited from the colonial period, and where local personnel sources have been insufficient to maintain them personnel has been supplied from France.

Senegal has one of the highest concentrations of French technical assistants and teachers in Africa, although she was considered to have been one of the two West African countries (with Dahomey) which could have exported public servants to some of the less well-endowed neighbouring countries at the time of independence. The explanation for this concentration of French personnel in Senegal lies as much with explicit Senegalese policy as it does with the continuation of French influence. It was the calculated cost of political stability in the years following independence. Senghor announced in May 1960

---

[1] France, Ministère d'Etat Chargé de la Réforme Administrative, *La Politique de Coopération Avec les Pays en Voie de Développement:* Rapport de la Commission d'Etude Institué par le décret du 12 Mars 1963 remis au Gouvernement le 18 juillet 1963 (known as the Jeanneney Report), pp. 80–1. 'Projects administered under F.I.D.E.S. gave priority to the infrastructure and provision of equipment, a long-term policy with sacrifices in the short-term. They were above all inappropriate to the type of aid required after independence.'

[2] J. Saxe, a paper written in October 1960 for the Harvard University Center for International Affairs ('The Legacy of Britain and France in West Africa'), cited in Teresa Hayter, *French Aid*, London, The Overseas Development Institute, Ltd., 1966, p. 40.

Technical Assistance

that he was firmly opposed to the use of Africanization as an ideological or political issue 'which risked becoming *africanisation au rabais*'[1] (cut-rate Africanization). To this end, he opted for the maintenance of Frenchmen in the administration in order to provide optimal efficiency and stability. And in education, he has clung to the classical French structure and curriculum, as the model for Senegal. Though French technical assistance is often referred to by Senegalese students and intellectuals as 'technical insistence', it would be an error to consider it as unilateral insistence on the part of France. In 1966, for example, the Senegalese government requested thirty more technical assistants than the French Secretariat of State for Co-operation was willing to supply.[2]

The original agreement[3] between France and Senegal which established the technical assistance programme in 1959 made reference to the 'provision of personnel estimated necessary for the functioning of the public services' of the Republic of Senegal. It mentioned certain prescriptions binding the technical assistants, such as conformity to the regulations and policies of the Senegalese government, abstention from actions which might be politically sensitive and the respect of confidentiality for information obtained in a professional capacity. Apart from this, however, there was no positive definition of the function of the technical assistant in the service of the Senegalese government, and this has not since been done at any official level. While it would have been very difficult to provide specific information on the very varied working roles filled by the technical assistants, the absence of any adequate definition of the scope and limitations of their responsibility or the nature

---

[1] '*Africaniser au rabais*' (author's italics) in placing incompetent civil servants at posts which require experienced technical skill is to move backwards: it is to introduce waste and inefficiency in the state services...' in a speech to the youth section of the *Parti de la Fédération Africaine* (the Mali Federation) published in *Nation et Voie Africaine du Socialisme*, Paris, Presence Africaine, 1961.
[2] Interview with H. Fralon, the French technical assistant serving in the President's office in Senegal for studies on the French programme.
[3] *Convention Relative au Concours en Personnel Apporté par la République Française au Fonctionnement des Services de la République du Sénégal*, signed in Paris, 14 September 1959 by M. Dia and J. Autin, roneo copy given to me at the Senegalese *Service de l'Assistance Technique*.

Origins and Structure of the Programme

of reciprocal interaction between the French and Senegalese in a professional capacity, has left interpretation open to debate. In Senegal, discussion has been institutionalized in annual 'Reflective Sessions' which have been attended by small groups of teachers, technical assistants, and Senegalese civil servants since 1961.[1]

In the initial phase of the technical assistance programme between 1959 and 1961, the Ministry of Co-operation, anticipating pressure for rapid Africanization withdrew more expatriate staff than many African governments, including the Senegalese, thought appropriate. Senegalese leaders were reluctant at the time of independence and subsequently to place potential political opponents in posts which had been previously held by Frenchmen.[2] So long as Frenchmen remained in crucial administrative or advisory posts, the administration was kept safe from political opposition and disorder. In this early stage of development, the French Ministry of Co-operation met the requests of the Senegalese government and reduced the rate of repatriation of colonial officers. Throughout 1964, Frenchmen remained officially in command posts in the rural and central administration as, for example, prefects, governors, and *directeurs du cabinet*. After this time, no such posts by name were held by Frenchmen and there were no longer any expatriates in the rural administration.

The first general review of the French programme of co-operation came in the Jeanneney Report of 1963.[3] It was followed a year later by a programmatic review of five years of Ministry of Co-operation activities in Africa, which recommended among other things abandonment of the idea of aid as an instrument of total economic integration into the French community and of the idea that there should be exclusive economic complementarity between France and her former

---

[1] Reports are published as République du Sénégal, Ministère de l'Enseignement Technique et de la Formation des Cadres, *Session d'Information du Personnel de l'Assistance Technique*.

[2] Ruth Schacter Morganthau, *Political Parties in French-Speaking West Africa*, Oxford, The Clarendon Press, 1964, p. 174.

[3] France, Ministère d'Etat Chargé de la Réforme Administrative, *La Commission d'Etude Institué par le decret du 12 mars 1963 remis au Gouvernement le 18 juillet 1963*.

Technical Assistance

overseas territories.[1] A more specific recommendation was for a reduction in the number of French technical assistants in purely administrative posts, as a step towards more rapid abandonment of colonial structures.[2] In Senegal this generated an attempt to shift expatriates from managerial to technical posts in the administration, a distinction which proved difficult to maintain in the actual working situation. The majority of administrative personnel at this time were formerly colonial officers; and shifting their established roles and experienced methods of work was as difficult for them as for their Senegalese colleagues, who had come to rely on them.

PLANNING AND EDUCATION

While French personnel remained in important posts in many sectors of the administration (and, in fact, their numbers increased between 1963 and 1967), the new policy had at least some effect on the redeployment of this personnel. First, there was an attempt to shift the emphasis from administrative to teaching posts. Second, within the administration an attempt was made to shift expatriates to certain areas considered more technical than purely administrative—education, health and production (the last of which included several ministries—Rural Economy, Plan, Commerce and Industry). While the total number of technical assistants serving in Senegal was increased in 1964, and continued to be through to 1966[3] (see Table 9, p. 188), the internal shift remained towards 'specialist' ministries or from managerial to specialist posts. In the Ministry of Finance, however, which was considered to be one of the more managerial than technical departments, the plan to reduce expatriate personnel in the years between 1963

---

[1] France, Ministère de la Cooperation, *Cinq Ans de Fonds d'Aide et de Coopération* (1959–64), Rapport présenté par M. R. Triboulet, Ministre délégué, chargé de la Coopération, 9 April 1964, pp. 5–8.

[2] *Ibid.*, pp. 22, 64–5.

[3] From Commission Mixte Franco-Sénégalaise, *Propositions Concernant le Personnel de l'Assistance Technique en 1964 et Provisions pour 1965 et 1966, 18 April 1964*, Dakar, roneo policy document provided by the Senegalese Service de l'Assistance Technique.

and 1966 was reappraised after a disappointment in the performance of their African replacements. Their proportion to local civil servants is higher in Finance than in most ministries and six serve on the *Cabinet du Ministre*, which has since independence been directed by a Frenchman (with Senegalese nationality).

The effects of French aid and personnel on the educational system is of very great importance. The time has not long passed when black children in Senegalese schools repeated to the rhythm of the teacher's stick, *Nos ancêtres, les gaulois*, a phrase which remains indicative of the depth of assimilation among the present generation of Senegalese policy-makers in the field of education. There has been only some attempt since independence to adapt the French system of education either to the economic needs of the country or its existing social and cultural environment. For the French-educated élite the *baccalauréat* remains 'one of the most powerful fetishes in Africa'.[1] French teachers provide nearly all of the staff for technical and secondary schools and French technical assistants in the Senegalese Ministry of Education ensure the continuation of policy in keeping with the French tradition (for total personnel see Table 9, p. 188).

Since the maintenance of good educational standards and the number of students in school are among the accepted indices of modernization, the French contribution in this sphere seems above criticism. Yet if one moves beyond the obvious value of education for its sake alone in countries which have had limited development in this area, the order of priorities in educational planning remains an often complicated and very difficult problem. In Senegal, as in many countries, the calculation of educational priorities for the maximization of economic development and manpower planning is far from a simple equation.

The initial policy decisions concerning education which were made in the first few years following independence favoured the French model for the development of primary education and the maintenance of classical French standards

[1] Teresa Hayter, *op. cit.*, p. 193. She mentions that Senghor in particular is one of the most fervent believers in this 'fetish'.

in the secondary schools, which kept the curriculum and examination structure within the metropolitan system, so that academic certificates, and in particular the *baccalauréat*, were mutually acceptable. With so few appropriately qualified Senegalese, the maintenance of the secondary school system was entirely dependent on the importation of French teachers. Most students follow the traditional *lycée* course in either general studies or classics in preparation for the *baccalauréat*. This highly developed system has already begun to produce a surplus of secondary school graduates, whose educational qualifications make them only suitable for posts in the already top-heavy administrative structure (or to compete for places at the University of Dakar).

The maintenance of French standards in the Senegalese school system is, of course, in the interests of all expatriate families and remains one of the main advantages of a post in Dakar. The replication of French educational aims and policies in Senegal is even better exemplified at the University of Dakar. Inaugurated by General de Gaulle in 1959, Dakar became the eighteenth university of France, and its curriculum remained entirely within the metropolitan tradition.[1] Despite its often cited official sub-title of 'the university in the service of Africa', Dakar has only recently added to its syllabus agronomy, agricultural or development economics.[2] The continuing impact of cultural assimilation has kept it much more French than Ghanaian or Nigerian universities are British.

The academic staff remains one of the least Africanized for universities in any independent country on the continent, despite Senegal's long history of élite education. There were no African professors in 1967 and only twelve non-French *maîtres de conference* (the next below professorial rank in the French system), nearly all of whom are in medicine. Two Senegalese who were, so it has been said, likely candidates for professorial

---

[1] Its administration and nearly all of its finance are the responsibility of the French Ministry of Education. A few years ago, the University became juridically a Senegalese public institution, for which a nominal contribution towards running costs was made by the Senegalese government to the French Ministry.

[2] Many of these changes occurred after the student demonstrations in May 1968.

posts,[1] received ministerial appointments. The political arena is regarded as being much more important in career terms than the academic sphere in nearly all African countries, but the continued French direction at Dakar has made the university even less attractive as a career for young Senegalese intellectuals. The largest group of non-French academic employees is at the level of *assistant*,[2] the lowest rank of employment in the French academic system. Many of these are Lebanese, Moroccan, Tunisian, Dahomean and Togolese, as recruitment of both students and staff is technically open to all French-speaking countries, while French staff, in fact, remain predominant at all levels. The French administration of the University[3] is regarded by certain members of the academic staff as being the major source of opposition to African advancement, although it is not clear that this opposition only resides here.

About one-third of the students in the University are of French nationality,[4] most of whom are the children of locally resident families (for statistical purposes these include many Lebanese with French nationality). A small group of the students at Dakar come directly from France principally for the opportunity of being in Africa, and have remained because they find that they have more personal contact with members

---

[1] The geographer, Assane Seck, and the historian Abdoulaye Ly.

[2] Of the total academic staff in 1967, 144 were of French nationality, and 65 'other' (mainly African, although not always Senegalese). There were apparently many Senegalese in university posts in France, who do not choose to return to Senegal. Of the 65 who were of 'other nationality', less than one-third were above the level of *assistant*, and all but one of these are in medicine and science. The faculties of letters, law and economics are the least Africanized. Université de Dakar, *Organisation et Corps Enseignant*, 10 January 1967, roneo.

[3] There was in 1967 only one Senegalese among the fifty-nine persons employed in administrative posts at the University. Among low-level clerical and maintenance personnel recruited locally, more than 25 per cent of the jobs went to French nationals—usually women serving as secretaries. Information obtained at the *Rectorat*, 1967.

[4] A large proportion of these are girls. The sons of local expatriates seem to prefer to remain in France in view of the greater variety of technical courses offered (Dakar does not for example have an engineering faculty), as well as the importance of being in the orbit of the metropolitan job market. Most of the French students at Dakar are in the Faculty of Letters, and more than half of these are girls.

Technical Assistance

of staff, owing to its limited size and the relaxed atmosphere of work, compared with the universities in France. The number of French students has in recent years been increasing in proportion to the number of Senegalese students, and at the expense of students from other African or Middle Eastern countries.[1]

As has been the case in *lycée* and university education, the planning and execution of programmes of vocational and technical training rely heavily on French technical assistants and have closely followed the French model. The syllabuses and structure of training in some vocational schools remain so dependent on metropolitan precedent that employees are at times technically unprepared for the environment in which they work. The most significant adaptation has been the addition of a high proportion of practical training in civil service courses, notably in the National Schools of Administration, Applied Economics and Rural Cadres, which are designed both for newly appointed civil servants and for in-service training for those already in posts, and have been well-integrated into manpower planning for the public sector.

Planning for the allocation of technical assistants to various ministries and educational establishments is worked out in joint Franco-Senegalese commissions[2] on the basis of existing expatriate personnel in each area and planning for forthcoming projects. In the Senegalese administration there is a permanent department, the *Service de l'Assistance Technique*, which co-ordinates these requests and deals with on-going personnel problems or policy planning relating to the programme. Basic disagreements with the local office of the Secretariat of State for Co-operation in Dakar, the *Mission d'Aide et de Coopération*, arise over conflicting interests. The Senegalese government

---

[1] Information from Université de Dakar, Bureau Universitaire de Statistique, *Statistiques des Effectifs des Etudiants*, Années Universitaires, 1961, 1962, and *Statistiques des Etudiants Inscrits*, 1963–64, 1964–65, 1965–66, roneo documents from the *Rectorat*. For further details on the University of Dakar see R. Cruise O'Brien, op. cit., 1969, pp. 311–14.

[2] These commissions meet at three-year intervals. The allocation in education is done annually in a joint meeting of representatives of the African countries concerned and a representative of the French Ministry of Education.

Assessment of the Programme

wishes to retain those technical assistants who have been long in service, are well integrated locally and considered thus of optimal effectiveness.[1] Nearly all are ex-colonial officers. The French administration, on the other hand, does not wish to maintain civil servants abroad too long because of the potential difficulties of professional reintegration when they return to France. Recent French policy has been to try to impose a maximum length of service abroad and to encourage contracts of only two or three years for new recruits. Education was the only area in which limits were actually set, although they were quite liberal. A maximum of fourteen years of service abroad was imposed in 1967, despite the opposition of both the Senegalese government and the French teachers already in posts.

The financial responsibility for the technical assistance scheme is naturally French, although the Senegalese government contributes a stipulated amount, which adds to already very heavy spending within the national budget on administrative salaries. All technical assistants are given a base pay of about £84 per month (50,000 C.F.A. francs) by the Senegalese government, which is about one-third of their average total salary, as well as furnished housing. The latter inflates the demand for scarce places, and the government commitment becomes, in effect, a subsidy of property in Dakar and the major towns of the interior, most of which is owned by French syndicates or Lebanese businessmen.

THE TECHNICAL ASSISTANTS AND AN ASSESSMENT OF THE PROGRAMME

Despite the growing preference among Paris officials for shorter contracts of service, nearly 60 per cent of those interviewed in the survey had been in the colonial service, having been grafted on to the newly defined programme of co-operation in 1961. They had, however, less colonial experience or length of residence in overseas territories than did their

[1] Interview with the Director of the Senegalese *Service de l'Assistance Technique*, November 1966.

Technical Assistance

compatriots in the private sector, and, indeed, 25 per cent of those interviewed had been recruited to Senegal during the three years prior to the time of interview.[1] Most of the latter were in teaching posts.

The most recent and highly mobile participants in the programme are the *militaires de contingent*, who were introduced in 1963. They are military conscripts with university degrees who substitute for their military service a thirteen month tour in co-operation schemes overseas. Their services were first offered free to African countries but after three years the same basic salary contribution was requisite for them, as for all technical assistants in the programme. Their monthly salaries (£100 or 60,000 C.F.A. francs) were only slighter higher than the stipulated Senegalese contribution, thus providing a considerable economy for France in making up the total number of personnel requested by each country. Since their introduction, the Senegalese have continually complained that the *militaires de contingent* have inadequate experience to act in an advisory capacity. Owing to the continued pressure on this matter nearly all of them are now serving in teaching rather than in administrative posts, although in this capacity also their lack of experience remains a source of discontent. That their military stipend is almost covered by the Senegalese contribution to salaries has deepened this discontent, which the most outspoken critics regard as an indirect Senegalese subsidy to the French armed forces. *Militaires de contingent* were 10 per cent or 150 of a total number, of technical assistants in Senegal in 1967, and 90 in 1970.[2] The French government has tried to increase their numbers annually while Senegalese officials feel that they are losing well-established and experienced

---

[1] Cumulative colonial experience of respondents:

	Total (250)	Technical assistants (60)
less than 3 yrs	10·4%	25·0%
3–6 yrs	12·8	18·3
7–10 yrs	12·4	15·0
11–14 yrs	16·0	8·3
15–20 yrs	24·8	16·7
20–25 yrs	8·0	5·0
more than 25 yrs	15·6	11·7

[2] *Le Monde*, 22 August 1970.

Assessment of the Programme

civil servants for young men who only remain in the country for thirteen months.

The professional and financial advantages of overseas service in the capacity of technical assistant have made recruitment to the co-operation programme fairly easy. Nearly two-thirds of all technical assistants interviewed wished to renew their contracts in Senegal although the proportion in this category was higher among teachers (83 per cent), and technical advisers (70 per cent) than the general average. They mentioned such specific reasons as the interesting and independent nature of the work, as well as the favourable aspects of working in a smaller, more relaxed environment, compared with the French administration. Those technical assistants who had been settled over a considerable period in Dakar gave this as an explanation for their reluctance to return to France, although unlike their compatriots employed privately their professional reintegration into the French civil service is assured by the Secretariat of State for Co-operation (a reasonable justification for the attempt to limit the length of contracts).

Technical assistants who wished to terminate their contracts included chiefly younger people, who wanted to pursue a type of career not available overseas. Some commented that 'life was too easy in Senegal', and that they feared the consequent risk of losing the 'dynamism' necessary to compete in the metropolitan professional environment. There was a certain group of young middle-aged technical assistants (who had served from ten to twenty years abroad) who were ready also to return before it was 'too late' to be successfully reintegrated into the metropolitan administration. A minority were ready for repatriation because of a sense of futility and ineffectiveness in their post or a decline of interest in the task to be performed. Among these were a number of keen developmentalists— interested in economic planning and modernization, who specifically sought overseas employment, either because of their own training and educational background in fields relevant to developing countries and/or because they were personally committed to the need to help such countries and their inhabitants. Many of these 'developmentalists' became very disillusioned with what they consider to be the prevailing inertia and inefficiency in Senegal, and after making efforts which they felt were unsupported by the Senegalese for a number of years, a number of them left Senegal in disgust, considering that their talents had been wasted.

Many more technical assistants than those who were leaving had extensive criticisms of the assistance programme in Senegal, and they found as much fault with Senegalese participation as with its organization in general. Certain of them felt that their efforts were not supported or that project funds were misused. Only about one-third of the total number of expatriates interviewed were willing to give the scheme unqualified support in its present form. The pattern of comment from Frenchmen outside the service ranged from an emphasis on the necessity for an aid and assistance programme because of the inability of the Senegalese to manage on their own, to pointed *ad hominem* criticisms about technical assistants themselves. Teachers in particular serve generally as a negative stereotype of insularity and miserliness, so resented in the business community, although criticism is not always confined to this profession. *Faux blancs*, as they are called, are widely accused by local French merchants and businessmen of abusing the privileges accorded to all technical assistants—specifically, of using large baggage allowance to import vast quantities of domestic goods and food, less expensive at metropolitan prices. One extraordinary and often heard story is worth recounting, as illustrative of the contempt for this type of Frenchman. Since *Perrier* (mineral water) bottles are not taken back for refund of deposit in Senegal, it is said that families pack cartons of empties (their annual consumption) and transport them back to France to retrieve the five francs deposit on each. The jealousy of those employed in the private sector is aroused chiefly by the fringe-benefits enjoyed by technical assistants, which not only give them special status, but also make their real income and potential savings even greater than their already relatively higher earning power.

There is a specific antipathy held by businessmen towards the younger generation of technical assistants because the businessmen consider colonial experience essential for an understanding of Senegal's problems. In addition to their lack of knowledge and understanding of the Senegalese 'temperament', these young

Assessment of the Programme

men are accused of having no sense of responsibility for the country. More specifically, they are ridiculed for trying to institute 'socialist planning which the older generation understands will be ineffective'; and they are personally disliked for dismissing all businessmen as 'capitalists' and 'colonialists'. One-quarter of the respondents in the private sector felt that the failure of the technical assistance programme lay with the individual technical assistants alone, and especially the younger, more recently recruited among them. In elaborating on this some said that they felt they had a better mutual understanding with those technical assistants longer established in Senegal, and a few felt, in addition, that they could rely on them to defend their interests. Certain acknowledged, however, that overt co-operation between French businessmen and technical assistants was not always successful:

> The minute a technical assistant turns his head towards us, he ceases to be listened to in his Ministry by the Senegalese; but the Senegalese themselves know that we understand them better than these new people who come and try to socialize everything.[1]

Despite criticisms, even the most hostile critics in the private sector acknowledge that the presence of 1,500 technical assistants within the general structure of French aid is in their interests. The advantages they derive from it are economic and political as well as social: first, the preservation of a local expatriate market (in spite of limited spending); second, a sense of political security because of French presence in the administration (even considering the political views of certain individual technical assistants); and third, the social advantage of maintaining a large local white population, (whether social interaction between members of the public and private sector is frequent or not).

The attitudes of Senegalese respondents towards the technical assistance programme were on the whole more favourable than their view of French activities in the private sector. One post-office clerk felt that the programme reflected 'the benevolent work provided by developed countries for underdeveloped

[1] Interview with the Director of Maurel et Prom, December 1966.

Technical Assistance

countries—this is the way we are able to train our cadres or to prepare them for the future'. Several respondents felt that because of the common French language the existing French system was preferable to any other type of foreign assistance programme. Special mention was made of the important role of technical assistants in education and training. A minority (mainly civil servants) who were critical of the assistance programme felt that there were certain basic problems built into its structure:

> It doesn't answer our problems, for it merely perpetuates the colonial relationship. Individually, technical assistants work well, and with great interest in the Senegalese; but this must be fitted into the larger framework, which seems to serve French interests.

One civil servant felt that 'it must not be eternal', and several others felt that it was the obviousness of the French presence which weakened projects and the efforts of individual personnel. Those with direct political criticisms of the present regime felt that technical assistants provided a framework of stability with certain direct and anticipated consequences on the part of the French government:

> The French are here because of the economic interests of French investors and in order to protect them. French aid is not disinterested—France gives nothing free.

Among French respondents, the government's programme of co-operation received unqualified praise from only half of the total, and only 25 per cent of technical assistants. Although critical of its specific aspects, hardly any of them would have been entirely opposed to a scheme, so obviously in their interests. General criticisms were chiefly of financial mismanagement, lack of financial control, miscalculation of projects and unnecessary expenditure. Only ten respondents had specifically political criticisms of a 'Cartieriste' variety[1]—

---

[1] A position on overseas aid derived originally from Raymond Cartier, 'En France Noire', *Paris-Match*, 11, 18 August 1956. It was revised when another series of articles were written by him in *Paris-Match* in 1964 after the publication of the Jeanneney Report.

suggesting that the reduction of expenditure on overseas dependencies would make more funds available in metropolitan France. Although the original formulation was essentially a conservative objection to overseas aid, those in my survey who were sympathetic to the general viewpoint mentioned a 'privileged class of French and African administrators', or 'social security before the burden of a former imperial age'. On the whole, judgements concerning the co-operation programme were made independent of political preference, for Gaullists were just as critical as others.

The possibility of a greater internationalization of aid and technical assistance was mentioned by only eight French respondents, who also felt that the financial commitment of France should be reduced. Internationalization has at least begun in one respect. Through French participation in the Common Market, former French colonies which have remained in the franc zone have been assigned associate status, which makes them eligible for the *Fonds Européen de Développement* (F.E.D.). One of the conditions of Senegalese associate membership was the gradual reduction of the external subsidy required to make Senegalese groundnuts competitive at world market prices, until recently paid by France. To this end S.A.T.E.C. (*Societé d'Assistance Technique et de Crédit Social d'Outre-Mer*)[1] was introduced in 1964, in order to increase groundnut production by intensifying the yield of the land under cultivation. With over fifty European agents in the rural areas, it has been distinguished as one of the most effective agricultural projects of either local or external origin. Thus at a time when the last French civil servants were withdrawn from the rural administration, they were effectively replaced by a wave of European agricultural agents.

THE WEAKNESS OF THE ROLE OF THE TECHNICAL ASSISTANT

The actual responsibility of a technical assistant, whose function

[1] It is now called SODEVA, *Société de Développement Agricole*.

Technical Assistance

may be to 'aid', 'assist', or 'train' is ambiguous in the context of a governing organization, and in the absence of any attempt to specify his function or role, other factors become extremely important. The personality of the expatriate, his length of experience and the relationship with the director or minister for whom he works are among the factors which determine his influence. In the absence of explicit delineation of responsibilities, this influence can be shaped by the political or ideological disposition of the technical assistant or his career pattern.

Since the Senegalese administrative structure is based so closely on the French model, the latter remains the obvious reference point for activity and assessment. Two-thirds of those technical assistants serving in administrative posts saw no difference between the jobs they did in France and those they were doing in Senegal, which would seem to indicate that a majority were still 'directing' or 'administering' rather than 'advising'. A technical assistant accepts that the Senegalese administrative system does function differently and that Senegalese administrative behaviour is considerably distant from his own, but retaining the French model, he is either disillusioned by the inefficiency, underemployment and corruption among which he works, or he uses it to assure himself that his services are indispensable.

Previous teaching experience has given French teachers a tendency to apply French standards and techniques with little respect for the cultural or social environment. Many ignore the fact that language and environmental factors may inhibit performance according to specifically French standards, measures of performance or techniques. Having been employed to perform a specific job, many explicitly admit that they see no difference between the work they do in Senegal and that which they had done in France.[1] The responsibility for this lies only in small part with the teachers themselves. They are working in a framework which,

---

[1] Teachers responded almost universally in the negative in answer to the question: 'Is the work you do in Senegal any different from the work you did in France?'

by explicit Senegalese policy-decision, remains French.[1]

In annual 'Reflective Sessions' between Senegalese and locally based French civil servants and teachers, an attempt has been made to cope with these and other problems relating to the structured work situation. While the discussions are frank and open, recommendations from them are never put into operational form, nor are they binding on the participants or any other parties. The same problems are brought to the fore year after year, with a slight alteration of nuance. Those who attend these discussions are usually the same core of people—young articulate Senegalese civil servants who generally share similar ideas with the liberal or radical Catholic elements among the technical assistants. Among the most conscientious members of their respective groups, they are the most likely to have discussed these problems outside the formal structure of a colloquium, thus leaving the majority on either side uninvolved in such reflections.

The indifference of most technical assistants to the milieu in which they work is often a conscious attempt to 'remain neutral', or 'not to mix in politics'. One of the interests of the Senegalese in these annual discussions is to point out how unreal is this view: 'to say that the counsel offered to the Senegalese administration must be technical and apolitical is unrealistic, since at all levels of the administration, a working decision can be political'. Because the technical competence brought to the study of a text is translated into decision by those who have authority, 'it is well that technical assistants recognize this and are aware of the consequences of decisions and the effect of their advice on them'.[2]

---

[1] A study conducted among African students in a technical school in Dakar (Lycée Delafosse) in 1962 was inconclusive as to overall preference for being taught by French or Senegalese teachers. Of those expressing a preference, 35·7 per cent of the students preferred French teachers out of respect for their professional and moral qualities, while 24·5 per cent preferred Senegalese teachers because of their better understanding of the personal and cultural background and the problems these raised for educational performance. Françoise Flis-Zonabend, *Lycéens de Dakar*, Paris, Maspero, 1968, p. 68.

[2] Sénégal, Ministère d'Enseignement Technique et de la Formation des Cadres, *Session d'Information et de Réflexion Sur la Coopération Technique au Sénégal*, Dakar, 4–5 February 1967, speech of Ben Madé Cissé, pp. 128, 136.

Technical Assistance

The expertise provided by technical assistants can become a form of authority in an administrative system, although it is rarely recognized as such and can be exercised with little knowledge of the environment and little responsibility for the consequences. In this situation the essential ambiguity built into the role of the adviser and his place in the organization becomes important. He may be counselling someone who is in a higher administrative position than himself, although a political appointee without the knowledge and expertise or the executive experience which he possesses. Is the technical adviser supposed to do only what his minister asks or may he disagree with him on the basis of his personal knowledge and experience? Does the technical adviser only prepare memoranda within the parameters of existing policy or may he initiate a new departure by suggesting a new programme or procedure? All of this seemed to be unclear, and practice varied widely from place to place within the administration.[1]

Technical assistants may be developmentalists or technocrats whose advice and counsel are made on the basis of technical calculation of cost, output and effectiveness, whereas local civil servants are constantly aware of extra-administrative considerations which may ultimately influence a decision. The location of a deep well, for example, might be optimally located near a densely populated farming area, whereas it might in the last resort be placed on the estate of a traditional religious leader whose capacity to supply votes is of importance to the minister. Such conflicts of interests exist in all countries, yet can be particularly dramatic in developing countries where resources are extremely scarce and the imperatives of the political kingdom so predominant.

Virtually all administrative decisions have political implications of some kind, even if they were formulated on a non-political basis. And it can be said that the decision made by a technical assistant to give advice 'A' rather than 'B' is in itself

---

[1] I was not able to do any specific research on the exact types of decisions taken, advice given or influence exerted by technical assistants in Senegal, which would have required a careful examination of their activities over a certain length of time. Without official sanction from both the French and Senegalese governments, such a delicate examination was impossible.

political whether formulated on an ideological basis or a technocratic, and ostensibly neutral basis. The influence of the technical assistant may be identified as the 'sapiential' authority he exerts in the organization. This authority which is perhaps intended to be neutral may be determined, in fact, by the experience of the given technical assistant (the technocrat) his political disposition (the ideologue) on his career interests (the Minister's 'yes-man').

There is only a fine distinction between technical assistants who are committed developmentalists and those who are progressives or socialists in the Senegalese context. Although at a national level ideological considerations are not of great importance, there are recognizable cliques of ideologues—both expatriate and African—in the administration. In Algeria following the revolution expatriate ideologues became known as *pieds rouges* (the successors to the settlers or *pieds noirs*), and while a new departure in terms of white participation in the Algerian setting, the Algerians found that these new Marxist advisers provided problems because of their lack of understanding of the traditional values of Muslim society.[1] In Senegal, their counterparts are called *pieds roses* because, although socialist in sentiment, they are generally of a more evolutionary or liberal persuasion (and often associated with liberal Catholic organizations). Their pre-fabricated plans for development are not popular in most circles.[2] While there is criticism among Senegalese civil servants of most technical assistants for not being responsible for the decisions on which they advise, there is also another fear that some may become an independent force, losing the perspective of 'assisting the nation', and directing it instead. The balance between these is a difficult one to maintain.

[1] Albert-Paul Lentin, 'La Situation de la Minorité Européenne en Algerie', *Le Mois en Afrique (Revue Française d'Etudes Politiques Africaines)*, December 1966, p. 44.

[2] 'He (the technical assistant) must not be so impressed by his tasks as to mix in internal matters, playing the role of the *eminence grise*—in the political context. He is often involved in intrigues which influence his decisions and the way he thinks, but which do not necessarily conform to the idea of what is good for Senegal.' Sénégal, Ministère d'Enseignement Technique et de la Formation des Cadres, *Session d'Information du Personnel d'Assistance Technique*, 19–20 February 1966, Dakar, p. 62.

Technical Assistance

In reality the French technical assistants have become an administration within an administration, partly because of the weakness of the Senegalese civil service. Frenchmen in each department tend to form a separate clique or team responsible to the minister or head of department. Expatriates are usually physically separated in an office or cluster of offices, often doing policy studies for which there are few experienced or qualified Senegalese civil servants. In the Ministry of Planning, for example, this function appears to carry with it considerable latent executive authority, yet there is no Senegalese working on the expatriate planning team in order to learn these skills. Experienced expatriate technicians and administrators sometimes have *militaires de contingent* wishing to learn a type of work as their assistants. In the Department of Urbanization and Town Planning in 1967, the principal technical adviser had working with him three young French university graduates, while Senegalese draughtsmen worked together in adjoining offices.

Decisions from one part of the administration to another pass often from one French adviser to another French adviser. And decisions within a department are sometimes made among senior civil servants and their technical advisers, without the knowledge or consultation of Senegalese colleagues.[1] Such a pattern is obviously more rapid and efficient, and senior civil servants have come to rely on the interlocking directorate of technical assistants rather than allow major decisions to be lost in the inefficiency of the regular administrative structure. Instead of coping with the difficulties of the administration, there remains the option of just ignoring it.

The disorganization and inefficiency of the Senegalese administration has inhibited the optimal employment of technical assistants. Talent or technical skills are often wasted on useless projects, red tape, or simple inactivity; and one of the main purposes of the scheme, the training of Senegalese *homologues* or counterparts, has been partially sacrificed by

[1] This practice was cited to me by a Senegalese civil servant in the Department of Rural Administration (Ministry of Planning), which contains many expatriate *idéologues* and Senegalese 'Diaists' and is generally regarded as one of the more successful combined French-Senegalese efforts.

The Role of the Technical Assistant

this. Individual technical assistants believe that training should be the principal role of the technical assistance programme,[1] yet they are joined by the Senegalese in acknowledging its obvious failure. In addition to the structural deficiencies of the scheme, the difficulty of promoting personal relations between most French and Senegalese inhibits good working relations. Because Frenchmen and Senegalese are mutually reluctant to share an office, each preferring to work alongside a colleague of the same race, the purpose of training the Senegalese in certain skills and techniques has in fact been abandoned. With little pressure from Senegalese sources, the expatriate administration within an administration persists. One of my Senegalese informants blamed this on the French themselves:

> Below the very senior, advisory level, Frenchmen consistently underestimate the value of Senegalese civil servants and maintain them purposely at an inferior level. Such Frenchmen want to preserve the idea that if they leave, nothing will work in Senegal, that everything will go to pieces.

Those civil servants interviewed were asked to comment on whether or not they thought that Frenchmen had a direct responsibility for decisions in the administration. Three (out of twelve) felt that this was not possible, since Frenchmen worked in a Senegalese administrative structure and would therefore require Senegalese approval or specific request in order to make a decision. One added, however, that if any Frenchman did exercise direct responsibility in the administration, he was certainly capable of exercising it. Three others felt that Frenchmen did have a direct influence on policy, which might consciously or unconsciously be exercised in the interests of France. The remainder thought it varied depending on the person, his longevity in service or the particular policy involved.

'It is in effect very difficult to pass concretely from a political phase of colonization to a political phase of co-operation,' as it was aptly put by the Director of Rural Animation in 1967.[2] In the context of the administration there remains the basic

[1] See question 68 for technical assistants only, Appendix 3.
[2] Sénégal, Ministère d'Enseignement Technique, *op. cit.*, 1967, p. 131.

Technical Assistance

problem of interaction between two groups which have for so long known one another in a superior-subordinate relationship. The basic ambiguity of the new role of technical assistant has tended to force both Frenchmen and Senegalese into behaving in terms of the residual relationship upon which the colonial service was built—the Frenchmen direct and the Senegalese are directed. One expatriate who served in the colonial administration used it as a justification for returning to the former situation in explicit terms:

> (The present system) could only be effective if the technical assistants directed things like a colonial administration, but the *dialogue* is ill-defined and doesn't work well, leading thus to confusion.
>
> Africans can only work with Europeans if they know that they are respected and commanded at the same time.

And Senegalese informants, when asked whether technical assistants work in good rapport with local civil servants have variously responded:

> There is a superior-inferior relationship built into the mentality of each; collaboration cannot proceed at an equal level. Since there are no 'human' relations between them, there is no professional rapport;

and

> The technical assistance is a common effort within the 'family'. We have the habit of working with them from the colonial experience.

The colonial framework remains obviously apparent in people's thoughts. And the tendency to return to the former structure of dependence, when faced with a new and potentially ambiguous situation, is manifest in the behaviour of certain Senegalese civil servants. While a Frenchman remains close at hand, the tendency of most civil servants is to pass the responsibility to him. Often when a special project is in progress, extra hours are put in by technical assistants while the Senegalese civil servants go home. There are two independent factors which affect this situation: differing cultural views of work and of the importance of work; and the size of the Senegalese administration. Since many civil servants are superfluous to the functioning of the administration, and much of the crucial work will be done by Frenchmen anyway, there is no compunction about missing work or arriving late, and at a higher level there may be no compunction either about the deliberate confusion of public and private funds.

Personal and family loyalties remain for the Senegalese much more important than a spirit of formalistic impersonality and reward commensurate with responsibility—which are regarded as essential to an ideal-type bureaucracy.[1] The confusion of norms of behaviour from a modern and a traditional context largely influences the functioning of the Senegalese administration, as it does that of many other African countries. The structure was criticized by French administrators for being weak, ineffective, heavy (a French legacy), disorganized, parasitic and anti-modern.[2] Senegalese civil servants were considered to be too preoccupied with family problems and other commitments. The majority of technical assistants interviewed were opposed to accelerated Africanization, because of the behaviour they had observed at work. The extent to which such behaviour is inevitable in a transitional stage of development or perpetuated by French presence (or a combination of factors) remains an open question. French aid, as most obviously manifest in the administration is an example of development generated from the outside at the cost of the modernization or improvement of the indigenous administrative structure. Instead of trying to come to terms with problems general to the bureaucracies of many nations in Africa, the Senegalese government has postponed the problem by relying on large numbers of French personnel. The irresponsibility of individual civil servants and the weakness of the general structure remains.

[1] H. Gerth and C. Wright Mills, trans. and eds., *From Max Weber*, New York, Oxford University Press, 1958, pp. 330, 341.
[2] 'Insofar as public administration systems fall short of the Weberian legal-rational model, they are said not to be modern.... Technical assistants have a tendency to go abroad with this (the attributes of this ideal-type) in tact, while we know that the respective bureaucracies of Britain and the United States (for example), when experiencing rapid economic change, conformed to the Weberian model much less than they do today.' Joseph La Palombara, *Bureaucracy and Political Development*, Princeton, Princeton University Press, 1963, pp. 10, 11.

TABLE 9

Technical Assistance Personnel (1963–1971, Proposed and Actual)*
(Secretariat of State for Cooperation)

	1963	1964	1965	1966	1971
Office of the President	22	18	15	10	
Ministry of Foreign Affairs	3	4	3	2	
Ministry of Justice	47	38	28	23	
Ministry of Finance	70	63	39	29†	
Ministry of Interior	13	18	16	14	
Ministry of Civil Service and Labour	7	3	1	2	
Ministry of Information, Tourism	62	57	52	44	
Ministry of Commerce and Industry	12	17	14	11	
Ministry of Plan and Development	9	13	13	26	
Ministry of Rural Economy	52	68	73	71	
Ministry of Energy and Hydraulics	9	17	17	17	
Ministry of Urbanism, Housing, Transport	55	52	45	37	
Ministry of Railroads	66	65	60	59	
Ministry of Ports, Commerce of Dakar	23	21	20	20	
Ministry of Merchant Marine	17	18	13	13	
Ministry of Health and Social Welfare	92	106	106	103	
Ministry of Education and Culture	589	634	665	701	891
(a) primary ed. and administration	—129	—115	—93	—80	
(b) extra-mural ed.	—129	—139	—144	—144	
(c) secondary ed.	—331	—380	—428	—477	
Ministry of Technical Education	289	300	313	319	
Ministry of Popular Education, Youth, and Sports	38	42	39	32	
Sub-total in education: (proposed)	(916)	(976)	(1,017)	(1,052)	
(actual)	(823)	(896)	(948)	(983)	
TOTAL (proposed)	1,475	1,554	1,532	1,532	
(actual)	1,380	1,414	1,499	1,523	1,209

(See note opposite)

Note: Part of the difficulty in comparing these figures successively for four years is that the Senegalese public sector had some minor administrative reforms which placed technical assistants in and out of several categories.

* Proposed estimates from Commission Mixte, Franco-Sénégalaise *Propositions Concernant le Personnel de l'Assistance Technique en 1964 et Provisions pour 1965 et 1966, 18 April 1964, Dakar,* roneo policy document provided by the Senegalese *Service de l'Assistance Technique.* Actual estimates from the *Mission d'Aide et de Coopération,* Dakar, 1967, and Secretariat of State for Cooperation, Paris, 1971.

† This was altered to 71 who were actually serving in 1966.

8. Expatriate Politics and Political Influence

The political apathy of the French in Senegal appears to have remained unchanged since independence, if the exercise of voting rights is used as the sole measure of political involvement. Because of the single-college electoral system of the colony which was dominated by the African majority, there was no traditional corporate political identity among Frenchmen. In the years leading up to independence, the participation of Europeans in the nationalist movement would have been to them unthinkable. Most remained entirely outside all political movements, although counselled by their countrymen on the right and the left to participate and thus show their support for the creation of a Franco-African community which would ensure their security in West Africa. A small group of local Frenchmen were, however, favourable to Senghor's political ideas and aspirations, and either provided finance or took an active part in his party, the *Bloc Démocratique Sénégalais*. They were appropriately rewarded with political posts, although their activities are now usually confined to membership in the Economic and Social Council, since the Law of Senegalese Nationality in 1961 excluded them from other representative institutions (see Chapter 4).

Following decolonization, there was even less incentive than previously for the creation of a corporate political identity among Frenchmen in Senegal, since expatriates obviously lost their voting privileges in Senegal but voted individually in their *départements* of origin in France. In spite of the loss of formal participation in local political institutions, however, the expatriate group continues to have considerable influence on the Senegalese political system. No longer having the familiar framework of a colonial administration, company directors have had to develop an entirely new series of channels and connections for protecting their interests. The political representation of economic influence is the principal political activity[1] of French company directors in Senegal. And although outside formal political institutions, both the form and the effectiveness of their influence are to some extent shaped by the dominant form of African political activity: the competition among a number of factions within the single party, the *Union Progressiste Sénégalaise*. These 'clans', as they are called locally provide the political support for a given notable in return for patronage and other rewards. The French form an interest group outside the party which derives considerable advantage from its coherence, unity, stability, and, above all, its financial resources. Considering the political fragmentation in the governing party, all of these factors enhance the potential influence of the European interest group. Operating within the framework of Senegalese political controversy, French interests seem to be balanced against the interests of the various African clans in the governing party by President Senghor, whose role as a political mediator is crucial not only to Europeans, but to the maintenance of the entire system of politics. This chapter will be concerned with an identification of personalities, groups, and methods of local French influence within this framework, after a preliminary discussion of French voting behaviour in the metropolitan political system.

METROPOLITAN POLITICS

Although Senegal remains within a sphere of French influence, geographical separation from France has tended to mute metropolitan political issues and debates for most expatriates.

---

[1] The significance of the local political activity of Frenchmen in Senegal has been rarely recognized by political scientists. For example, W. J. Foltz, usually a reliable source on Senegal, has written: 'As a group, neither (the Lebanese nor the French) has at any time since the war played a significant role in Senegalese politics. . . . On the level of official governmental policy, the French unquestionably do exercise influence, but this influence comes directly from France not from the French residing in Senegal.' From 'Senegal', in J. Coleman and C. Rosberg, eds., *Political Parties and National Integration in Tropical Africa*, Berkeley, University of California Press, 1964, pp. 49, 50.

Expatriate Politics and Political Influence

While about half of the Frenchmen I interviewed said that they followed political events in France closely, only about a quarter of the total group voted in the Presidential election of 1965.[1] Part of the explanation usually given for low electoral participation is the complicated procedure of registration for Frenchmen overseas and the need to delegate someone in France personally to cast the vote of the absentee, thus negating the secrecy of voting preference. According to the account of a number of persons interviewed, French social gatherings in Dakar rarely touch on the subject of politics—not only because of substantial lack of interest, but also quite deliberately because of a reluctance to mar the ambiance with a potential political quarrel in such a restricted social environment. Interest in metropolitan political subjects is naturally greater among those more recently arrived than those long distant from the metropolitan political scene. Those respondents more recently arrived in Senegal (in the three years preceding interviews), said at least that they followed political events in France closely,[2] as compared with those who had been in Senegal for a longer period of time. Those in Senegal for more than fifteen years showed little interest in affiliation to a particular political party, and those who had been resident in Senegal for nearly all of their working lives (twenty-five years or more) seemed vague, distant and unconcerned with contemporary French political events. Technical assistants on the whole maintained closer contact with metropolitan politics than others,[3] partly because of their shorter terms overseas. Higher electoral participation may also be a reflection of their occupation and their generally higher educational standard,

[1] This was the last Presidential election before the time I carried out the interviews. Twenty-eight per cent voted in the 1965 election and 65 per cent did not (the remainder being not abroad at the time of the election). The percentage of those voting in France in the same election was about 85 per cent of the registered voters (information from the French Embassy in London).

[2] The interview question: 'Do you follow political events in France closely?' allowed the respondent to give an entirely subjective response which did not necessarily correlate with voting behaviour. (See qs. 41–42, Appendix 3).

[3] In contrast with 55 per cent of all respondents who said they followed political events in France closely, 70 per cent of technical assistants said they did.

Metropolitan Politics

compared with expatriates in the private sector. A large proportion of technical assistants seemed to keep in contact with metropolitan affairs by reading *Le Monde* regularly. Among the total group of respondents only 65 per cent read any metropolitan newspaper regularly. The tendency to identify with socialist or generally left of centre political movements was higher among technical assistants,[1] although the total proportion of those in this category in Senegal was much lower than the national average for France in 1967:

	France (Nov. 1967)[2]	Senegal (Feb.-May 1967)[3]
	%	% of those expressing a political preference
Left	44	29
Fifth Republic	41	40
Democratic Centre	} 15	10
Other Right Wing parties		8 (3% = other)

One-quarter of those interviewed in Senegal had no political preference at all and the number of those who gave the Communist Party as their preference (4 of 250 respondents) was much lower than the metropolitan support for the Party.[4] The latter can be partially explained by the absence of a local French working-class or trade union movement. Both the social structure of the local group and its perception of its interests as outposted Frenchmen would seem to affect

[1] Half of the technical assistants who responded to the question on political preference put themselves in the category 'socialist or left', while only one-sixth of the interviewees in the private sector placed themselves in this category.

[2] The data on French voting preference is from a poll conducted by *The Société Française de Recherches et Études Sociologiques* (S.O.F.R.E.S.) a French public opinion study organization. It was published in *L'Express* on 1 April 1968.

[3] From the results on political preference in my questionnaire survey. Since 26 per cent of respondents expressed no political preference, and there was no such category in the French metropolitan poll, these proportions were adjusted to make them comparable. For a precise statement of political preferences among my respondents, see question 43, Appendix 3.

[4] The national electoral support for the French Communist Party in 1968 was about 20 per cent.

the formation of political preferences. But the most certain factor of all concerning their political behaviour remains the general apathy to the metropolitan political scene, except with regard to decisions which may directly affect their future, (that is, policy decisions of the Ministry of Co-operation or a parliamentary debate on overseas aid).

INTEREST GROUPS AND POLITICAL PERSONALITIES

Frenchmen are not at all agreed that there is any particular person, group or institution which defends their interests in Senegal. Responses to direct questioning on this produced various suggestions depending on the individual's interpretation of 'defend', which was often understood in the context of labour-employer relations, thus making employer's associations a frequent suggestion; or in the legal or diplomatic sense, which made some suggest the Consulate or Embassy as the appropriate defending body.[1] It was only through further questioning of various leaders in the local community that the organization and purpose of informal expatriate influence became clear. It is perhaps indicative of the effectiveness of these informal means of influence that no single formal institution could be located as a recognized spokesman of business interests.

The political background to the nationalization of groundnut marketing in 1960 and the influence of Mamadou Dia were discussed in Chapter 5 in the context of its anti-business implications. Since Dia's fall from power, certain French company directors seem to have a more direct influence in the political sphere, especially those who have the personal favour of the President. One of the most significant aspects of politics in Senegal in general is the continuity of personalities (both Senegalese and French) from early post-war political activities to participation in or influence on the present political system.

One means of trying to analyse this influence is by examining the role of certain local French personalities known to be

[1] See questions 70, 71, Appendix 3.

Interest Groups and Personalities

associated with politics. Not all of them are leaders in the French community, nor would they be recognized as its representatives. A few such as Jean Rous, Special Presidential Adviser on Foreign Relations, have no connection with the local expatriate community. Rous is very little known, even by the Senegalese,[1] although thought to have considerable influence on the Senegalese delegation at the United Nations and on foreign affairs generally. Recruited to Senegal in 1961, chiefly because of his political activities in support of decolonization in North Africa, his experience of Senegalese politics is relatively recent. Guy Etcheverry, who had been active in local politics for a long time, was, like Rous, grafted on to the technical assistance structure at the request of the President. Despite his long residence in Senegal and other countries in West Africa his left-wing opinions and participation in African political activities have cut him off entirely from the expatriate community.

The Minister of Finance, Jean Colin, a Frenchman who has adopted Senegalese nationality, is very well regarded by local company and bank directors,[2] and considered very valuable because of his close personal relations with the President. While a useful ally, he cannot be considered a representative of local business interests, which must be balanced against many considerations bound by national priorities and financial agreements with France.

The only Frenchman who remains in the Senegalese National Assembly is Robert Delmas, who regards himself as more of a 'technician' than a 'politician' (in the sense that he can claim expertise in military affairs, for example, and other parliamentary matters, and is not allied to any political clan within the

[1] In contrast with some of the other Frenchmen in the President's entourage, he rarely appears on social occasions and generally remains in the background. A long-time member of militant left-wing movements in France, he was a secretary to Trotsky as a young man. Since the war he was involved in militant activities in support of the independence of Tunisia and Morocco in particular, through which he has built personal and political ties throughout the Maghreb and the Middle East, as well as throughout Eastern Europe. Interview with *Le Monde* correspondent, Dakar, March 1967.

[2] 'Senghor understands very little about economics and finance and is happy to have a capable Minister of Finance.' Interview with the Director of the *Banque Internationale de Commerce et d'Industrie*, Dakar, April 1967.

U.P.S.). A member of the Delmas family which dominated trade and shipping in Senegal since the mid-nineteenth century, he joined Senghor's political movement in the nineteen-fifties. Despite the large business holdings of his family, he does not consider himself a representative of European interests. His seat in the Assembly seems to be rather a reward for personal political loyalty by the President than a recognition of his power or influence in the business community. To the extent that he may serve these interests, it is in an indirect personal capacity, the actuality and importance of which was difficult to gauge. He is a rather elderly gentleman, and probably no longer as vigorously effective politically, as he might once have been.

Paul Bonifay, for thirty years a lawyer in Dakar, and very active throughout this period in politics, is perhaps the doyen of the European community. His career best fits the pattern of continuity from early political activities to present political influence on behalf of local European interests. He is the Vice-President of the Economic and Social Council, and expands the importance of this post through his long experience of political channels in Senegal, and the amount of personal contacts he has with Senegalese politicians and senior civil servants. He is one of the few Frenchmen in Senegal who is familiar enough with the 'clans' within the ruling party, for example, to be able to use them to advantage. He is generally recognized as a leader of one of the informal expatriate interest groups, which brings together business executives, and professionals, and a few old S.F.I.O. militants who form a caucas for the purposes of exerting influence on the political system, as an informal lobby of the Economic and Social Council. Bonifay's group meets socially several evenings a week at his home and is locally known as *L'Abreuvoir* ('The Watering Trough'). Including a number of important industrial executives as well as a number of his old colleagues from the S.F.I.O., the style of this group is largely set by its younger members. It is considered to be the informal lobby for European interests on the Economic and Social Council, and because of its exclusiveness and the secrecy of its discussions, it is regarded by technical assistants and Senegalese civil servants as an extremely important informal caucus. Outside the political sphere, its members are very active in the French mutual aid society (*Association d'Entraide des Français du Sénégal*), of which Bonifay is the honorary President.

THE CHANNELS OF POLITICAL INFLUENCE

If the study of politics is fundamentally the study of influence and the influential, as Lasswell suggests, then the local French both in the public and the private sector merit consideration in political terms. Lasswell defines the influential as 'those who get the most of what there is to get', through their ability to manipulate the environment owing to their control of violence, goods or symbols.[1] The economic leverage or influence on a political system which is based on the control of goods remains, however, usually in reserve. This potential for influence can be positively or adversely affected by the fact that the private sector is foreign-owned and directed, as it is in Senegal. In addition to the control of goods and capital, the French alone possess the skills and knowledge for making the industrial sector function in the present framework. The benefits which French businessmen seek to derive from exercising influence on the political system are, in some cases, contracts for supply to the government, but more generally, assurances on market stability and influence on such matters as licenses, quotas, price controls, company taxes and import duties. Should they not maintain a certain amount of potential influence or leverage on government decisions regarding such matters, the position of business would be considerably weakened, possibly making investment insecure.

The amount of influence exerted by various French company directors can be differentiated according to the size and importance of the company they direct and the sector of the economy in which it is situated. Those in the industrial sector are more important than those in the commercial sector, on the whole. It is not only the size and type of investment, but the amount of technological skills required for the operation of a particular firm, as well as its links to metropolitan holding

[1] Harold Lasswell, *Politics: Who Gets What, When, How?*, New York, The World Publishing Co., 1966, p. 73.

companies which contribute to its potential for influencing government policy. Thus, for example, the directors of groundnut oil refineries have considerable power and influence, while the directors of traditional trading companies were unable to prevent the nationalization of groundnut marketing in 1961. While trade can be Africanized relatively easily, the skills and knowledge required for a 'takeover' in the industrial sector present quite a different problem. This variance between the industrial and commercial sector generally is reflected in the style of politics and political influence exerted by each.

The owners of small enterprises and the directors of traditional trading houses have relatively little direct influence in the political sphere, and rely usually on their employers' associations to represent their interests. The directors of larger firms exert varying degrees of influence, which depend on the company's size, resources and complexity of operation, as mentioned above, but are also affected by the personal style and influence of the director himself. Although this personal influence is often bound by the present power and future potential of the company in the local context, it can also have an independent effect on them. Certain directors have been more adept and successful at asserting themselves than others. Some who have long colonial experience in Senegal have used their familiarity with local personalities and channels to their advantage, while others of the same experience have found it difficult to adapt personally to the demands of the new political and economic environment. Some who have recently arrived to take up directorial posts find the whole political environment as well as the structure of business so different from France that they cannot easily locate the patterns of influence or interaction required of them, while others who are also relatively new to Senegal find their non-colonial background an advantage over longer established colleagues. The older generation are usually attached to formalities and honours, to taking part in official functions and concentrating on their personal recognition in the local context, while the younger university-educated businessmen (technocrats as they are called) are uninterested in the formalities of public life, being concerned only with efficiency and the viability of the investments they direct.

A few particularly important local company directors whose personal influence in the political sphere is worthy of note are: Harel of Peyrissac, who has been in large measure responsible for the company's sizeable turnover and its close relations with the government; Dupont of SONADIS who was recruited from France to manage a now rather successful commercial experiment of mixed private and government finance; Bourbel of CITEC, the local representative of a large French textile manufacturer, whose twenty years of experience in Indo-China in a similar business gave him some useful knowledge for successful competition in the local market; Crémieux of SOCOSIM, the Cement Company of Rufisque (a mainstay of local heavy industry), who was one of a handful of Frenchmen who adopted Senegalese nationality in 1961; Forrestier of S.E.I.B. (a multiple industrial installation in the provincial town of Diourbel), who receives favourable audience in governing circles because of the location of the firm outside Dakar and its importance to the development of a provincial labour and supply network, and whose advice is sought on rural development and technical assistance programmes for the area. Four out of five of these directors are members of the Economic and Social Council.

The economic framework within which local French influence is exerted is one of nearly total dependence of Senegal on France for aid and capital investment. Senegalese concern for the maintenance of French aid to some extent perhaps restricts the Government's scope for action towards the French companies, thus providing a kind of residual protection. Although official French interests and those of the local companies are not always the same, a general attack on French business might be expected to lead to official sanctions. And this expectation might have concrete political effects on decisions of the Senegalese government, (all of which would have been too difficult and too delicate to try to assess in the course of my study).

The actual channels through which local influence is exerted on behalf of expatriate-owned enterprise are as follows: first, the regular sessions of the Economic and Social Council; second, planning commissions in which Frenchmen participate; and third, the activities of employers' associations; and fourth,

Expatriate Politics and Political Influence

direct personal intervention at high level. Perhaps a fifth form of influence can be seen in the presence of technical assistants in the administration, which provides a stability in the public sector, thus maintaining the *status quo* and bolstering the existing political regime. Their contribution to the maintenance of political stability is, of course, an important service to the French private sector. Both technical assistants and French company executives shared in the leadership and membership of a variety of drafting commissions for the First Economic Plan (1961–64), and the Second Economic Plan (1964–67). It is obvious from the total membership of these commissions, which ranged from about ten to about twenty-five, that the actual drafting of the various parts was done by a core group of French and Senegalese among them, rather than by all the members of each commission. Among the drafting commissions of the First Plan, Frenchmen were in the majority on four out of six sections. Technical assistants were numerically predominant over either Senegalese participants or other Frenchmen in the Commissions for Industrialization, Education and Training and Rural Economy (see Table 10, p. 213).

A list of the participant members of the commissions from the private sector provides an indication of which occupational roles in this sphere carry at least potential political influence:

1. *General Commission*—President, Chamber of Commerce; and Director, Central Bank;
2. *Rural Economy*—Vice-President, Chamber of Commerce who is also Director of Assn. of Market-Gardeners of Senegal;
3. *Industrialization*—Director, *Printania* (a department store in Dakar, owned by one of the largest French retail chains); and Director, Bank of West Africa;
4. *Transport–Commerce–Urbanization–Tourism*—Director, shipping company; Director, electricity company; Director, *Air-France* in Senegal; Director, Water Commission; Director of port construction. Their importance remained, however, only potential in this capacity, as, like most economic plans in recently independent African states, that of Senegal remained an interesting declaration of purpose which was not reflected in achieved goals or subsequent policy. This was particularly true

of the First Plan which was discredited with the fall of Dia at the end of 1962.

Despite official efforts to ensure co-operation with the private sector by co-opting company directors to the first drafting commissions, for example, this provided no assurance of co-operation between the government and private firms in its implementation. The First Plan included provisions for the industrial sector 'which did not correspond to the plans of foreign firms and were consequently ignored'; according to a recent study on industrial labour in Senegal. 'As long as no new relationship between Government and expatriate firms develops, it might be realistic for national planners to exclude industry from their plans. The government does not have significant influence on decisions to invest, to recruit and to train.'[1]

The divergence between the published document and the plans of the private sector became so obvious that a revised plan was begun in 1963–64. This became the Second Economic Plan which was drafted by commissions with about an equal division of French and Senegalese members (see Table 11, p. 213) although even larger in total membership and more unwieldy than those for the previous plan. Representatives from the Chamber of Commerce and employers associations (*syndicats patronaux*) were predominant from the private sector. The new plan renounced further interest in nationalization and was heralded in business circles as the explicit statement of a 'new spirit of liberalism'. Company directors congratulated one another on the renewed confirmation that the threat of socialism and rigorous economic planning had been eradicated with the disappearance of Diaist influence in the government. In an editorial on the Plan, an author in the local expatriate news magazine, *Les Echos de France*, wrote that the role of French enterprise 'remains important to the extent that it eradicates the uncertainty about the nature and the importance of the intervention of the state'.[2]

[1] G. Pfeffermann, *op. cit.*, p. 252.
[2] The plan was finally published in 1965. The editorial was called 'Les Français en Face de l'Economie Sénégalaise', and appeared in April 1965, unsigned, pp. 3–4.

Expatriate Politics and Political Influence

BUSINESS ORGANIZATIONS

The institution in Senegal with the longest history of defending the interests of private capital is the Chamber of Commerce. It became a Senegalese public body in 1963 with an official consultative role and obligatory membership for all registered French firms. Its structure follows precisely the metropolitan model, as does its source of finance which is raised from national tax revenue. While a record of its activities would amount to excellent historical documentation on the growth of trade and industry in Senegal, its political role as a representative of European business interests had by 1967 become nearly irrelevant. It did not have the confidence of the majority of the business community, because it had ceased to provide an effective channel of influence on the government. It was ignored by most company directors who used instead either their employers' association or their personal contacts through the Economic and Social Council, or, if they were sufficiently important and powerful, made individual representation to the Minister, working party, technical assistant or study group concerned.

There are two main reasons why the Chamber of Commerce had lost the confidence of the French business community. First was the archaic and unrepresentative nature of the institution: the membership of the working committee or *bureau* of the Chamber in Dakar has not been renewed for over a decade (less than half of its members in 1967 were still alive or in the country). The second reason lay in the person of its President, Gallenca, who, although largely ineffective as a representative of business interests, was a loyal client of President Senghor. The role he played seemed best described as that of a kind of 'diplomatic representative' of the business community to the government, the frequent recognition of which on formal occasions concealed to some extent its lack of intrinsic importance in political terms.

There had always been a basic paradox in the formal role of the Chamber of Commerce as a Senegalese public institution which represented the interests of a foreign-owned private sector. The charter which allowed for only membership of French and Senegalese nationals was designed specifically to exclude the Lebanese. While revealing a basic weakness in the organization, it obviously revealed its latent function as an anti-Lebanese stronghold, especially since it provided the government with information about Lebanese practices or lobbied for price controls and other decidedly anti-Lebanese measures (a vigilance provided also by employers' associations).

In its formal capacity the Chamber of Commerce prepared briefs for government departments and commissions and maintained substantial staff and documentation. It advised the government how to make a particular proposal for private investment attractive to prospective investors. In this capacity as adviser, it chiefly represented the interests of more traditional French companies. In the words of the Secretary-General in 1966:

> When the government wishes to initiate a new enterprise or extend a certain area of commerce or production, we urge them not to forget *les anciens*; not to create too many investments in one sector, so that existing ones suffer because that factory cannot operate to capacity, given the size of the market.

Its bias towards defending the interests of local French enterprises, no matter what their potential for growth and role in the economy, was regarded as unrealistic and inward looking by most of the French directors in industry. Its irrelevance, above all, was reflected in its public image among businessmen themselves, many of whom regard it as an unreformed colonial institution.

The Africanization of the Chamber of Commerce had been a subject of discussion since the independence of Senegal, although the official position of Gallenca and the central office of the Chamber remained unchanged: Africanization which was not commensurate with ownership in the private sector would render questionable the role of that body. Those few African members who did serve in the Chamber (five of twenty-nine members of the bureau) seemed to have been chosen more for their loyalty to France than their importance

Expatriate Politics and Political Influence

and activity in the sphere of African business. Africanization of the Chamber was never taken up by any of the groups in Senegal interested in promoting it in other sectors. Radicals, in particular, argued that African membership would give a power base to local bourgeoisie with a vested interest in protecting their own or French private capital. In the first decade after independence, it also seemed that the leadership of the U.P.S. was not so keen to support Africanization, since a capable Senegalese President could have used the Chamber as a power base from which to play 'clan' politics with the financial backing of French investors. While this was a view which appeared to prevail through most of the Sixties, various federations and consortia of African businessmen[1] had begun to become active in demanding a place in the Chamber of Commerce. Although most Senegalese business is hampered by a shortage of capital, difficulty in raising credit, and consequently confined chiefly to small scale activity in the commercial sector, local businessmen have at least been able to press for the appointment of an African president of the Chamber of Commerce. The appointment of Amadou Sow, the director of the *Union Sénégalaise des Banques*, in 1969, requires a new look into the political role of the Chamber of Commerce which is beyond the scope of this study.

French employers' associations are very active in Senegal in providing information and preparing studies for their members, as well as engaging in direct influence and political activities on their behalf. They keep abreast of all official proposals for policy which might affect their constituents. Although sometimes included in official working parties or consultative committees on particular issues of interest to them,[2] most of their direct contacts are made though their full-time secretaries with the civil servants or technical assistants in the Ministries of Finance, Industry and Commerce. Through these channels

---

[1] For a description of their organizations and activities, see Samir Amin, *Le Monde des Affaires Sénégalais*, Paris, Les Editions de Minuit, 1969.

[2] SCIMPEX, for example (see below), is represented on a number of consultative committees in the Ministries of Public Works, Ports, Finance, and Commerce and Industry. It also has a member on policy commissions concerning price regulation and stabilization.

Business Organizations

of contact are made mutual requests for information or documentation on a given problem or policy. They also are the means through which the employers' associations make formal suggestions or protests on behalf of their members, which would be decided at a regular meeting of the association.

A particularly active employer's association is the *Syndicat des Commerçants, Importateurs et Exportateurs de l'Ouest Africain* (SCIMPEX), which was founded in Dakar in 1943. Owing to the declining importance of traditional French trading houses in the economy, however, SCIMPEX is no longer very influential in the local political context. Most of those associated with it were trying somewhat in vain to protect their declining role in the economy, and their perceptions of the political framework and channels of influence were coloured by this. This was indicative in the attitudes of the Administrative Secretary of the organization who felt that the Senegalese were much more influenced by socialist ideas, as were the technical assistants, whom he described as having no sympathy for business interests either. His readiness to attach the labels of 'socialist' and 'communist' to either or both of them was perhaps indicative of his sentiments and expectations, rather than his understanding of political reality.

There are several employers' associations which are grouped into federations, the largest and most important of these is UNISYNDI (*Union Intersyndicale d'Entreprises et d'Industries*), representing nine associations in various sectors of activity.[1] While providing common services and information to its members, some of its constituent organizations are sufficiently influential to go outside the offices of UNISYNDI for matters

---

[1] A complete list of member organizations is provided in Chambre de Commerce, d'Agriculture et d'Industrie de Dakar, *L'Economie du Sénégal*, Dakar, April 1961. Other employers' federations include UFISCA (*Union Fédérale des Syndicats Industriels, Commerciaux et Artisanaux*) which was established in 1937, and served as a distributing agent of rationed goods during the war. Many of its members own small retail businesses which were considerably affected by the post-independence economic decline. Like *SYPOA*, also founded in 1937 and also serving independent businessmen, most of its current activities and political influence are directed through the Chamber of Commerce or the Economic and Social Council. Information derived in interviews with representatives in January and February 1967.

of specific interest to them. An example of this is the *Syndicat des Huiliers*, the association of groundnut oil manufacturers, which has its own paid administrative director. It can be a powerful instrument of concerted influence on the government, partly because groundnuts and groundnut oil account for about 80 per cent of the country's export receipts[1]—the life-source of the economy; and partly because the companies in Senegal have been able to work closely together for their common interests. It was the directors of the oil companies collectively who set the date of the 1968 national election.[2] They were concerned that the date did not interfere with the opening of the groundnut trading season, lest trouble for the government be forthcoming and the trade be thus in question. Unlike the SCIMPEX Secretary's attempts to exert political influence on behalf of importers and exporters, the administrative director of the *Syndicat des Huiliers* relies on the assistance of certain key French technical advisers in the administration to put forward the industry's proposals. It is the size and power of the industry in contrast with the relative unimportance of the commercial sector which makes the chief difference in its influence and the response to it both on the part of technical assistants and Senegalese politicians and civil servants. The Secretary of the *Syndicat des Huiliers* prepares notes for the Ministry of Commerce and Industry which, by his own account, are often 'drafted as official policy with only a change of phraseology'.

THE ECONOMIC AND SOCIAL COUNCIL

The Economic and Social Council in Senegal, which was founded by Presidential order in 1961, was modelled on the institution of the same name in the Fifth French Republic. Its formal purpose as a consultative assembly is 'to assure the representation of different professional categories among the members and to discuss their participation in the economic and

---

[1] Sénégal, Conseil Economique et Social, *Note sur la Situation Agricole du Sénégal*, Dakar, roneo, 1966, p. 37.
[2] Information from M. Fauvel, Secretary-General, *Syndicat des Huiliers*, in an interview in April 1967.

The Economic and Social Council

social life of the nation'.[1] It is composed of five categories of members including employees, bankers and merchants, industrialists, technical assistants and certain well-known personalities chosen for their competence in a given field. Frenchmen are represented in all the commissions based on these categories, except that of employees, and they are naturally predominant among merchants and industrialists. While in France, the purpose of the Economic and Social Council is to provide technical advice to the government which is not influenced by political parties, in the Senegalese context it is the institutional expression of the '*dialogue*' between the Senegalese and the French, and both officially and informally is recognized as an extremely important arena of discussion and influence. For economic purposes, the government uses it as a sounding-board for intended policy changes which would affect private investment; and businessmen use it to initiate proposals of their own or defend their own interests on proposed government policy. To a certain extent, its success is based on the effectiveness of rapport between the French and the Senegalese members. The Council also serves as a point of introduction for younger businessmen both to the realm of government and to individual Senegalese with whom they might later develop useful professional contacts.

President Senghor suggested in a speech to the opening session of the Economic and Social Council in 1967 that it might be given more powers, even though it could not become a second legislative assembly, because of the non-nationals among its members. He added that 'its composition offered a realism which was often lacking in other special government organizations', and most pointedly at a time of political turbulence in the senior ranks of the party, that 'it kept its distance from ministers . . .'.[2] In the context, this seemed like a lightly-veiled warning that if differences within the Cabinet could not be resolved, he might look to the Council as a 'new cabinet'.

In its present role, an example of the way in which the

[1] Sénégal, Journal Officiel, 20 July 1963, *Ordonnance No. 63–08 du 4 Juillet 1963 portant loi organique fixant la composition, l'organisation et les règles de fonctionnement du Conseil Economique et Social, p. 982.*
[2] Reprinted in *Dakar-Matin*, 16 March 1967, p. 3.

Economic and Social Council operates was provided by a discussion on the distribution of commercial activities (*réforme des circuits commerciaux*) in the interior, which dominated the debates in 1965.[1] This provoked intense activity among the directors of French trading companies to whom it seemed to suggest an implicit threat of the possibility of state intervention in the market process once again. The prelude to the debate took place as early as 1963, but at this time, discussion never reached the floor of the Council. In that year a government proposal was made for the creation of a federation of consumer co-operatives throughout the interior. Sufficient pressure was brought to bear directly on the Minister concerned by French businessmen who were represented by their employers' associations and the President of the Chamber of Commerce, so that the project was shelved.[2] Independent political factors seem, however, to have been crucial in facilitating its rapid demise: it was a Diaist proposal which no Cabinet member was interested in sponsoring so short a time after the alleged coup.

A suggestion for a complete reform of the commercial circuits of the interior was again raised early in 1965 in the Council. The purpose of the reform was to promote African commerce and, above all, to fill the so-called commercial vacuum (*vide commerciale*) created by the withdrawal of the French trading companies from many marketing depots in the interior, following the nationalization of the groundnut trade in 1961. This left the distribution of consumer goods in an unsatisfactory situation, according to the government, and created a commercial vacuum which could be blamed in part on the private trading companies. It was to this accusation that the business community felt compelled to rise in its own defence. Looking outside the Council for information on the matter, the Vice-President (Bonifay) sent a letter to the Administrative Secretary of SCIMPEX, which asked for its members' views on the condition of marketing circuits in the interior. The text suggested that the problem or potential problem must be solved

[1] These are reproduced in the following document: Sénégal, Conseil Economique et Social. *Etude sur les Circuits Commerciaux dans l'Intérieur du Sénégal*, Dakar, 9 November 1965, roneo.
[2] Interview with a French technical assistant at the Ministry of Planning, February 1967.

The Economic and Social Council

by the co-operation of the trading companies, the co-operatives (set up for buying groundnuts) and the government. It explicitly asked if the source of the problem was in their view 'the co-existence of private enterprise with a certain amount of government ownership, in the form of a co-operative sector',[1] which seemed, by implication, to wish to involve them in a general debate about the nature of the Senegalese economy itself. After responding to the technical aspects of the distribution of commercial activities in the interior, it was to this general issue that SCIMPEX, joined by UNISYNDI, devoted most of their formally submitted documentation.

The final report of the Council on the entire matter of the organization and improvement of commerce in the interior analysed the information provided and suggested certain measures which might be taken, none of which were seriously contrary to the interests of private investors. Towards continued Africanization in the commercial sector it advised that 'private commerce had its role to play in creating new wealth by reasonable profits, and in training men who would be more convinced that their activities must produce positive results, as their errors and their weaknesses would be automatically sanctioned'.[2] Thus, the report seemed to reaffirm its faith in the existing marketing system of free enterprise (with African apprenticeship in French firms as the means of providing more African participation). The report was presented to the government as the official assessment and recommendation of the Council concerning the problems of interior marketing. No further action was taken either towards the creation of consumer co-operatives or towards implementing the recommendations of the report. At the conclusion of the affair, it is not entirely clear what was the purpose of raising the matter and taking it to the Economic and Social Council in the first instance. It may possibly have been an indication of dissatisfaction among certain elements in the U.P.S. with the conduct of private trade and an opportunity for the trading

[1] Letter from P. Bonifay to the President of SCIMPEX, 1 February 1965, on behalf of the Liaison Committee of the Economic and Social Council.
[2] Sénégal, Conseil Economique et Social, *Etude sur les Circuits . . ., op. cit.*, p. 167.

companies to defend their existing activities. It may, on the other hand, have been a warning from more neutral political elements within the party that such dissatisfaction might arise, and an opportunity for the trading companies to make their position known officially or to 'put their houses in order', and thus forestall any overt opposition.

While the Economic and Social Council can exert considerable influence on the government on economic matters, its recommendations must always be weighed against those emanating from other branches of the political and administrative system. Thus, while the sanctions available to those who control major economic resources are important, they may not be decisive. An example of this was contained in the same Presidential speech in March 1967 which proposed the extension of powers of the Council. This was a rejection of one of the proposals made in the Council's report on commercial circuits: to divide the *Office de Commercialisation Agricole* (O.C.A.), into two branches, one for commercial and one for developmental purposes. The President reminded the Council members that the existing structure of the O.C.A. 'was in keeping with our socialist option, and that there was never a question of reversing its achievements'.[1] This seemed to provide an obvious example of the balancing of 'clan' interests and French interests by the President, through which the French proposals had to be sacrified in favour of certain elements within the U.P.S.

THE ROLE OF PRESIDENT SENGHOR

Frenchmen interviewed seemed to consider that their continued presence in the country depended particularly on the stability of the present government. Most had a much higher regard for President Senghor and a few of his Ministers, than for the rest of the Senegalese in positions of political or administrative authority. Some considered that the problems of the country could be partly explained by the corrupt and incompetent supporters on whom Senghor had to rely. To the question of whether or not Senegal's leaders had grasped the

[1] *Dakar-Matin*, 16 March 1967, p. 3.

The Role of President Senghor

problems of economic development, a frequent response was: 'Only Senghor, not the rest.' Implicit in reasons given to explain this was quite often the assumption that Senghor was really 'European' and that most Senegalese remained 'unlifted from their primordial African ways'. For many local Frenchmen, he is the only one in whom they have confidence or trust. They were particularly alarmed in the spring of 1967 (a period through which I was interviewing), because of an assassination attempt on the President. Many felt that the future was entirely uncertain without Senghor and reflected with unease on the casualty rate of African governments around them. This was revealed also in answer to the question as to whether or not they, as expatriates, followed political events in Senegal closely. More than 80 per cent said that they did, and many reasons given for this attention were related to the uncertainty of their future. A high proportion of respondents mentioned the stability of the President in office as the crucial factor involved, although only few recognized explicitly that this importance lay in his capacity to respond to and reconcile the inherent conflict between their interests and those of various African interest groups, including the 'clans' within his own party. Their own reasons for their reliance on Senghor was his personal attachment to France, his French demeanour, his status as a poet and statesman in France, but, above all, his desire for Senegal to remain in the French sphere of influence politically, economically and culturally.

While the maintenance of close Franco-Senegalese relations was felt by a majority of respondents to lie deeper than immediate political considerations or personalities; and while they felt that the long-standing connection between France and Senegal penetrated beyond short-term political changes, a real disquiet remained. This chiefly concerned their own presence in Senegal, the permanence of which they related more specifically to a kind of mutual political commitment, and a style of Franco-Senegalese politics which might or might not be perpetuated. Part of France's strategy for maintaining the stability of this political alliance is the conspicuous presence of 2,200 French troops in Dakar, stationed only a few miles from the Presidential palace. The fact of their presence and their occasional manœuvres in and around the city are so much an accepted reality in Senegal that few people any longer mention it when discussing the stability, viability or future of the Senghor government. Whether or not they would actually intervene in the case of a serious threat to the regime is an open question. But the potential, at the very least, remains and has made opposition movements wary of such attempts, thus maintaining political stability without the need for active intervention.

TABLE 10

Planning Commissions of the First Economic Plan*

	FRENCH MEMBERS			SENEGALESE MEMBERS
	T.A.	P.S.[1]	Total	
1. General	1	3	4	5
2. Rural Economy	8	1	9	2
3. Industrialization	9	3	12	6
4. Transport, Commerce, Tourism	6	7	13	6
5. Education and Training	11	2	13	8
6. Health and Hygiene	6	0	6	9

Note: The leadership of each commission included presidents, vice-presidents and secretaries who were in total thirteen Senegalese and eight Frenchmen.

* Sénégal, Ministère du Plan et Développement, *Commission du Plan*, 14 September 1960, a document communicated by a French civil servant who formerly served in the Ministry of Planning in Senegal, Paris, 1966.

[1] T.A. = technical assistants and P.S. = representatives from the private sector.

TABLE 11

Planning Commissions of the Second Economic Plan*

	FRENCH MEMBERS			SENEGALESE MEMBERS
	T.A.	P.S.	Total	
1. Rural Economy	9	5	14	15
2. Mining and Energy	7	7	14	14
3. Hydraulics	7	6	13	8
4. Commerce, Tourism	3	4	7	12
5. Health and Social Affairs	6	3	9	16
6. Transport, Communication, Building	6	7	13	17
7. Education, Training, Information	8	0	8	21
8. Aménagement de Territoire	11	0	11	10
9. Finance	11	1	12	14
10. Structures of Development	7	0	7	12
11. Religionization	4	0	4	12
12. Studies and Research	18	0	18	3
13. Synthesis	9	0	9	13

Note: The leadership of the commissions was shared by fourteen Senegalese and twelve Frenchmen.

* Sénégal, Ministère du Plan, *Commissions du Plan*, June 1964–April 1965, untitled roneo document communicated by the Technical Adviser, Ministry of Planning, April 1967.

9. Expatriate Social Structure and Social Life

ORIGINS

Throughout the colonial period, Frenchmen in Senegal were required to make little cultural accommodation to the environment of their working life:[1] their roots and terms of reference, with few exceptions, remained entirely in France.[2] The size of the resident French minority and its continuity did, however, over the decades generate a kind of local folklore. And although almost without exception Frenchmen in Senegal now eventually retire to France, there are a number of 'old-timers' still in residence, and many who at the age of sixty-five take back with them to France the memory of a whole working life. Among those 'old-timers' there are a few who consider themselves 'more Senegalese than French', but they remain only a picturesque minority who are not even known to most of the new arrivals. The characteristics of the small colonial community in Dakar,

---

[1] Unlike the white settlers of Jamaica, for example, they did not become alien to their country of origin, 'more influenced by the demands of the plantation and slave system than that of their origins. . . . The (Jamaican) colonists, like the slaves, were a product of a culture foreign to the island; both had lost part of their former way of life in transit, and in the new and strange environment. The adjustment required something which was for one not quite African and for the other not quite European.' Philip Curtin, *Two Jamaicas*, Cambridge, Mass., Harvard University Press, 1955, p. 42.

[2] And unlike the whites of Algeria who were of varied Mediterranean stock, they never developed a new cultural identity with its own dialect and folklore, while at the same time trying to retain an affinity with metropolitans. 'The population in Algeria before the war were for a long time considered French citizens of the "second zone". To compensate, they created a kind of unreal nationalist spirit, maintained by a local folklore and self-isolation from metropolitan news.' Pierre Nora, *Les Français d'Algérie*, Paris, Julliard, 1961, pp. 52–3, 135. And of the whites of Algeria, it has also been said, 'despite a pride in their identity, however, they were always seeking to be understood and accepted by their metropolitan brothers'. Jacques Chevallier, *Nous, Algeriens . . .*, Paris, Calmann-Lévy, 1958, p. 23.

Origins

which were already rapidly disappearing in the nineteen-fifties, are now all but entirely eradicated.

The varied geographical origins of the present group were different from the traditional areas of colonial recruitment. In securing trading agents and other company employees for the colony, the commercial houses of Bordeaux and Marseilles originally recruited principally from the poor, unindustrialized areas of the southeast and southwest. The establishment of the Ministry of Colonies at the end of the nineteenth century did distribute the recruitment of civil servants more widely throughout the French provinces. Among those who were privately engaged for overseas service, however, there remained a disproportionate representation from the southeast and the southwest even into the nineteen-fifties,[1] despite the sizeable migration of labourers from all over France following the war. An examination of the geographical origins of the present expatriates still reveals a rather high proportion (33 per cent) from Bordeaux, Marseilles and the rural southern regions of France, although 28 per cent are now also recruited from Paris. This in part reflects a shift in the sources of investment from the south to Paris, where a high proportion of business firms with overseas interests now have their head offices, as well as a preference for recruitment in the large and varied labour market of the capital. In both the public and private sectors, the increasing need for more specialized and highly-trained expatriate personnel has tended to favour recruitment either from the capital or from other large cities. Among those respondents from non-urban provincial areas (26 per cent), most were found to be teachers recruited for the technical assistance programme. Those expatriates who had been recruited from Paris were found to have the highest level of educational achievement, especially in advanced technical studies and university training, and those from the rural southeast and southwest, the lowest. A higher proportion of those with only primary or secondary education

[1] A census of the French serving in French West Africa in 1951 indicated that twice as many came from the southwest and southeast of France as from the central and northern parts of the country. Haut-Commissariat de l'Afrique Occidentale Française, Service de la Statistique Générale, *Recensement de la Population Non-Autochtone de l'A.O.F. en Juin 1951*, Dakar, Table 4–1, p. 38.

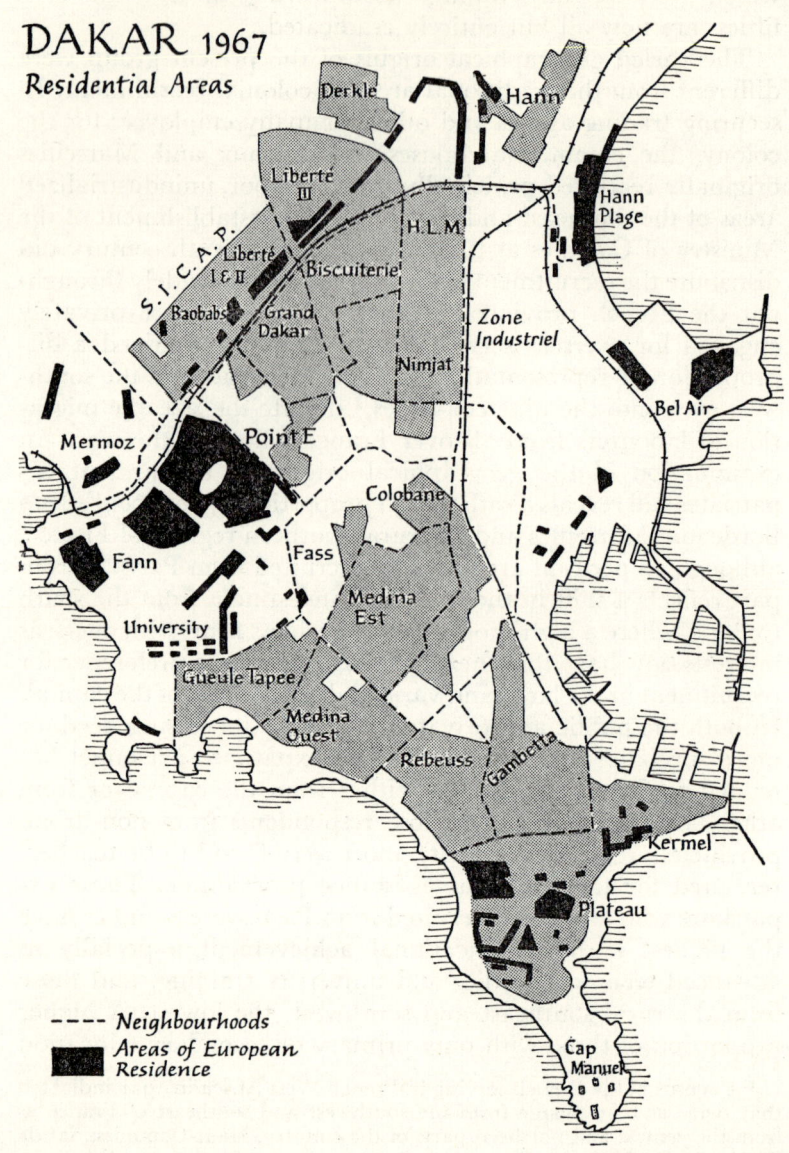

had been more than fifteen years in the colony, while there were more university graduates among new arrivals.

CLASS, SOCIAL STATUS, AND OCCUPATIONAL DISTINCTIONS

The important changes in geographical recruitment and educational achievement among expatriates have had a significant effect on the social structure and the whole of French social life in Senegal. While Dakar continues to retain something of the atmosphere of a provincial town among older or longer

---

European Residential Areas of Dakar in 1967

The *Plateau* area has added to its multiple dwellings a number of luxury apartment blocks built since 1955. The *Kermel* sector is no longer predominantly European, as it still was then, but predominantly African, largely because the dwellings are in an even poorer state of repair than previously. Most Europeans from this area have moved into dwellings in the Plateau. Recently, however, a few properties (both flats and private dwellings) have been converted by the government for housing expatriate technical assistants.

While Europeans spread into a number of mixed areas just off the Plateau during the housing shortage of 1955, many of those who would have remained would probably have moved into the newer SICAP area. These formerly mixed areas therefore contain very few Europeans any longer.

Hann, Fann and *Point E* have all undergone additional development of private villas. *Fann* has become a quarter of diplomatic residences, and *Hann* (along the sea front) and *Point E* remain almost exclusively European.

SICAP (*Société Immobilière du Cap Vert*) has been considerably extended since 1955, nearly trebling the number of small and large bungalows as well as flats available at moderate rents. While the area is mixed (European and Senegalese), there tends to be an inner segregation based on cost of dwelling or flat, with Europeans occupying the more expensive ones and Africans the cheaper ones.

Other developments in town planning which have not affected European residential patterns have been the building of H.L.M.s (*Habitation et Logement Modéré* or French-style public housing) along the main thoroughfares of the Medina and in H.L.M. I & II. The open area between *Grand Dakar* and the *Zone Industrielle* has been completely filled in by the extension of the shanty town, owing to continually high rural exodus.

established Frenchmen, wherein particular people are readily identified: 'Ah, yes, he is the painter', or 'He is surely the builder', this sense of community and familiarity is being eroded by new overseas career patterns, rapid turnover of personnel and increased anonymity. What is left of the receding core of old colonial Dakar is engulfed in the rapid comings and goings of the majority of expatriates. Technical assistants on short-term contracts are replacing ex-colonial officers. And the personnel departments of metropolitan companies advise that expatriate employees are more effective on the job if they are employed for only limited time periods overseas.

New employment patterns dictated by the end of French colonial administration in Africa and the reorientation of private investments had reduced the number of employment grades for which Europeans were considered suitable. This in turn reduced the range of socio-economic or class distinctions among expatriates. Expatriate society is now essentially middle class. And although expatriation is still considered to be synonymous with upward job mobility, increased earning power, and increased social status as it was during the colonial period, the amount of possible mobility in social or professional terms is now more restricted. This is, in part, because present metropolitan recruitment is almost exclusively confined to those of middle-class origin in France, who have achieved a certain educational or professional level which makes them suitable for overseas employment. Cases of dramatic mobility, such as an apprentice or trading agent rising to become a company director, thus largely eradicating his metropolitan class origins, no longer arise. Gone also is the opportunity of making a fortune overseas and endowing one's family with an entirely new status in France as one of the *grandes familles coloniales*.

Within certain prescribed limits, however, relative upward professional and social mobility are still assured by expatriate service. The jobs for which Frenchmen are recruited are almost always of a higher grade and responsibility than those which they had previously occupied in France. Thus provincial branch managers become company directors in Senegal, and middle-level civil servants become ministerial advisers. Sometimes this elevation in professional status can be transferred back to France, as is the anticipation of young company employees who specifically seek overseas posts as a means of professional mobility. Professional status and responsibility cannot always, however, be transferred to an equivalent job in France, which makes many older expatriates somewhat reluctant to return to the prospect of a rather ordinary job. The financial advantages to be gained from overseas employment, are usually now transferred into savings. Savings may be thus later used to acquire material items associated with high status upon return to France. The combination of various financial and professional advantages, as well as the fact of shared expatriation itself, tends to reduce the importance of status distinctions in the local context.

There are, none the less, certain identifiable strata within the expatriate middle class, which in terms of salary and employment grade could perhaps broadly be designated as: an upper-middle class, including company directors, executives, senior civil servants or technical advisers, lawyers and doctors; a middle-middle class, including technical assistants, teachers, low-level managerial personnel, and certain entrepreneurs and merchants; and a lower-middle class, which would be confined to the private sector, including small shopkeepers, clerical employees, technicians, foremen and factory supervisors. These distinctions have some reference to differing social interaction, notably expressed in different types of leisure activities. Membership in social clubs, for example, still tends to be based on status groups, as does participation in certain forms of recreation—of which golf, yachting and tennis are largely confined to the upper-middle class, and the Mediterranean game of *boules* to the lower-middle class. There continue to be, however, a number of mitigating factors in the local context which make social interaction and hospitality groups much less restricted by class or status distinctions than would be the case in France.

Class distinctions among Frenchmen in Senegal were felt to be much less marked than in France by 70 per cent of my respondents. Eleven per cent felt that they were more marked largely because of the concern for local status competition in a restricted environment. The remainder felt that they were much the same as in France. Nearly all of those who felt that class distinctions were important—that is, either more marked or the same as in France—were employed in the private sector, where internal stratification is more pronounced, and their lower educational standard might have made it more difficult than for technical assistants to generalize about their own situation. Technical assistants, who almost universally regarded class distinctions as less important, are recruited, of course, from a much more homogeneous class and professional background. Their relative lack of concern with local social activities would also make them less conscious of status competition and less concerned about it.

Many local Frenchmen felt that residual social distinctions were unimportant because of the ambiance of expatriate life, attributed partly to the tropical climate and casual nature of social activity, and partly to the feeling of solidarity which existed among foreigners outside their own country. A few expressed the need to 'stick together' because of potential hostility from the black majority. Others felt that the common desire to live abroad was what bound expatriates together, and that their high qualifications muted minor differences. A technical assistant said that he knew many more important personalities in Dakar than he would have if he had remained in France. And a number of employees in the private sector declared simply that: 'I go out with the boss.' Most felt, however, that it was the high salaries and greater buying power shared by all which made the differences of employment grade seem unimportant.

In spite of the number of levelling factors and the predominantly middle-class character of expatriate society, there is an identifiable social élite in Dakar. Owing to the fact that the expatriate socio-economic structure is transposed on to the capital city and centre of an independent country, rather than remaining affixed to a metropolitan town of equivalent size, the status of this élite is raised to national status.

The expatriate élite consists chiefly of company and bank directors, the members of the diplomatic corps, the Rector and Deans of the University of Dakar, certain senior technical advisers who have been in Senegal for a long time, and a few of the local doctors and lawyers. It is on the whole much less socially exclusive than during the colonial period, when the equivalent élite included the whole range of colonial officers and resident naval and army officers, as well as the directors of trading companies, and others. Membership in the present social élite is usually associated with membership in the local Lions and Rotary Clubs or a few exclusive recreational clubs, and provides the French guest list for national receptions and embassy festivities. On the whole this social élite represented the older and longer established elements in Dakar, for whom high status in the local context was either personally important or essential for business. A number of respondents (among the 11 per cent who felt that local class distinctions were more marked) commented on the existence of this élite, its status and the origins of its members, and concluded that social status and its achievement in the local context by those who did not enjoy the same status in France gave rise to petty snobbery. Some felt that the real basis of social distinctions was to be found in the differences between older, more established local residents and new arrivals: 'Those with high salaries who have been in Senegal for a long time play the *petits seigneurs*.'

Despite comments about local social pettiness, the relative unimportance of class distinctions among most expatriates seems to have enhanced occupational distinctions and the animosity therein contained. The resentment of those in the private sector of special privileges accorded to technical assistants, as well as their widely scorned miserliness explains much of this animosity. The traditional rivalry between merchants and administrators in the colony appears thus to have become important again in the present context.

About 60 per cent of those interviewed observed that there was only infrequent contact between technical assistants and those employed in the private sector. This was in part accounted for by the fact that places of work furnished the largest reservoir of acquaintances, but also that the leisure time activities of the two groups and their styles of life were quite different. Technical assistants and teachers cared less, on the whole, for local social activities, wishing to transfer locally earned financial gain into status after their return to France, rather than having the satisfaction of giving local receptions or joining local clubs in Dakar. Teachers, in particular, lived rather frugally, often sharing household items among a number of families and going only to the beach or to the cinema for recreation: they were rarely seen in the restaurants or cafés of Dakar. Technical assistants who had been rather a long time in Senegal, and particularly those who served in the colonial administration, seemed to have much more in common socially with business executives and professionals than with their own colleagues. There are, of course, a few high-ranking ministerial and presidential advisers who are members of the expatriate social élite in Dakar. But, on the whole, technical assistants keep to themselves.

A general observation concerning social intercourse among Frenchmen could be made in the following terms: the relative unimportance of class distinctions in the local context seems to have enhanced occupational distinctions and the animosity therein contained. The resentment of those in the private sector of the special privileges accorded to technical assistants—higher salary allowances than are given to executives and employees, assured housing, importation of automobiles without customs duty, unlimited baggage allowances for travel, and other fringe benefits—as well as for their widely scorned miserliness explains much of this animosity. A number of technical assistants themselves felt that this resentment and jealousy was the reason why there was so little contact between technical assistants and French company employees. Among those in the private sector who offered a specific explanation for the lack of contact across occupational lines, three-quarters attributed it to the fact that technical assistants lived separately from the rest of the community and 'with one foot in France', or that they were a 'privileged caste', who were only interested in making money. Although it is technical assistants who bear the brunt of remarks about their narrowly defined interest in overseas service for its financial remuneration alone, or their exclusive concentration on what can be gained later in France from expatriation, this has become a much more general phenomenon among Frenchmen in Senegal than the somewhat stereotypical views held by a large number of expatriates in the private sector would suggest.

ADVANTAGES OF EXPATRIATE LIFE

Expatriate life seems to revolve around annual leave and frequent trips to the airport to fetch friends or colleagues, closing down homes for the rainy season, and making arrangements for the holiday in France. This constant movement is found to be disruptive to marital and family life, although such negative aspects are generally outweighed by the favourable climate, casual life style and leisure activities which are felt to be the great advantages of expatriate residence in Dakar. Not only newly emerging career patterns, but also the increasingly dominant pattern of annual leave seems to underscore the extent to which members of this group can only be considered temporarily outposted Frenchmen.

The motivations which draw French expatriates to Senegal today lie in a series of inter-related professional, social and financial advantages. These are considered by most to be significant enough to keep them there—a majority of respondents who had been in Senegal for more than three years wished to remain as long as possible. Advantages of living in Africa were considered to be the relaxed pace of life, the leisure and the 'favourable ambiance'. Dakar was considered particularly advantageous for several reasons—its size and diversity, its cosmopolitan character relative to other posts in West Africa, its 'Mediterranean' climate, and, above all, its large expatriate population which demanded various facilities and comforts, including the maintenance of a good educational system. An unusual advantage of expatriate life was felt by some to be the relative unimportance of materialism or the acquisition of material goods in the local context. A middle-aged couple who had lived in Dakar for twenty years told me that they gradually found the concerns of their relatives in France to be entirely different from their own. They scorned what they considered an exaggerated concern for home improvement and the acquisition of furniture among them: 'Life is much simpler

Expatriate Social Structure and Social Life

here ... one is not bound by intense social competition. We feel ourselves to be so much younger and more adventuresome than those of our age group who have remained in France.'

Some older and more settled respondents were quite explicit about their desire to live outside the confines or *'cercle'* of France, 'where one could escape from family or social origins', and the frenzied pace of metropolitan life. Those who were most attracted to expatriate life were, of course, those who had spent much time in the overseas territories or who are from traditionally colonial families. Most of the labourers and *petits blancs* recruited to Senegal during the post-war period have now returned to France with the exception of those few who were able to secure better employment or a more stable business situation. Such a case is a former *pied noir* from Algeria who has a thriving small enterprise in the sale and repair of pens and cigarette lighters, which is largely patronized by the Senegalese middle class, 'who', he explained, 'are fond of acquiring such prestige items and keep them in excellent running order'. There is a group of retired officers from the army who sought also to remain in Senegal after being relieved of military duty: a captain in the colonial services for example, from the Midi who served in the Casamance from 1928, 'making peasants into soldiers', has now been engaged by an employers' association as a labour overseer for 2,000 dockers at the Port of Dakar. He explained that he had tried, but could not get used to life back in France for he no longer had any friends there and found it difficult to re-adapt. The wife of a retired navy captain mentioned a similar feeling of *déracinement* from metropolitan life:

> We have many pleasant memories of our life in St. Louis. My husband was in charge of river navigation, and was everything—doctor, fireman, teacher—for the local people (at a village at the mouth of the Senegal River). The Frenchmen who come to Senegal today are not the same—they have no feelings at all for the country—if it weren't for the C.F.A. (franc), there would be none here at all. This is really *our country*. We return to France only to see the family and get a little cool air. We certainly feel *dépaysé* when we are

there. People no longer have the same ideas or way of life that we remember.

And the seventy-year-old former vice-president of the Chamber of Commerce, Jean-Baptiste Graulle, put such sentiments even more graphically. Upon being asked for an interview, he replied, 'I am Senegalese and can only tell you about the European community from afar':

My grandfather was a doctor in Aude in the southwest of France, near the Ariège. He had five or six sons, and since there wasn't sufficient inheritance for all of them my father decided to strike out on his own. He came to Senegal in the 1880s and set up as a trading agent in Kébémer. Several years later, he helped his brother come out and establish at Koungheul.

I arrived from my studies in Bordeaux in 1922 to take over my father's business in Kébémer. I was 18 at the time and had never before been to Senegal, as I was raised and sent to school by my father's family in France. From 1922 to 1928 I remained in the interior—it was the life of a pioneer—I lived with the Africans. The only other European was the local police commissioner. All our daily life centred around our work: There was nothing else to do.

After 1928, I settled in Dakar where life was very casual and friendly among the small closely-knit European community. All the invitations and receptions helped to make up for the long periods of separation from France.

In 1942, I became interested in market-gardening on the Cap Vert. It was war-time and we needed the money, in addition to which my wife was pregnant and owing to wartime shortages we couldn't get any fresh fruit and vegetables for the baby. I began with only a thousand square metres, but built it into a very large business after the war, because all the new European arrivals wanted these vegetables and fruits which were only supplied at very high prices from France. I encouraged a number of African farmers to take up irrigation and truck farming also on the Cap Vert and today we have a farmers' association, SYNJAMAR, of which I am the President, and still the only European member!

Expatriate Social Structure and Social Life

A similar life story was told by an old Ariègeois who had a part-time job at the Chamber of Commerce:

> Our rugged hardworking background prepared us for life in the colonies. We came from poor farms in the countryside of France, and the lack of comforts one met in Africa did not disturb us.
>
> My uncle arrived in Senegal in 1900, and brought my father out in 1909 as an agent for a large Bordeaux trading company.
>
> From 1915, my father worked as a mason, and laid out all the main streets and squares of Dakar during the big building boom just preceding the Great War.
>
> In 1919, he opened a small cement factory in Rufisque, but it went bankrupt because the cost of transport from Rufisque to Dakar made the price higher than cement imported from France.
>
> You know, I have been here a long, long time. This is my adopted country. All my memories of youth and adulthood are bound to Senegal. I am happy and content to stay.
>
> The economic situation is not good, but Senegal is a young country with many problems. People are impatient now: they come here and ask why this or that is not being done; they don't have the patience to wait. A young country must make mistakes, but it learns by them. The problems of need and growth are enormous and cannot be resolved all at once. We have to give the Senegalese a chance for they are new at running the government, the administration and the economy.

There was tendency among such 'old-timers'—with twenty-five years or more of colonial experience—to exhibit a greater receptivity to Africanization, the policies of the government and the general state of affairs in Senegal today. This is a distinct reversal of the tendency for more negative attitudes to increase with the number of years colonial experience among the total group of respondents with less than a quarter century of overseas service. This reversal may perhaps be attributed to a kind of 'mellowness' which these old colonials felt after being in Africa for so many years, a certain resignation to accept things as they were and to cease to compare them with France or Europe, in part because of the dimness of contact and experience against which to compare them. To this may be added the occasionally expressed feeling that they were a part of Senegal 'for better or for worse'.

PROBLEMS OF EXPATRIATE LIFE

Several of these 'old-timers', whose ties with France are somewhat remote and most of whose family and friends are long since dead, do not return for annual leave. This is also true of the small minority of colonial families whose children may have been raised in Dakar and also remain year after year. For this younger generation, however, being so accustomed to the pace and style of expatriate life in Africa may involve a long-run disadvantage: that of having eventually to return to France to find re-integration made difficult by old habits and preferences.

Even a technically or professionally qualified person who can command an excellent salary and working environment in Senegal finds it difficult to keep abreast of new working methods and techniques in the industrial and business world in France. This has in recent years become an important consideration among expatriates whose standard of education and technical expertise is much higher than it had been among those serving previously. It is particularly important for engineers, chemists or skilled technicians working in private companies, for they do not return to a protected place, as do civil servants, although some among the latter group expressed similar feelings. Several respondents told me that they spent a part of each annual leave keeping up with developments in their respective professions. Among my respondents, 60 per cent said they wished to remain as long as possible in Dakar, but 34 per cent had definite plans to terminate their period of overseas service, usually because of the anticipated difficulty of professional reintegration or their dissatisfaction with children's education in Senegal.

There was a great deal of expatriate concern about the local educational system. While the level of local secondary education has been maintained up to French standards by large numbers of French teachers, increased Africanization of the staff at the primary level has, according to respondents, lowered standards considerably and put their children at a disadvantage for being reintegrated into metropolitan schools. Several suggested that although they personally wished to remain in Senegal, they felt that it would be detrimental to their children's future. For some, concern about clearly defined problems in the educational system was enlarged to include the general 'moral' climate in which children were reared in Senegal. The presence of servants and the general ease of life were felt to provide an atmosphere which had a negative effect on children, not only in the family environment but also in their capacity for keeping up in terms of maturity and intellectual development with their peer group in France (a concern which was particularly prevalent among young business directors).

The potentially debilitating ease of life was, however, felt to have an even more profound effect on women than on children, who are occupied at school during most of their annual stay in Dakar. A state of recurrent depression is recognized among women, which psychologists attribute to loneliness, boredom and lack of activity.[1] Nearly all French women have servants to look after their home and children, which engenders a sense of futility among them, although depressions seem to be especially acute for women who are outside the capital, where the relatively varied social and leisure distractions of Dakar are not available. A company director from Kaolack mentioned the tendency for employees' wives to 'vegetate' and become unhappy as one of the most important sources of personnel problems and turnover: 'an executive has two choices after working here for a number of years—either he resigns or he is divorced'.

The disruption of family life, often involving the separation of women and children from the male head of household, seems to contribute to most major disorders among women. Doctor Henri Collomb calls attention to this in an interesting study on suicide and attempted suicide among the non-African

[1] Interview with Dr. Le Guerinel, psychiatrist at the Centre Hospitalier de Fann, Dakar, in April 1967.

Problems of Expatriate Life

population of Dakar.[1] The attempted suicide rate among French women in Senegal is considerably higher than for women in France.[2] When seasonal variations were studied, it was observed that more than 60 per cent of these attempted suicides occurred in the three months between August and November, or just after the annual leave, and many of these concerned adultery or imagined adultery during the period of separation.[3] Allusion to moral laxity among expatriates was made by a number of people in interviews.

The human and physical environment of Africa may contribute to the difficulties of adaptation resulting in psychological problems. The sudden contrast upon arrival from Europe can have dramatic effects upon personality and behaviour; and the geographical surroundings can also be an inconvenience or disadvantage, providing considerable restriction on mobility outside of city or town. The potential problems of the human environment do not affect all equally. Those respondents who said they felt a particular hostility on the part of Africans usually had a combination of other concrete financial, family or career problems. Such remarks as 'Africans are the chief disadvantage of being here', or 'Africans hate Europeans and want to show that they are the bosses', occurred only in a few interviews. It was found that hostility to Africans can be strong and occasionally obsessive[4] among women with psychological difficulties, but that this was not the principal cause of disturbance, which remained the anxieties of the marital and family situation.

Uncertainty about the future was a continuing disadvantage and constant source of anxiety to a small number of respondents —most of whom were self-employed businessmen, the managers

---

[1] H. Collomb, J. Zwingelstein and M. Picca, '*Les Conditions suicidaires à Dakar en Milieu Non-Africain*', Faculté Mixte de Medicine et de Pharmacie de Dakar, Centre Hospitalier de Fann, Dakar, n.d. roneo (about 1962). This study was conducted with the records of those hospitalized for attempted suicide, of which non-Africans were 60 per cent, despite their very small proportion of the total population.

[2] In 1962, for example, it was nearly four times the national average for France, *ibid.*, p. 55.

[3] *Ibid.*, p. 50.

[4] Interview with Dr. Le Guerinel. See further discussion on women and racial prejudice in Chapter 10.

of declining trading companies or among the small proportion of expatriate employees who remain under local contract. Among those interviewed, only 15 per cent did not take regular leave to France which was chiefly attributable to a relatively meagre financial situation. They are almost unnoticed amid the dominant affluence of the expatriate minority. They include a number who have remained since the nineteen-fifties in the hopes that they could be re-employed under local contract. Only some have been successful, as, for example, a rent and property inspector in a predominantly African housing estate, whose biography is indicative of those who set out to seek their fortune in West Africa after the war:

> I was wounded during the war and after spending three years in the hospital I decided I must get out of France, and thought there might be some excitement in Africa. I got a job as a magazine salesman in the A.O.F. and travelled a great deal, which appealed to me. I liked the free and easy life of the bush and felt suffocated each time I returned to France.
>
> I was in Guinea and Togo from 1950–1955, which was a very difficult period. Africans were aggressive, they called Europeans names and even spat on them. But they failed to realize that they could not be trusted and were incapable of doing anything relatively complicated.
>
> In 1955, I came to Dakar and set up a chicken farm. I worked all alone and was my own boss, which was very important to me. I have a distaste for supervision and a formal relationship of employment to someone else. I had an exclusively European clientele, and they were all my friends. For ten years I never took a vacation or returned to France. But in 1965, my chickens were decimated by disease, and I hadn't enough money to start again. So I was obliged to look for other employment. I originally came to Senegal because I felt the work situation for Europeans was better than elsewhere in West Africa, but things have changed completely now and the future is uncertain for us.

Employment under local contract does not include any guarantees of compensation if the firm closes down. And thus, there were in 1967 about sixty European heads of families

Problems of Expatriate Life

looking for work in Dakar,[1] including former office employees, clerks, labourers and shop-owners who tried to make a new start and remained until all their funds had evaporated. The social worker at the French Consulate and the secretary of a French mutual aid society (*Association d'Entr'aide des Français du Sénégal*) are together concerned with providing assistance to such people. The *Association d'Entr'aide* was founded by a group of local lawyers and company directors and provides a reservoir of potential contacts towards employment, but there are very few jobs available any more for semi-skilled Europeans, either because of closure or increased Africanization.

Most social work among the French is concerned with initiating the process of repatriation for individuals by providing funds and trying to ensure through metropolitan agencies that the repatriate will be given a new start. Under the auspices of the French consulate or the *Association d'Entr'aide* about 150 persons a year are repatriated. In addition to those who have lost their jobs, these include old people who have spent their working lives in Senegal and have no retirement benefits, and others who have returned to Senegal after an unhappy initial retirement to France and found themselves without the means of help or support. While most people have some family or friends to help them in France, some become the responsibility of the metropolitan authorities. The French Consul at St. Louis followed up the cases of twenty families repatriated from that town since 1960, and found that all had returned first to their region of origin, while a few subsequently went to another part of France to seek work. In principle all repatriates are given priority on the metropolitan labour exchange and in public housing, but both accommodation and employment can only rarely be provided in their region of origin, thus complicating the social and psychological problems of reintegration. At the beginning of the Algerian war, a Ministry of Repatriation was created to deal with the reintegration of French refugees from Africa. From its inception, however, these services were only available to people who had actually been expelled from a country, and could not be

[1] Interview with the Secretary of the *Association d'Entr'aide des Français du Sénégal*, January 1967.

extended to those who had lost their jobs or businesses because of post-independence recession or Africanization. Since 1960, a group of Frenchmen in Dakar have been working on proposals for the extension of these regulations and facilities for repatriates from Senegal, but with little success.[1]

In addition to its activities in the area of personal aid and assistance, the French mutual aid society acts as a local pressure group for the general interests and welfare of the resident French minority. It sponsored a campaign for the improvement of hospital facilities and the standards in state primary schools, and it tries to deal with complaints concerning anti-French practices in the courts and elsewhere. Much of its efforts are turned to social activities for which its bulletin, *Les Echos de France*, provides a monthly chronicle.[2]

SOCIAL ACTIVITIES

Club membership and social activity seem to be much more highly developed among Frenchmen in Senegal than would be the case for the same group in France. Respondents attributed this increased activity to the atmosphere of sociability and the pleasant climate in Dakar, and noted that entertaining at home was also much more common than they were accustomed to in France. Regional ties and communality are maintained locally through a number of *amicales* (friendly societies) in which people of the same region of origin—Basque, Breton or Corsican, for example, join together for folklore festivals, annual banquets or the sponsorship of sporting events as they did before the war.

The most prominent European clubs in Dakar, some of which were founded as early as 1910, have tennis and swimming

---

[1] Because French repatriates from Senegal are not, for example, considered under repatriation benefits, they are not awarded social security or health payments in the first six months that they are back in France, which is when they most need them, 'Accueil et Reinstallation des Français d'Outre-Mer', *Journal Officiel de la République, Française*, No. 1215, 1964.

[2] It also provides information on metropolitan events of interest to expatriates, stock exchange reports and advice on retirement plans. The Association participates in the *Union des Français à l'Etranger*, which was founded in 1927 for the purposes of providing services and information to all Frenchmen abroad.

facilities and are similar to suburban country clubs. There used to be a fairly high proportion of naval officers and senior colonial administrators among members, but now such clubs are dominated by businessmen, bankers and professional people, and only draw about one-third of their membership from among technical assistants, most of whom have been in Dakar for a relatively long period of time. Because of the pleasant year-round climate, and the proximity of these clubs to member's homes, European families spend a great deal of time at them. They organize special activities and facilities for women and children, and are especially crowded each evening at the *'heure de l'apéritif'* when male members have finished at the office. Membership is restricted by numbers, and there is usually a fairly long waiting list for entrance. The fees for membership are between £50 and £75 per year for an adult, and well above the means of those expatriates who are interested in saving a good proportion of their salary. These clubs represent, on the whole, the social life and style of older residents in Dakar.

The most striking feature of any of the social and leisure activities in Dakar is that they are almost exclusively white. Of club members interviewed, nearly all belonged to clubs which had no Africans or only one or two, as occasional participants. This is explained partially by different cultural, social and leisure interests among the two groups, but also by fees of membership which would be prohibitive for even a Senegalese with a relatively high salary. Nearly all expatriate club presidents said that they annually tried to recruit Senegalese to join, but that even those few who did occasionally join did not remain long because they felt ill at ease. The only clubs which have made any progress towards a racial integration of leisure activities are the sporting and athletic associations which have a considerable proportion of Lebanese as well as Senegalese and French members, and which are confined mainly to young people.

The two civic clubs in Dakar, Lions and Rotary, provide a focal point of the activities of the expatriate social élite. By profession, the highest number of French members are company directors and the remainder are lawyers, doctors, bankers and diplomatic personnel. There are only a handful of technical assistants in these clubs, and about eight or ten Senegalese members. A group of young French businessmen founded a Junior Chamber of Commerce in Dakar in 1958 with the specific purpose of promoting activities together with young Senegalese on matters of civic interest. It launched several enthusiastic projects which were found to be too ambitious for the time and financial resources of its members, and most of the Senegalese gradually lost interest. Most young Europeans involved in such activities remain rather demoralized by their failure or the difficulty of contacting like-minded young Senegalese. Their efforts are largely self-defeating and their altruism somewhat self deceptive in the present environment.

Those Europeans who come to Senegal with good intentions about getting to know Africans are often 'corrupted' by the exclusively white atmosphere of expatriate life of Dakar, and some of the prevalent negative attitudes about Africans. Others of good intention who persevere for a longer time often find that they cannot break out of the dominant atmosphere of separation of the white and black communities, and give up trying after a while. Some do have a few Senegalese friends who share their developmentalist viewpoint or are interested in a common effort, but most of these friendships are found to be not as close or as deep on either side as those shared with friends of the same race. For a few expatriates the lack of social contact or intercourse with the Senegalese has become a disadvantage of life in Senegal.

Some expatriates regarded the dearth of local cultural opportunities as a considerable disadvantage of their life abroad. For young people, there are a number of recreational, social and cultural clubs at schools and at the University, and although they are racially mixed, they tend to contain sub-groups or cliques which are drawn on racial lines.[1] There are a number of amateur theatre groups and a Cinema Club in Dakar, which have multi-racial membership, but their leadership and

[1] Most of this information was derived from an unpublished paper by L. V. Thomas, former Dean of the Faculty of Letters of the University of Dakar, and from subsequent conversations with him. The paper, which was prepared for a conference of the *Institut Fondamental d'Afrique Noire*, Dakar, was entitled 'Les Fonctions Culturelles de Dakar'.

Social Activities

organization tends to be dominated by young Frenchmen, with Senegalese members maintaining varying degrees of passive interest.[1]

While a considerable number of expatriates complained about the relative cultural deprivation in Dakar, activities are plentiful compared with the virtual vacuum of social and cultural distractions outside the capital. Europeans who live in the provincial towns of the interior use Dakar as a weekend oasis, if they are near enough to make the journey. The old colonial capital at St. Louis remains as a crumbling monument to its earlier history and grandeur. Its resident French population has declined steadily since 1960 when the colonial administration and naval base were dismantled: 3,200 in 1960, it had dropped to 800 by 1967. The present French minority is composed of two-thirds technical assistants, nearly all of whom were teachers, and one-third who are employed in the private sector as trading company agents, shopkeepers or hotel owners.[2] The foundation of the old social structure which was dominated by an élite of *métisse* families, has given way to a new order dominated by technical assistants and teachers and an annual influx of hundreds of Senegalese children for the school term (there are four large *lycées* in St. Louis).

The small group of 400 French expatriates in Ziguinchor, the capital of the Casamance region, are more isolated from the central part of the country than expatriates in other towns in the interior. As a consequence one of the most popular local activities is the Aero-Club which provides weekend trips to Dakar. There is only one expatriate social club in the town itself and a colony of weekend huts and cottages, used by nearly all the group, at the seaside about forty miles away. The present French population of the town includes about sixty teachers and forty employees in local processing plants and commercial enterprises.[3] Kaolack, Diourbel and Thiés also have European residents who are almost exclusively teachers and company employees. Diourbel and Thiés are company towns

[1] For residential distribution of Europeans in Dakar and a description of predominantly white neighbourhoods, see Map and Notes, pp. 216–217.
[2] Interview with the French Consul in St. Louis, April 1967.
[3] Interview with the French Consul in Ziguinchor, May 1967.

235

Expatriate Social Structure and Social Life

which are distant from the sea and have a sparse geographical environment and debilitating climate. Because of the absence of local diversion or entertainment, employees tend to work long hours. Life is simple and monotonous with only a few games or sports to combat the boredom. It is in this type of situation above all that the most dramatic problems for women are apparent. Many children of French families living in the interior attend boarding school in Dakar. One still finds a handful of Frenchmen resident in the interior who live there by preference, because, having come to Africa 'to get away from it all', they find Dakar a replica of what they left behind. They are naturally much fewer in number now than they were in the early days of the colony or at any time during the colonial period.

READING ON AFRICA

Eighty per cent of those Frenchmen interviewed said they had read books on Africa, although only a minority could remember the titles of them, suggesting perhaps that either the books they read made very little impression on them or that they felt an affirmative answer was the expected one (that is, that people who live in Africa should have read at least a few books about it). Rather than a source of attitude formation, the selection of books seemed to reflect already established attitudes and interests among expatriates. Technical assistants, for example, said they had read a number of books on the political and economic situation in Africa, although fewer on sociological or anthropological subjects. A significant minority of technical assistants had also read a series of African novels particularly by the Senegalese authors, Ousmane Sembène and Birago Diop. These would have been roughly the same group who also read progressive magazines and weeklies on Africa, including *Jeune Afrique* and *Afrique Nouvelle*, and had among their metropolitan selection, *L'Express* and *Nouvel Observateur*. Respondents in the private sector were more inclined to suggest novels about Africa written by whites as their chief source of reading material, although a number of them also mentioned an interest in French colonial history, books on hunting in the tropics and books about the present economic situation in Africa. René Dumont's *L'Afrique Noire est Mal Partie* was mentioned very frequently in interviews, although it seemed obvious from a few probe questions (off the questionnaire schedule) that respondents had often not read the book themselves but were struck by the appropriateness of its title or had heard about it from friends.

A few novels were suggested to me again and again as things I should read if I really wanted the background on Europeans in Africa, or to provide some flavour for my study. They had obviously made a considerable impression on some respondents, usually those with rather limited education and negative or potentially hostile attitudes towards Africans. They shared a certain similarity of theme. The following is a brief summary of the three most popular ones. *The Empire of Baksheesh* (*L'Empire du Bakchich*, Anon., Paris, Denoel, 1962) is a satire on independence in Africa, the local political élite, the empty palaver of nationalism, the persistence of African traditions, foreign aid programmes and the diplomatic corps. *The Savage State* (*L'Etat Sauvage*, Georges Conchon, Paris, Eds. Alban Michel, 1964) describes an expatriate community in Central Africa, which is obsessed by the problems of racialism. It is a rather laborious account of a U.N. civil servant who arrives in a central African capital to learn that his wife, from whom he had been separated, is the mistress of an African minister. It describes how the local whites watch him day by day becoming more and more affected by the suffocating and disturbing local atmosphere in which the blacks 'become the centre of anxiety, the very anathema of existence'. Of those interviewed who had read it, most were quick to comment that it was not true of Senegal, nor did they think it a valid portrait of whites elsewhere in Africa.

The most popular of the novels in this group was *Aziza de Niamkoko* (H. Crouzat, Paris, Presses de la Cité, 1959), a rather curious satire on colonial society, which ridicules whites and blacks alike, though with a marked difference in tone. The principal characters are fictional stereotypes: Aziza, the *métisse* who dreams of being white, as a salvation from her past; Akon, the embittered black who leads a nationalist movement, after an unsuccessful marriage to a French girl; and Villevieux, the old *colon* and dubious hero of the novel, who beats blacks and has fantasies of hunting them like beasts, but who remains a loner in colonial society and eventually saves Aziza from the scorn of local whites by offering to marry her. While the satire of white society is gentle and slightly mocking, the view of African society which the author presents is openly contemptuous and hostile. The negative view of Africa and Africans presented in this popular literature is, however, to be considered as more of a reflection of views held by its readers than a factor in their formation.

10. Race Relations

The limitations of relying on a questionnaire survey for the collection and analysis of attitude data on such sensitive matters as race relations became obvious through continued contact with the milieu in which the French survey was conducted. Familiarity with respondents or potential respondents made apparent the discrepancy between information given in a formal interview situation and actual 'off the record' opinions and feelings. My experience in Dakar was that Frenchmen tended to be much more moderate or reasonable about matters of race when answering formal questions than when talking among themselves or sharing an explanation or assessment of African behaviour with a white newcomer (myself) in casual conversation.

Questions concerning social contact with Africans caused particular unease among French respondents in the interview situation. Many of them tended to become defensive on the subject and most of them seemed to exaggerate the amount of contact they had, (by their own admission in some cases, this was based on servants alone). In some interviews, the initial unease created by the series of questions on race relations, which were unfortunately clustered together, seemed to be reduced as the interviewer was accepted into confidence as a fellow European. In other interviews a feeling of ease was renewed when the interviewer did not react with disfavour or surprise to the embarrassed answers or the accompanying side remarks. In most interviews, however, it was difficult to probe beneath attitudes 'for public consumption', with the fixed schedule of questions. With only a small minority of interviewees did one have the feeling that they were sufficiently obsessive about blacks to discard self-censorship and provide actual feelings without a probe. It would perhaps have been more

Race Relations

useful to have used a probe technique and responded to ideas and answers to open questions, but the impossibility of standardizing the interview situation made this method unviable.

The predominantly negative reaction to mixed marriage and the extensive range of reasons given for it seemed to be more indicative of true expatriate feeling on racial matters than answers given to other questions. The questions on mixed marriage themselves seemed less embarrassing to respondents on the whole than those concerning social contact between the races. Respondents seemed to be quite accustomed to discussing their feelings on mixed marriage and had definitely formulated ideas about it, which they were not reluctant to share, whereas their lack of contact with Africans was perhaps felt to be an element in their life style about which they should be defensive.

SEPARATION AND INTERACTION: ENVIRONMENT, WORK, SOCIAL LIFE

'Something which would strike a foreign visitor to Senegal is that, despite a liberal colonial tradition and long contact with France, there is almost no contact between the European and African communities.' These are the words of Paul Bonifay (in December 1966), a French lawyer in Dakar, whose career is closely bound to recent Senegalese political history. There is not, nor was there historically, a legal colour bar in Senegal (except during a brief Vichy period). There are, however, socio-economic, religious, cultural and educational factors which keep contact between Frenchmen and Senegalese restricted to a minimum outside of the working situation. In Dakar, there has never been official residential segregation, but the separation of dwellings based on income or class continues to have a racial referent. The original colonial quarter near the port has fallen into decay and houses a high density of African families, including many mulattoes from the Portuguese Cape Verde Islands; the city centre is dominated by luxurious blocks of flats designed for expatriates; new dwellings outside the centre are separated by income and *de facto*, therefore, by race. The location of the Medina, which is bounded to the east and west by wide roads, as well as the 'cosmetic' effect of building new dwellings along its periphery, keeps European visual contact with African urban life at a minimum while travelling from residence to work, to the club, to the beach or to school. Dakar still bears the obvious marks of accommodation to European tastes.

The working environment is the most frequent field of contact between the races in Senegal. Interaction is, however, in a structured superior-subordinate relationship, rarely one of colleagues, and only in the administration is a Senegalese even formally in a superior role. The executive hierarchy of French companies and the inter-locking roles of technical advisers in public administration usually provide an exclusively white network of interaction. Only about one-third of those Frenchmen interviewed had most of their contact during working hours with Senegalese (one-quarter had about equal contact with French and Senegalese), which places in question the training function assumed to be a part of the expatriate role in the public as well as the private sector. Senegalese respondents were also asked to estimate the number of Frenchmen with whom they worked (as an index to understanding labour relations). Those who worked with 'many Frenchmen' included office employees, transport and travel agents in French firms; those who worked with only a few Frenchmen were civil servants and State Bank employees; and those who worked with no Frenchmen were municipal civil servants, including policemen, court clerks and post office employees. Though the number of Senegalese interviewed was small (25), there seemed to be a distinct difference in attitude towards working with the French between those who worked with a lot of Frenchmen and those with only a few. Those in the latter category expressed more individual self-confidence about their work than those who were surrounded by Frenchmen at work or constantly under their direction. Expressions of the need for French direction or feelings of dependence, insofar as they existed, were found most markedly among those for whom French direction was a part of their real work situation.

Race Relations

A European manager in the work situation has a dual role for the African subordinate. In addition to being an executive superior in organizational terms, he is a member of a group which maintains a self-conception of cultural, social or racial superiority. The view, held by most expatriates, that work in Senegal must at the present time be directed by whites with black subordinates is a nearly accurate description of the extant situation in the private sector, and this situation leads to the formulation of certain patterned reactions and expected role behaviour. A European executive rarely expects to be confronted with an African in a similar role. An example which illustrates this was provided by a Senegalese executive: 'On business errands in Dakar, I am treated like a messenger or clerk who delivers a communication, but has no authority to discuss it. Although I have explicit instructions to discuss certain aspects of company policy, as an African I am ignored. Even, however, if my status is made quite clear by my managing director on another occasion, the reaction often remains the same (with perhaps added politeness), and matters continue to be verified with the boss'.[1]

Belief in the need to perpetuate expatriate direction because African performance is sub-standard in European terms is founded on an element of truth in the work situation. Nearly 90 per cent of respondents felt that the work output of Africans was inferior, which was for most the basis of their conviction about African inferiority. 'A stereotype can originate from a nucleus of truth which can be perpetuated because it does not differ sharply from everyday perceptual data',[2] according to two American social scientists. They found that increased contact (other factors remaining constant) changed the image of the group and thus concluded that the stimulus of social contact produced the change. Owing to the absence of social stimulus in the Senegalese situation, the nucleus of truth concerning work output tends to reinforce certain less verifiable beliefs about Africans.

[1] Interview with an accounts executive of the *Société Commerciale de l'Ouest Africain* (S.C.O.A.) in March 1967.
[2] E. T. Prothro and L. H. Milikian, 'Studies in Stereotype: Familiarity and the Kernel of Truth', *The Journal of Social Psychology*, Vol. 41, 1955, pp. 3–10, esp. p. 4.

Separation and Interaction

The difficulty of communication between white and black on the job, as well as behaviour resulting from this, can serve to reinforce the idea of African inferiority. An African worker, for example, may be too intimidated to ask for the repetition of a command from a European foreman, whether misunderstood for linguistic or other reasons.[1] He might be afraid to insult the European, or to have abuse heaped on himself, for admitting that he did not understand.[2] He may therefore act from guesswork, making the efficiency or exactitude of his work questionable, thus behaving as if the pervasive European view of African inferiority was a self-fulfilling prophecy. Such a situation is particularly evident among domestic servants in a European household, who are under the constant surveillance and command of their employers, and whose knowledge of French may be very limited in the initial stages of employment and even later. If the situation in which the African remains inferior or makes mistakes which seem to reinforce his inferiority is convincingly defined as real, it can be real in its consequences. As Merton has put it:

> Men respond not only to the objective features of a situation, but to those which have an ascribed meaning.... When Negroes are tagged as incorrigibly inferior because they don't manifest certain virtues (dictated by the dominant group), this confirms the natural rightness of their being assigned an inferior status.[3]

The influence of the self-fulfilling prophecy on behaviour is further described by Allport in *The Nature of Prejudice*: 'Ask yourself what would happen to your own personality if you

---

[1] Although the number of workers who do not speak French is declining rapidly in Senegal, there remains a large proportion of unskilled labourers who are over thirty-five and understand at best only rudimentary French commands. There are very few French foremen any longer who speak Wolof or have taken the time to learn it. Such linguistic difficulties are more prevalent outside of Dakar.

[2] Such a situation was found to be operative in the Gold Coast (G. Jaboda, *White Man: A Study of the Attitudes of Africans to Europeans in Ghana before Independence*, London, Oxford University Press, 1961, p. 74), and in the mines of Central Africa (Hortense Powdermaker, *Copper Town: Changing Africa*, New York, Harper and Row, 1962, p. 75).

[3] Robert K. Merton, *Social Theory and Social Structure*, Glencoe, Illinois, The Free Press, 1962, pp. 422, 430.

heard it said over and over again that you were lazy, a simple child of nature and had inferior blood? . . . What people think we are is bound to some degree to fashion what we are'.[1] This can lead to a kind of protective behaviour in which the object of derision does not necessarily believe what is said about him, but finds it simply easier to act that way.[2] I have found this type of protective behaviour particularly obvious among certain older, uneducated Senegalese and domestic servants in the employ of European families.

The relationship between the expatriate and his domestic servant is very basic to inter-racial contact, since it is for many expatriates the only source of interaction they have with Africans outside working hours. Among those Frenchmen resident in Africa for a long time, a paternalistic relationship with servants, many of whom have worked for the family for many years, is most common. The operative factor for differentiating the treatment of servants seems however as much related to the class and status of the white employer as to his length of residence in the colonies. Upper-middle class women on the whole behave more politely towards servants than the wives of clerks or foremen, who probably had never had servants before living in Africa, and were both unsure of the appropriate role and anxious to assert newly acquired status associated with expatriation. Studies in another context have demonstrated that there is a direct causal relationship between status-seeking or status-conscious groups and prejudice,[3] which would seem to be relevant here. One of the

---

[1] G. W. Allport, *The Nature of Prejudice*, New York, Doubleday, 1958, pp. 7–8.

[2] This has been called 'clowning', *ibid.*, p. 144. In the American south it was known as the Sambo personality and in Jamaica as 'quashee'. For a penetrating analysis of it in the context of Jamaican slave society, see Orlando Patterson, *The Sociology of Slavery*, London, McKibbon and Kee, 1967, pp. 175–80.

[3] It was established that the greatest amount of prejudice is found not only among those who are status-minded, but in particular among those who have suffered status loss. F. Silberstein and M. Seeman, 'Social Mobility and Prejudice', *American Journal of Sociology*, 65, 3 Nov. 1959, p. 261. This is relevant in this context because of at least potential status loss: many lower-middle class whites are now uncertain about their future in Senegal and thus the maintenance of status acquired in the overseas context.

manifestations of prejudice can be the attempt to deny differentiation within the group which is the object of prejudice. This is apparent among certain expatriates who employ the common European designations for domestic servants, 'fatou' and 'boy', in a wider context as synonyms for African woman or man. It would appear to indicate a view of Africans as an undifferentiated mass within which the characteristic role is that of maid or steward.

Housewives, who have nearly all their contact with Africans restricted to servants, showed markedly less tolerant attitudes than women who had additional contact through a work situation.[1] Intolerance may in this case be related to the lack of interest or activity in the lives of non-working women, causing them to harp on what they considered to be the most obvious defects of their environment. It may also be explained by a generally low educational standard among such women, making them less apt at censoring their feelings or disguising them behind euphemism and explanation. There are occasionally complaints from Senegalese servants about their treatment which reach the labour exchange in Dakar or trade union headquarters, but usually, because of the presence of so many job-seekers in the towns, and the relatively good wage scale for domestic employees in an expatriate household, complaints are few.

Contact between a Frenchman and his Senegalese servant, or a French manager and Senegalese worker, remain quantitatively the most important sources of interaction between the races, and perhaps therefore the most important sources of attitude formation. An examination of the reasons for limited social contact is important, for which purpose it may be helpful to refer to the socio-economic strata within the expatriate middle class which were identified in Chapter 9. The upper-middle class and in particular its 'social élite' of company directors, prominent lawyers and technical advisers has the most opportunities for social contact with the Senegalese through Rotary and Lions Clubs, official receptions and diplomatic parties. It was mentioned to me on a number of

[1] An unsystematic comparison of open responses found in questionnaires of fifteen non-employed and fifty-three working women.

occasions, however, that such contact tends to remain rather formal and is rarely the source of lasting friendships or close personal relationships. The middle-middle class have, on the whole, less opportunities for social contact with the Senegalese. Within this stratum interaction is generally restricted to religious or charitable activities, liberal or radical political groups, and certain intellectual circles. Most expatriates taking part in such activities are technical assistants. Specialized religious or political groups are very small in number, and usually contain a substantial proportion of non-Senegalese Africans who are resident in Senegal (Togolese and Dahomeans, in particular). Certain expatriates have used such examples to indicate that contact with the Senegalese is more difficult than with other Africans, which they explain either by the fact that the Senegalese are Muslim, and therefore less deeply Westernized, or because they are anti-white. Such explanations were most common among lower-middle class expatriates, whose social contact with the Senegalese was practically nil, as was apparent in the oft heard remark: 'Such things (viz. contact with Africans) are for my boss, not for me.'

The occupational distinction between technical assistants and all others, however, seemed to be a more crucial determinant of participation in social activities with the Senegalese, than distinctions among socio-economic strata (as is also the case for attitude formation on racial matters and a number of other general themes in the survey). Only one technical assistant, for example, said that he never had any contact with Africans, whereas 29 per cent (50 respondents) of those in the private sector placed themselves in this category. Forty-four per cent of the total sample estimated that they had more than 'rare' contact with Africans outside of working hours, although many appeared to exaggerate the amount of contact they had as revealed in certain parenthetical remarks like 'I see them on the streets', or 'I see my "fatou" every day'.

It became apparent, therefore, that the schedule of responses concerning contact with Africans served perhaps less as a measure of the actual contact experienced by the respondent (owing to the wide interpretation of the word contact itself), than as an index of the awareness of the 'appropriate' or expected response. Those groups in the population which were particularly positive about the importance of contact with Africans included the same people who indicated that they had more contact with Africans than the norm. They had also exhibited an accumulation of broadly liberal or moderate attitudes. Included in this group were young people, technical assistants, those with relatively little overseas experience, those with more liberal or left-wing political affiliations, and those with relatively high educational achievement (this last being the common denominator of all the others). This could be in part explained by the fact that it was precisely these groups who would be most sensitive to the 'appropriate' reflex on such matters or the need to conceal negative behaviour.

Following a similar tendency among French respondents, Senegalese informants defined personal contact between the races in Senegal in the broadest possible terms. Less than half felt that there was a lot of contact between the French and the Senegalese, however, which they considered essential to the exchange of ideas and experiences, 'the basis of human relations'. About an equal number thought that the opportunity or frequency of contact depended on the individuals concerned. Some suggested that among the young, and in particular those who had been to France and were therefore accustomed to cafés and other European entertainments, there was a greater possibility than among others. What inhibited further contact was felt to be the differing modes of life and, for some, the mutually closed circles of African and French society in Senegal.

Only about half of the Senegalese informants felt that there should be more contact with the French, and they gave many of the same reasons for this as those Frenchmen who felt similarly:

'Better human relations promote better working relations.'
'We must understand each other better for the sake of human brotherhood.'
'Human contact is the best weapon against prejudice.'

One Senegalese informant thought that making a special effort

Race Relations

to get to know Frenchmen was a kind of inverted racism, an observation shared by a single French informant.

A fairly high number of Senegalese respondents (seventeen out of twenty-five) said that they had French friends, although several modified this by adding that they were not really as close as African friends, 'only pals (*copains*) with whom I work.' One respondent spelled out in detail the difficulties of building a truly close friendship with a Frenchman:

> I don't go to cafés after work, or to the beaches on Sundays. We have a collective family life which takes up most of our free time. The French never 'drop in' to see us, and we feel that we can therefore never go to see them, but must wait for a formal invitation. This formality is not our way of doing things, and it inhibits our feeling of friendship.

Fifteen respondents said that they had been invited to the homes of Frenchmen, and that they had similarly invited Frenchmen to their homes. One got the impression, however, that this was a rare or occasional occurrence.

Of those Frenchmen interviewed who considered contact with Africans to be important (65 per cent of total respondents) the reasons given were primarily 'a better understanding of the people or the country' in which they were resident. Several respondents mentioned that it was perhaps the only way of combating racial prejudice. And others who had been in North Africa (all of whom were technical assistants) expressed concern about the limited contact they had, considering the personal rapport they had built with local people in places like Morocco. A few of them considered this lack of contact to be a disadvantage of their residence in Senegal. Some respondents, on the other hand, defined the need for inter-racial contact from a position of strength or superiority, mentioning that the Senegalese were 'flattered to have contact with Europeans'. Among those who said that inter-racial contact was important (obviously as the appropriate thing to say), for example, six of them had said in another context that Africans were biologically inferior, and five, that they were 'big children' who needed direction.

Older respondents were on the whole less concerned about making contact with Africans. 'Old-timers', however, (those

Separation and Interaction

over fifty-five years old or with more than twenty-one years of colonial experience) at least said that they had more contact with Africans than was in keeping with the generally negative correlation between increased age and contact. It often became obvious from subsequent information (usually self-provided) that the contacts which they had were generally confined to old employees or 'clients' who were once perhaps a part of a trading network, and for whom they felt a kind of paternal responsibility. One retired trading agent put it as follows:

> Contact with the Senegalese is now easier and yet more difficult. Although Africans have an educational standard nearer to a European one now, the closeness that was once achieved is no longer possible. During the old days of the groundnut trade there was greater human interaction. Each peasant carried a card in which his sales were marked and on the front of which was a photo of the European he traded with. Such a confidence or intimacy no longer exists!

Although 'old-timers' had more favourable views than most expatriates towards African leadership and recent developments in the country, their attitudes concerning direct contact with Africans remained firmly fixed in the past. They were considerably above the average in their opposition to mixed marriage, for example.

Those with the least interest in contact with Africans or making what seemed to others an appropriate gesture were employees under local contract,[1] many of whom were women. Women in general showed a fairly high resistance to the necessities of appropriateness in their attitudes towards Africans,[2] especially those who were interviewed at home and were therefore freed of the outward sense of propriety often

[1] Twenty out of a total of forty respondents under local contract admitted to never having any contact with Africans outside of working hours, and about the same proportion thought it was of no importance.

[2] Women said they had consistently less contact with Africans than any other sub-group in the sample, and did not think on the whole that there was any need to increase it. For example, while only 16 per cent of men interviewed had never had any personal contact with the Senegalese, 43 per cent of the women interviewed were in this category. And while about 70 per cent of the men said they felt that it was important to have such contact, only half of the women did.

required in the working environment. The minority of respondents who declared that they did not feel that it was particularly important to make contact with Africans seemed to accept the separation of the two groups as something natural or appropriate:

> I am not interested in them. There are enough whites here.
> I see them enough at work.
> It doesn't worry me—we live in a completely different manner—they don't want it either.
> We live separately and harmoniously.

Despite the apparent lack of contact between the French and Senegalese, the existence of a *dialogue* between the two cultures is an idea which was introduced into Senegalese political rhetoric by President Senghor. Beginning with his concept of negritude, the dialogue becomes a philosophical dialectic through which black and white cultures are mutually enriched. While a majority of Senegalese respondents (nineteen) thought that such a dialogue existed in their country, most understood it to mean only the basis of policy between Senegal and France, and did not interpret it as communication on a personal level between individual Frenchmen and Senegalese. Only two informants thought that they participated directly in the dialogue. The others were either unsure if anyone participated in it, or felt that it was reserved either for leaders, the élite, the governing class, senior civil servants or ministers ('I'm only a simple employee, how could I participate in the dialogue? I haven't the competence.') One very critical young man said that 'it was President Senghor who created the dialogue, and only he who participated in it'.

FACTORS WHICH REINFORCE SEPARATION

The concept of social distance[1] was developed for the purpose

---

[1] A statement of it appears in R. E. Park, *Race and Culture*, Glencoe, Ill., The Free Press, 1950: 'Not only is it true that we have a sense of distance with whole groups of persons, but it is also true that "race" and "class" consciousness frequently interferes with, modifies and qualifies personal relations', p. 257.

Factors which Reinforce Separation

of analysing inter-group relations in terms of everyday social life. Its principal components, all of which exist to a considerable degree in the relationship between Frenchmen and Senegalese are: first, the preponderance of certain types of social relations, notably those between a superior and a subordinate, a senior and junior, and between people of comparable social standing, but potentially conflicting obligations; and second, negative attitudes deriving from unfavourable ideas about the members of another group. Distance also indicates a relative absence of common interests or experiences, usually a reflection of cultural differences between the two groups.[1]

According to Senegalese respondents those things which prevented members of the two groups from knowing each other better were felt to be the cultural differences and mutual social isolation in the local context. They also felt that there was a sense of mutual embarrassment which derived from the uneasiness felt on either side, making social rapport therefore unrelaxed and extremely difficult. Only two respondents thought that the Senegalese in general wished to have more contact with the French. A few were critical of those Senegalese who made a special effort to get to know Frenchmen: 'They think it gives them a social importance.' It was noted that Senegalese who accorded special importance to contact with Frenchmen were rather poorly considered by their compatriots. The implicit suggestion was that such people were trying to reach for something which they considered superior to themselves, and were therefore accepting an essentially European assessment of African society.

Expatriate explanations for lack of contact with Africans were based on both the objective factors of stratification and cultural difference, and certain more subjective impressions or negative attitudes: 'Contacts between those of varying standards of living are always artificial, and Africans have an inferiority complex—for they would like to be whites.' Recognition of all the objective factors which inhibit contact between the races in Senegal, as well as an explicit suggestion of European superiority, were combined in the following

[1] *Ibid.*, p. 316.

statements by a French member of the Chamber of Commerce in Dakar:

> Africans and Europeans are two separate communities; their customs are entirely different, as are their leisure activities. Africans are much more bound to their family at large as their social circle. To enumerate the basic differences: they are Muslim, their women are not up to our standard. And they don't need us for friends. There is no reason for either European or African to penetrate the circle of the other. Africans are not exactly like us; there is no need to force this.
>
> A white loses his dignity if he goes too far to penetrate into the African milieu. Why should they be forced to? The separation of the two communities living side by side is ideal. Why should we mix?

Some respondents went into greater detail in hypothetically assessing what a friendship with a Senegalese would be like:

> I have nothing to say to them—they think they know it all. If I were friends with an African, my home would never be my own. They would be all over it with their family and friends.
>
> It is not out of racist sentiments that we avoid such friendships, but because inevitably they only become the means for the solicitation of money.

It may be the size of the French minority itself which accounts for the limited interaction between white and black in Senegal. The white community provides a vast reservoir of white acquaintances and does not therefore encourage any resident expatriate to attempt to overcome the barriers which separate the two groups. The infrequency of social contact between them does not, of course, inhibit the facility with which generalizations about 'all Africans' are made by Europeans. The fact that European social occasions with rare exceptions are exclusively white can lead to an unceasing exchange of information about blacks (often reinforced by the desire to educate or initiate the newcomer to the group). As an evening among friends wears on, the polite conversation or amusing anecdotes about local matters which are exchanged during the *aperitif* often degenerate into obsessive discussions about Africans or the situation in Africa in general in the most fierce derogatory terms. What was most striking perhaps in this context was the obvious discrepancy between the 'attitudes for public consumption' as provided on the questionnaire by some company directors, professional people and even technical assistants, and what can be heard behind the closed doors of a French sitting-room after dinner. Certain respondents volunteered the information that they felt there were considerable obstacles to inviting a Senegalese to their homes: 'Religious practice prevents most Senegalese from drinking alcohol; and others are embarrassed to bring their wives, since the wives often do not speak French and are timid in the unfamiliar social environment.' The standard of education of most Senegalese women is extremely low and their inferior status, in general, in a Muslim society is a considerable problem in any type of social contact in which wives are supposed to be involved. Apart from a small élite, social life among the Senegalese is divided rigorously: women are not included when men get together socially, and would not expect to be. To be invited as a couple therefore leads to a somewhat artificial situation. European hostesses also complained that the Senegalese often did not respond to invitations, thus making social contact practically impossible.

About one-third of my respondents said that they had never invited a Senegalese to their home, and slightly more had never been invited by a Senegalese to his home. Certain Frenchmen complained that although they made an effort towards initiating social contact, the invitation was hardly ever returned. Nearly all members of the Senegalese educated élite lead a kind of dual life in European terms. They behave in a certain manner in the working environment, and do not wish to jeopardize professional relationships built on this basis by inviting European colleagues to their non-European home environment. Although a European and African may have similar professional status, the large discrepancy in salary scales, plus the low importance accorded to home adornment as a measure of status by most Senegalese, makes the necessity of a return invitation usually awkward. In such cases a Senegalese often prefers to entertain impersonally in a restaurant in town, if he can afford it, thus also saving the embarrassment of having to present his wife or wives.

Even members of the Senegalese élite (excluding perhaps ministers and senior politicians) are usually too involved with family responsibilities to participate in a European style social life (or to afford it). The financial burden of polygamy and support for an extended family may be accepted by the educated élite because, though highly placed according to a scale of Western achievement, and accepting certain symbols of this prestige, they also feel bound by the symbols of prestige of their 'traditional' origins. And in any case, most Senegalese, including many who share a European style of life, are not particularly interested in local expatriate leisure activities, clubs, cafés and dinner parties. Paradoxically, social contact between French and Senegalese fellow employees may be easier where clearly defined ranks rule out any assumption of equality. French executives are very often invited to traditional marriages or baptisms by rather junior employees. Some of the invitees find this rather embarrassing because members of the party all speak in Wolof, and as invited foreign guests they are usually treated as a spectacle, seated prominently on a chair, perhaps, while the rest are on mats. This type of experience was shared very widely among Frenchmen (even those with very negative attitudes about Africans as a group) and serves to reinforce certain Frenchmen's notion of their own superiority.

In the secondary schools and the University, where the opportunity for contact between Frenchmen and Senegalese of similar interests and similar intellectual status exists, there remains remarkably little interaction of this kind. In one of the big *lycées* in St. Louis several years ago, a minor disciplinary incident became a major school scandal when a French teacher was accused by one of her pupils of being racist. The breach which ensued between the French and Senegalese staff (a by-product of which was the formation of separate professional associations) could have been avoided had there been good working relationships between colleagues. One explanation may be the slow pace of Africanization. The University of

Factors which Reinforce Separation

Dakar is so widely regarded as a European enclave, according to a Senegalese lecturer, that 'vendors and workmen appearing at the campus homes of African staff members asked to speak to *madame* or *le patron*'. A French faculty member explained the lack of contact between African and Senegalese staff by a kind of personal fatigue:

> After fourteen years, I find contact with Africans on a personal or friendly level more difficult. I think it is a personal view rather than a function of the times. In order to maintain contact with an African family, one must keep at it, keep inviting them, cultivate them. Now I am actually less enthusiastic than I was when I arrived, and so I have lost contact. I am too busy with my work and it is easier to just maintain those friends who are around me.

A specialist in African studies admitted with a degree of resigned sadness:

> After eighteen years here, I have not one African friend. It is not a question of racism, but that the two *milieux* live apart in this context. The only real personal contact that I have maintained is in the rural area where I did my fieldwork, but such relationships are not the same as a genuine friendship with an equal, of which there are many around me here.

While the secondary schools, especially those in Dakar, have a racially-mixed student body, they do not provide a locus of integration, but rather a reflection of the separation between the adult communities. Sporting activities are among the few shared by black and white students, but most other social cliques, clubs or friendship groups tend to be exclusive to one racial group or another. A university professor, whose children were born in Senegal and have always been in local schools, told me that they never invited Africans to their parties because they said they really did not know any. As with adult cultural or social activities in Dakar, it has been found that at the University as well as in schools, when clubs are dominated or directed by Europeans, Africans only maintain varying degrees of passive interest.

FRENCH ATTITUDES TOWARDS THE SENEGALESE

Contempt for African values and the African way of life (almost inherent in the relationship of colonizer and colonized) may be reinforced by the continued reliance on French personnel in crucial spheres of activity in Senegal. Its persistence is consistent with the negative feelings which most whites have about non-whites in a much wider context. Progress and efficiency, in the minds of both Europeans and Senegalese remain synonymous with the French standard. There is a constant comparison between the efficiency of the colonial administration (or the existing expatriate network) and the present Senegalese regime. The notion of progress remains almost entirely European-bound in definition, which makes European contempt for African values much easier—despite the ideological efforts of President Senghor. This is in part a testimony to the success of French assimilation of the Senegalese élite. French colonial policy denied explicitly any racial referent, allowing men of all races in overseas colonies to be assimilated to French civilization on equal terms. Having denied the 'improvability' of Africans in their own cultural environment, and having now closed the channel for advancement through a French system, it seems more difficult for Frenchmen to construct any respect for Africans or African society on their own terms.

The chief determinants of white antipathy or prejudice to Africans and the African way of life are similar to those discussed earlier in the context of inter-racial contact and its importance. Those expatriates who have been in Senegal for a relatively short period of time were on the whole freer of prejudice towards blacks than others, although they were also younger, and better educated on the whole, than longer resident expatriates (which factors may have helped to form their less prejudiced attitudes). For most of them, overseas employment was a temporary professional expedient, which made their concern for what older residents regard as the personal and institutional weaknesses in the local environment much less acute. Length of overseas residence appeared to be on the whole a more important determinant of prejudice than occupational grade. Although executives had fairly moderate opinions in many areas of questioning, a number of them made some surprisingly hostile comments concerning Africans. In the context of attitude formation of whites in Senegal, the finding that socially 'stationary' groups are almost consistently less intolerant than mobile groups is particularly important in the Senegalese context.[1] Those expatriates who have arrived in Senegal relatively recently are recruited largely from the middle class in France, and can anticipate only marginal change in social position or status during their residence overseas. Technical assistants are the most stationary of all expatriate groups in social terms and they also show consistently more tolerant attitudes and less susceptibility to prejudice. But in addition to the factor of relative social mobility or lack thereof as an attitude determinant, the high educational achievement of technical assistants relative to the rest of the group must also be taken into account.

The main components of prejudice in the local context are views based on a belief in the racial or biological inferiority of blacks, or the cultural inferiority of African customs and African society. Prejudice is frequently manifest in the denial of status differences among the Senegalese, and, in particular, in contempt for the élite. The generalization of characteristics believed to be those of a race or out-group to all its members, regardless of objective facts, is one of the essential characteristics of prejudice. It is particularly pronounced among those Frenchmen who exhibit frustrations concerning the discrepancy between their own beliefs and the real situation: a personal conviction of black inferiority in co-existence with the reality of black authority and power in the local environment, for example, produces a frustration which may be expressed in occasional outbursts of racial hostility. A policeman may thus be treated with paternalism or a stylized gesture of obedience. In 1965, a French woman was repatriated after an incident at the airport which began when she was told by a Senegalese

---

[1] See J. Greenbaum and L. I. Pearlin, 'Vertical Mobility and Prejudice: A Socio-Psychological Analysis', in S. M. Lipset and R. Bendix, *Class, Status and Power*, Glencoe III, The Free Press, 1961, pp. 483–5.

policeman that (in a swimsuit) she was not properly dressed to enter the building. She responded (using the familiar form of '*tu*'), 'Who do you think you are? Your grandmother walked around stark naked!' Such outbursts are infrequent and sufficiently unusual to remain a subject of discussion. (This story was repeated to me several times.) The difficulty of accepting African authority seemed to go along with certain deeper personal, financial or social frustrations in most cases.[1] Many of the most hostile comments about Africans were made by respondents whose security of employment and social status was threatened by the uncertainty of their future in Senegal. Such frustrations were also prevalent just after independence, when the declining business situation could be readily blamed on the new African government, or by extension on any African.[2] For some, it has had a lingering effect: 'I hate Africans. It was worst just after the Fifties when they thought that they would take over our jobs, but now they realize they can't.'

A conviction of African inferiority may in an extreme form even deny the possibility of improvement through contact with French civilization:

> Since Faidherbe there have been schools here, and they have produced nothing. We are paternalistic and try to help them, but they haven't changed.
>
> You left out a very important question in your study. You don't ask about the success of the French civilizing mission. I don't think it has been at all successful. All Africans have learned is to wear smart suits. They have not bettered themselves or their standard of living.

Certain respondents openly suggested that behaviour was

[1] Psychiatrists working at a hospital in Dakar found this to be so. H. Collomb *et al.*, 'Les Conditions Suicidaires a Dakar en Milieu Non-Africain', Faculté Mixte de Medicine et de Pharmacie de Dakar, Centre Hospitalier de Fann. Dakar, roneo, n.d. (about 1962), p. 54.

[2] G. W. Allport, *op. cit.*, pp. 7–8. Hostility towards a certain group can, according to the conclusions of a study conducted by Bruno Bettleheim, be (1) a function of the hostile individual's feeling that he has suffered deprivations in the past, or (2) anxiety in anticipation of the future, as inferred from expectations of deprivation. B. Bettleheim and M. Janowitz, *Dynamics of Prejudice*, New York, Harper, 1950, pp. 2–3.

determined by stable, inherited characteristics which made the race inferior:

> We can never know how much a black man suffers because he is black. He knows that he can never attain the same level as Europeans—psychologically, he is different.
>
> They are big children who have no ability to work which is partly explained by the climate, but also by the fact that they do not have the same brain that we do.
>
> Underdevelopment is inherent to individuals—it is a state of evolution. On a national level, underdevelopment means a nation of people all of whom are mentally underdeveloped.

Some respondents did not subscribe to the belief that Africans were racially inferior, insisting that inferiority *vis-à-vis* a European standard lay in specifically cultural characteristics. These normally prefaced their remarks with a somewhat self-conscious denial of racism, and were usually of a higher educational or professional level than the average respondent, thus perhaps being aware of the public importance of denying explicit racism. Their observations included:

> The Senegalese are not logical. They do not know how to think because Koranic teaching, which is done by repetition, mutes their powers of thought.
>
> They lack a sense of civic-mindedness—it is because they are allowed to run wild as children—and are never subjected to discipline and therefore must be under surveillance all the time to keep them at work.

The absence of certain patterns of behaviour associated with industrialized society (such as thriftiness and punctuality) was also attributed to African inferiority. Occasionally a reflection on the hierarchy of races or cultures led to a specific judgement on the nature of African inferiority: 'They are a decent flock of sheep: they don't react in the same way as we do, they are good boys, but I prefer the Arabs who are vicious.' A favourite topic of experienced colonials was that of the cultural differences among Arabs, Chinese, Indians or other colonized peoples, the conclusion of which usually reflected negatively on the place of Africans in the hierarchy of colonized cultures.

The general attribution of negative characteristics to all

members of a group regardless of objective differences in rank or status may be extended to the attribution of particularly negative characteristics to those of high status:

> As they rise the ladder of employment, they become lazy, less conscientious and more pretentious.
>
> I have more respect for the 'fatous' and 'boys' of this world, than all the Senegalese office employees—they have more spirit and are less pretentious than the others.

In Senegal, the word 'pretentious' is often used, as in this context, to apply to an African who is stepping out of what certain Frenchmen consider to be his appropriate place.

SENEGALESE ATTITUDES TOWARDS FRENCHMEN

Differences in educational achievement among Senegalese respondents seemed to be an important determinant of attitude formation concerning Frenchmen. Attitudes appeared to fall within a range from uncritical adulation by those with the least education to sharp criticism by those whose educational achievement gave them sufficient knowledge or personal security to do so, and who might also see themselves as competitors with Frenchmen in various contexts. Although differences in perception were obvious when comparing a primary school leaver and a university graduate, there was little discernible difference between informants from primary and secondary schools (largely because the sample was too small and the questions too general). In a study done among labourers and university students in Senegal concerning their attitudes towards the European way of life, it was also found that those furthest from Europeans in terms of social distance and education were the least critical, while students were specifically critical of the absence of family and community life, lack of hospitality or, more generally, 'a life impregnated with individualism'.[1]

[1] See P. Fougeyrollas, *Modernisation des Hommes: L'Exemple du Sénégal*, Paris, Flammarion, 1967, pp. 102–3, 138.

The religious affiliation of Senegalese informants provided an interesting basis of comparison which may be related to social distance. Although only three of the respondents were Catholic (and one of these a mulatto, which had added significance in terms of attitude formation), there was an apparent difference in viewpoint between Muslims and Catholics on certain issues which was obvious from explanations given in the text of open responses. In general, it seemed as if Catholics were more susceptible to the norms and values of a European value system, whereas Muslims retained a stronger sense of pride in and identity with African traditions, which gave them a greater self-confidence in their culture and their past.

While critical of certain aspects of European life, those Senegalese with relatively high educational achievement were found to be less susceptible to *stereotypical* views of Frenchmen and were better able than less educated respondents to discern readily differences between individuals and various types. Those few who had been to France, usually for the purposes of study, were aware not only of a broader class framework among Frenchmen than those locally resident, and more widely varying patterns of behaviour, they were also able to make general distinctions between those types attracted to colonial service or expatriate life and the rest of the metropolitan French population. Simply being exposed to life in France did not seem, however, to be an altogether crucial factor in promoting a greater sensitivity to different types of Frenchmen, for the attitudes of those few respondents who had been to France as soldiers or labourers did not necessarily reveal such an awareness. One informant who had served in the army in France tended to have an unusually uncritical respect for all Frenchmen ('The Senegalese must realize that they owe everything to the French'); while another who had gone to France as a labourer developed an uncritical hostility as a result of the experience ('All the French think we are imbeciles').

Although it was held by a number of informants that Frenchmen generally came to Senegal only for the purpose of making money and returning to France, three-fifths of those interviewed felt that the local French 'knew Senegal and the

Race Relations

Senegalese', which was explained primarily by the length of French contact with the country during the colonial period. One informant made the observation that the colonial officers who remained in Senegal got to know the country better than those who now came for short fixed periods and remained mainly in Dakar. But he did not feel that this alone was sufficient:

> The French who served in the colonial regime and remained a good part of their life here knew Senegal—its villages and bush. They knew the Senegalese very well, too, but their actions weren't in the interests of the people. The recent recruits may arrive with good ideas, but they never stay long enough to know Senegal or the actual life and problems of the people. And because they remain in the spot where they arrive, their ideas are Dakar-based.

A question asking whether or not respondents felt that all local Frenchmen had the same behaviour, or whether they shared the same attitude towards the Senegalese, was designed to elicit stereotypical reactions, or to see if respondents subscribed to such stereotypes, and, if so, what they were. An antipathetic minority suggested that none had confidence in the Senegalese, and that 'despite their "official" behaviour at work, disguised racism was usually obvious'. There seemed to be a consensus among respondents, however, that technical assistants shared on the whole more positive attitudes and behaviour towards the Senegalese, ('they are nicer, less haughty, more approachable'); although some felt that this was only because they were aware that they worked for a Senegalese public institution and that such efforts must be made at least publicly. Four stereotypical Frenchmen were designated by one informant, who added the characteristic behaviour of each with great amusement:

(1) progressives, who come with the idea that they are going to redeem the faults of their predecessors (the colonial officers);

(2) *faiseurs de C.F.A.* (money-grubbers) who flatter all blacks to keep their jobs;

(3) old colonial officers, who have changed only their official titles;

(4) paternalists, who have changed only their manner of expression—their basic ideas remain the same.

It was not, however, the differences in occupation between technical assistants and businessmen, but the variable of colonial experience which the largest number of respondents felt to be the most important influence on French attitudes to Africans. Only one respondent (the oldest member of the group) felt that French colonial officers were preferable 'because they gave presents to our children'. Most agreed that the more recent arrivals were more communicative and more concerned with training Africans, but a few felt that, 'although they were nice on arrival, they were usually corrupted by the European milieu'. Those with colonial experiences were generally criticized for retaining negative colonial attitudes and being 'more racist, more demanding, more hostile or more severe'.

When asked directly whether they felt that most Frenchmen were racists, ten Senegalese responded in the affirmative, although some qualified it by saying that such people could not show it openly any longer. Some felt that it was quite natural for Frenchmen to underestimate blacks and consider them inept: 'It is something practically natural as far as they are concerned; they have always underestimated the black race and continue to think that it is inferior.' One felt that '90 per cent of them were affected by a philosophy of life which considered that all races were different and that blacks were inferior to all the rest'. Others felt that only a few '*ignorants*' were genuinely racist and behaved accordingly. One felt that racism was basic to human nature. Denying that the label of racist was appropriate, others felt that while the French in Senegal preferred to live separately from Africans, this in no way compared them with those whites of explicit racist sentiment, as could be found in South Africa or the United States.

Respondents were asked to estimate the feelings of the Senegalese in general towards the French. Having thus depersonalized the discussion, general hostility to Frenchmen became more apparent than it had been in personal assessments. Some mentioned that the respect which a few Senegalese accorded to Frenchmen occasionally questioned the authority structure in which such a Senegalese had a role: 'As a police agent I have seen Senegalese policemen on the beat give greater consideration to Frenchmen than to Africans in the course of their duty—this indicates the problems of those who have an inferiority complex towards whites.' Asked to comment on whether old and young Senegalese had similar or different views of the French on the whole, most informants thought that the older generation was more devoted and less critical than the younger generation. In the view of some young respondents:

> We feel more equal; whereas the old are still susceptible to the paternalism of the French.
>
> The oldest *bons nègres* are more French than de Gaulle! Especially those who were in the army, and who submitted to French authority as if it were something natural. The younger Senegalese on the other hand, feel free to question the whole framework on which the colonial situation was built.

'INTERMEDIARY' GROUPS

Neither the mulattoes nor the Lebanese can be considered cultural or social intermediaries between the French and the Senegalese. The Lebanese have quite a lot of contact with the Senegalese: they were often born in Senegal and nearly all speak Wolof. With very few exceptions, however, they have little contact with the French. There are several groups of mixed racial background in Senegal, the most important of which included the old *métisse* families of St. Louis, whose members identified so strongly with the French that their attitudes towards Africans seem to remain a caricature of certain negative premises of French colonial policy towards blacks. They have retained a kind of stilted French chauvinism preserved intact from the past, which seems to conclude in a denial of their partially African heritage.[1] Many of the older

[1] For comparison, see John Peterson, 'The Sierra Leone Creole: A Reappraisal', in C. Fyfe and E. Jones, eds., *Freetown: A Symposium*, Freetown, Sierra Leone University Press, 1968.

members of these families have retired to France, and others have never returned since they went there for university studies. A few members of the old St. Louisian élite hold important professional, political and administrative positions in the Senegalese government. Many of them have a select group of French friends and acquaintances, who are quick to point out that 'they are not really Senegalese'.

A second group of mixed race includes those who are called the *'Portugais'*, Catholics from the Cape Verde Islands, many of whom settled in Dakar and the coastal towns to the south more than one hundred years ago. Some among them who are poorly educated behave in a rather servile manner towards the French, owing perhaps to their relatively marginal position in the society. Others are respected for their abilities as secretaries, clerks, and craftsmen, and are regarded by many local Europeans as distinctly superior to the Senegalese in such positions. They have almost no social contact with the French, except perhaps through the Catholic Church.

Mixed couples resident in Senegal are now nearly all composed of a Senegalese man and a French woman, while before the war when there were few European women in the colony, the opposite was the case. Since 1945, the number of African students in French universities has risen steadily and they have often sought French wives because there were no African girls of their own level of education. Initially many of them remained in France, but towards the end of the Fifties, as the opportunities for jobs in Senegal became more numerous, this new generation began to return home.

Sixty-two per cent of those Frenchmen interviewed said that they knew mixed couples, although 'knew' was interpreted very widely and was certainly not necessarily indicative of continued social contact or of a lasting personal relationship.[1]

[1] The lack of clarity in the responses is in some way a reflection of the vague wording of the question: 'Do you know any mixed couples?', which was meant to indicate whether respondents knew personally or were acquainted with any mixed couples. It seemed, however, that most respondents interpreted it to mean something like: 'Have you come across or heard of any people who were married to someone of another race?' Providing no real measure of the amount of contact between mixed couples and Europeans, the question did however serve as an introduction to the rather bald enquiry about attitudes towards mixed marriages.

Most of them were acquainted with only one partner and had usually met them at work. A number of prominent members of the Senegalese élite, including the President, several ministers and senior civil servants are married to French women. They are in contact socially only with the few expatriates of similar status, and remain completely unconcerned by the views of most of the local white population to mixed marriages. Since most of the Senegalese who are married to French girls have university degrees, they are therefore in a relatively secure income position in the local context, and are largely middle class. The original metropolitan social origins of their French wives may vary somewhat more widely. Some Senegalese students or other Senegalese who have been employed in France have married French girls of predominantly lower-middle class or working class origin. These girls would be largely excluded from contact with local expatriates, most of whom would be of higher status at least in the Senegalese context. Those expatriates who are of similar status originally are almost universally opposed to such marriages and would probably consider that they would be lowering themselves to associate with such women (see comments below). Certain Senegalese marry French girls who were their fellow students at University—and are predominantly middle class. But both the intellectual and political interests of such couples would naturally exclude them from interest in or contact with most expatriates, except the local intellectual élite. A few have friends among technical assistants and university academic staff. Most mixed couples in Senegal live in a somewhat detached manner among themselves, being neither fully accepted by Africans nor Europeans. The amount of cultural accommodation to both worlds which they adopt individually varies from family to family.

MIXED MARRIAGE: THE FRENCH VIEW

Negative attitudes towards mixed marriage were shared very widely by French respondents. Only 15 per cent said that they approved of mixed marriages, although a number of these added that while they were not *a priori* against such marriages, they had a number of reservations because of the difficulties involved. Those with relatively high educational achievement (*baccalauréat* and above) were more favourable than those with just a primary school certificate; but the most distinctive finding was the marked increase in the number of conditional responses ('it depends') with increased educational achievement.[1] As on matters of inter-racial contact, technical assistants showed a more favourable attitude to mixed marriage than respondents in the private sector, which correlates directly with their relatively higher educational achievement.

Among expatriates who said they were opposed to mixed marriage (60 per cent of the total), reasons given could be classified into a number of categories. The first (thirty responses) included those who felt a kind of instinctive opposition, in which its 'abnormality' or the natural inferiority of blacks was the principal focus of the response. This occasionally led to expressions of physical repulsion; even the introduction of the subject of mixed marriage in the interview in some cases provoked anxious mannerisms and modes of speech. It seemed somehow to be the suggestion of the closeness of the two groups which was most irritating to these respondents. Such sentiments were not, however, necessarily confined to the least educated or most marginal of the group and occasionally were made by respected figures in the community, who felt that they spoke with a certain authority. Nearly all of them seemed to be fairly idiosyncratic responses:

[1] Attitudes towards mixed marriage according to educational achievement:

Education of Respondent	Approve %	Disapprove %	Conditional %	Total Number
primary school	21	63	12·5	24
technical school	15	84	0	13
secondary school	8·5	73	13	59
baccalauréat	16	51	31·4	51
university studies*	38·5	54	8	13
university graduate	12·5	53	25	32
doctorate	44	11	44	9
advanced tech. studies	13	47	31	38

* Attended university, but did not complete degree course.

Race Relations

> I find it entirely distasteful. I have physical discomfort at seeing a white and black together.
>
> I could never stand the thought of a black head on white sheets.

The suggestion of inter-racial sexual relations seemed to be most distressing for some. One banking executive, however, gave the following rather cautious explanation of the culturally bound qualities of love:

> Love has been a part of European culture since the middle ages, but Africans don't know about it. 'Dear' doesn't exist in their language (*sic*). They try to imitate love *à la mode européenne* from what they learn in the cinema, but they return to their original ways. They don't make love the same way we do.

Implicit in the expression of 'their original ways' was the suggestion of inferiority. Certain respondents were more explicit about it:

> The white race diminishes with each mixed marriage. A mixed race is inferior to the white race. It is also a degradation of white women that they should have mulatto children in an underdeveloped country. In so doing, they lose their place in white society.
>
> When a white woman marries an African, it is her downfall. It repels me—a woman is an imbecile to mix with blacks. The wife often must work to support her black husband.

An instance of a community feeling of contempt for such women was perhaps illustrated when the French Mutual Aid Society in Dakar refused to repatriate the French wife of an African who, according to the Society's secretary, no longer had any interest in supporting her since he had taken on another wife. The explanation of the organization's spokesman, who participated in making the decision, was as follows: 'We knew that if she returned to Paris, the first black that she would meet on the Boul' Mich' (Boulevard St. Michel in the Latin Quarter), she would sleep with and quickly be off to Africa in a similar situation'. A young French priest in Dakar expressed opposition to mixed marriage in reflecting on the

Mixed Marriage: The French View

number of mulatto children who must be repatriated each year because of their sub-standard living situation in Senegal: 'They (the Africans) may be our "brothers" but let them not be our brothers-in-law!'

The second category of reasons for opposition to mixed marriage were the cultural and religious differences between the Senegalese and French (fifty-four responses). Specific elaboration on the value of African civilization or the typical aspects of its family and community life usually contained an implicit suggestion (often in phraseology or tone of delivery) that the differences were not considered in the framework of cultural relativism, that the African was inferior. Those who opposed mixed marriage for basically cultural reasons mentioned that the family ties or closed milieu of the extended African family and the Muslim religion, which condoned polygamy and conferred an inferior status on women, were all great obstacles to the success of such marriages. The general basis of cultural differences became more focused on the specific implications for mixed marriage as respondents explained fully the reasons for their opposition.

> The European wife will be invaded by the African family. Many Senegalese lie about their situation here, and their wives are therefore not ready and terribly disillusioned when they arrive.
>
> I do not object to mixed marriage itself, but to their (the mixed couple's) residence in an African milieu, the difficulty of which is the social and cultural imbalance.

The third category (forty responses) was somewhat more varied: disapproval was based on certain observed problems believed to be inherent in all such marriages. These included the problem of the children of such families, the difficulty of adaptation in the local context (especially for the French wife), and the assessment that marriages were difficult enough anyway without the addition of extra problems. It is in this category that Senegalese and Frenchmen share the most common ground for their opposition to mixed marriages. Since most Senegalese who are married to French girls have a relatively high income, it is expected by his extended family that they will share in his good fortune, especially if the couple is resident in Senegal. This seems often to provide the crucial test of such marriages. A young couple may be expected to offer board and lodging to poorer cousins for some part of the year, or pay for their education, or to make a contribution to the support of elder family members. These demands, which are integral to status and its responsibility in Senegalese society, are thought of as 'parasitic' by Europeans. It is difficult for a French woman to accept easily such responsibilities, since it is her nuclear family which instinctively comes first. Even when money is scarce, however, as it is when trying to live *à l'européen* in Dakar on a Senegalese salary, something usually is dispensed to a member of the family who may be in need. The couple is compelled to make a decision as to how many of these demands can be accepted, and how they can best cope with the outcome. An obvious solution for European observers seemed to be that the African husband should cut himself off from the traditional milieu of his family, if he chooses to live in Senegal with a French wife.

Those respondents who expressed a conditional attitude towards mixed marriage usually stipulated that, if the educational levels of the two partners were similar, or if they were of the same religion, or if they remained in a university environment, perhaps such marriages would be easier. They felt that certain factors militated against success, but were not *a priori* opposed to such marriages on other grounds. Several emphasized the necessity for an unusually strong personal relationship between the partners, so that they could accommodate the cultural differences and the pressures from both the French and Senegalese in the local context. Others added, with resignation, that really only if the couple remained in France would the pressures which existed in the local environment not be disruptive to their relationship.

MIXED MARRIAGE: THE SENEGALESE VIEW

It was the value placed on family and social life in Africa which formed the basis of Senegalese attitudes towards mixed marriage, whether entirely negative or only reservedly so. Asked whether or not they approved of such marriages six of my respondents said that they did, seven that they did not, and ten were reserved in their attitude. The chief obstacles to such marriages were felt to be differences in religion ('The Koran is against it—Islam is a very distinctive way of life'), as well as differences in cultural background and ways of living. Informants seemed, above all, to prefer an African wife for the purpose of managing the home in a way to which they had been accustomed, that is, maintaining the integration of the family and traditional values. Respondents also mentioned frequently the disapproval of relatives: 'I would find the rupture with my family too great.' But there was also a more general concern for cutting oneself off from friends or African circles in general by marrying a white woman. A reservation, which was shared by certain French respondents, was the plight of the children of such marriages, who were fully accepted by neither white nor black.

Students from the University of Dakar (interviewed in a survey in 1962 and again in 1965) exhibited more concerted opposition to mixed marriage than those interviewed in my study. Religious differences seemed to be a less important factor in student opposition than it was among my respondents. One of the most important reasons for student opposition was that they felt the couple would be exposed to extreme disapproval, a factor, no doubt, which they could observe rather closely, since mixed marriage is almost exclusively confined to university graduates. A second reason which differed from those mentioned by my respondents was that Africans who married white girls were 'lost for Africa', a reflection according to the author of the study, on the problem of acculturation in the colonial and post-colonial context.[1] It also seemed to be an indication that among some students at least, close association with Europeans was felt to be detrimental to the wider group purpose.

More than half of my informants thought that the Senegalese in general were opposed to mixed marriage; only one (a

[1] Pierre Fougeyrollas, 'Phénomènes d'Acculturation Chez les Etudiants de la Cité Universitaire de Dakar', *Revue Française de Sociologie*, 1963, Vol. IV, p. 417.

mulatto) felt certain that they were in favour of it. Others believed that perhaps the strength of the marital relationship between individuals could overcome the social and cultural pressures against the success of such marriages. Young men were, on the whole, more favourable to mixed marriage than older ones, and Catholics more favourable than non-Catholics. The mulatto informant, who throughout the interview showed more uncritical admiration of the European way of life than any other respondent, said of mixed marriage: 'I approve entirely—if ever I were given the chance to marry a Frenchman, I would not hesitate.'

Many of those, however, who were otherwise quite favourable towards French presence in their country, or who felt that the French contribution was generally beneficial to Senegal, remained opposed to mixed marriage. Only two felt that such marriages had a general chance of success, while equal numbers of the remaining respondents were either pessimistic or very reserved because of the number of cultural, family and religious problems involved. One thought that '50 per cent of such marriages were a failure, because European women never adapt themselves to the African way of life'. Most of their opposition to mixed marriage was relatively neutral on the matter of cultural superiority or inferiority. A few seemed to be implicitly on the defensive, while most were just expressing what seemed to be a natural preference for remaining among their own kind.

The French wife of a Senegalese civil servant described the predicament of her 'isolation from both worlds':

> The French are more racist here than in France—they have a colonialist temperament. In France, we were invited often to people's homes, here, we are not. I have been living in Senegal for seven years, and have never once been invited to the home of any of the people with whom I work in the bank. Most of the French people we see are technical assistants who work with my husband, and these are few. Contact with the Senegalese is difficult for me because when men come to the house they never bring their wives, and they converse in Wolof which I do not understand.

Mixed Marriage : The Senegalese View

The dilemma of this woman reveals the limited extent of common ground between the two principal groups, even when education and life style are rather similar. Its effects are, of course, particularly dramatic for mixed couples. Whether or not the distance or separateness of the two groups lies in an historical, cultural, social, economic, or psychological explanation, or some combination thereof, it is to some extent exacerbated by the racial prejudice of certain Frenchmen. This pervasive pattern of racial separation often inhibits others with good intentions from making the effort to counteract it. Some expatriates, for example, arrive with the intention of getting to know the Senegalese, but can be taken in by the exclusiveness of the white community and the attitudes of some of its members. Some find the need to cultivate African acquaintances or the effort it takes to try to establish a really mixed circle of friends is too time-consuming. And others simply give up trying to combat the dominant separation of the two groups and, while remaining rather dispirited about it, confine themselves like all others to predominantly white circles.

Appendix 1. French Population of Dakar, and of Senegal, 1909-1970

with total of the Lebanese minority and global population, compiled from several sources—cited below

	DAKAR			SENEGAL (including Dakar)		
Year	French	Lebanese	Total	French	Lebanese	Total
1909	1,899[2]	109[1]	9,894[2]	4,229[9]	281[1]	1,173,000[10]
1916		668		3,559	1,116	1,248,000
1926	2,488	709		5,545	1,962	1,354,000
1931	4,989	1,389	53,892	8,638	2,988	1,638,000
1935	4,941	1,269	92,634	8,399	3,829	1,738,000
1940	6,513	1,600 (approx.)	140,787			
1941	18,233[3]	1,600 (approx.)	165,188			
1945	12,000	1,900 (approx.)	175,000	16,432		1,872,000
1948	15,498	2,000 (approx.)	228,000			2,158,140 (1951)
1955	26,516	3,591[4]	231,000[4]			2,255,669 (1958)
1960[5]	30,000	10,000		38,000	15,000	3,110,000[12]
1966	29,023[6]	12,000[11]	457,297[8]	31,797[6]	18,000[11]	3,580,000[12]
1968	27,500[7]			29,500[7]		3,760,000[13]
1970[14]	27,500			29,000		

1. From J. G. Desbordes, *L'Immigration Libano-Syrienne en A.O.F.*, Poitiers, Imp. Moderne, 1938, p. 19 for 1909–35.
2. From Haut-Commissariat de la République, Afrique Occidentale Française, *Annuaire Statistique de l'AOF*, Edition 1949, Tome 1, Tableau XLIX, p. 90, for 1909–48.
3. The rapid rise of 12,000 in the French population from 1940–41 is explained by the mooring of the French fleet at Dakar. The

275

French population remained inflated throughout the war by the presence of varied military personnel.
4. From République du Sénégal, Ministère du Plan, *Recensement Démographique de Dakar*, 1955, Résultats Définitifs: 2ème fascicule, Paris, 1952, p. 3 annex.
5. From L. Verrière, *La Population du Sénégal* (Aspects quantitatifs), Thèse pour le Doctorat en Sciences Economiques, Université de Dakar, July 1965, pp. 31, 33.
6. Estimated by the Consul of France in Dakar, 30 September 1966. This estimate includes about 2,200 French military personnel plus their families, scaled down from 5,000 military personnel which inflated the total French population of Dakar to approximately 37,000 between 1960 and 1965 when the troops were concentrated from the rest of French West Africa (information from the French Consul at Dakar).
7. This estimate was made on the basis of information from the *Mission d'Aide et de Coopération* and the French Consulate in Dakar in 1968. The French population in towns outside Dakar was estimated as follows in 1966: St. Louis—800; Kaolack—500; Thiès—500; Ziguinchor—75; Diourbel—50. From the French Consuls in Dakar, St. Louis, Ziguinchor.
8. From Sérigne Lamine Diop, Groupe d'Etudes Dakaroises: 'La Situation Démographique et son Evolution', March 1966, roneo from the Government Department of Statistics, Dakar.
9. From *Annuaire Statistique de l'AOF*, Edition 1949 (see above), Tome 1, Tableaux XXIII–XL, pp. 79–81, for 1909–45.
10. From J. Lombard, Etudes Sénégalaises, No. 9, *Connaissance du Sénégal*: Fasc. 5 *Géographie Humaine*, Senegal, Centre de Recherche et de Documentation Sénégalaise, 1963, pp. 21–22 for 1909–58.
11. Estimated by the Economic Attaché of the Lebanese Embassy, Dakar, 1966.
12. From United Nations, *Demographic Yearbook*, New York, UN, 1967, pp. 120–1.
13. Estimated on the basis of United Nations projected annual population growth from above.
14. Estimated by the French Embassy, Dakar, Senegal, spring 1970.

Appendix 2. Sample of Frenchmen in the Technical Assistance and Private Sector

Technical Assistants
    Dakar   50 (see details following)
    Outside Dakar   5
        (Lycee teachers, St. Louis, Kaolack)
    University   5
        (Four professors and one member of the administration)
        T.A. sub-total 60

Employees in the Private Sector
    Dakar   164
        including 45 women } see detailed
                   114 men   } sample following
        in general business sector
        plus   2 lawyers
                   2 doctors
                   1 dentist

    Outside Dakar   11
        Kaolack   2
        St. Louis   3
        Diourbel   2
        Thiès   2
        Ziguinchor   2
        P.S. sub-total 175

Non-Employed (Women)
    Dakar   15

Total
    Dakar   235
    Outside Dakar   15
                          250

Sample of Frenchmen

SAMPLE FOR THE PRIVATE SECTOR (DAKAR)

(Based on a distribution of the labour force in that city in 1964 by origin and sex of employee, and sector and grade of employment, as presented in Table 7, p. 159.)

Sector and Grade of Employment	No. of Interviews	
Manufacturing Industries	men	women
Directors	2	
Management, Executives	7	
Foremen, Supervisors, Technicians	15	1
Clerks, Secretaries, Accountants	2	5
Labourers (skilled)	1	
Building, Public Works		
Directors	1	
Management, Executives	4	
Supervisors, Foremen, Technicians	7	
Clerks, Secretaries, Accountants		2
Labourers (skilled)	2	
Utilities (Water, Gas, Electricity)		
Directors		
Management, Executives		
Supervisors, Foremen, Technicians	3	
Clerks, Secretaries, Accountants		
Labourers (skilled)		
Commerce, Insurance, Banks		
Directors	7	
Management, Executives	15	1
Supervisors, Foremen, Technicians	15	2
Clerks, Secretaries, Accountants	6	16
Labourers (skilled)	2	
Transport and Entrepreneurs		
Directors	1	
Management, Executives	7	
Supervisors, Foremen, Technicians	6	1
Clerks, Secretaries, Accountants		2

Appendix 2

Sector and Grade of Employment	No. of Interviews	
	men	women
*Services**		
Directors	2	1
Management	4	1
Supervisors, Foremen, Technicians	2	1
Clerks, Secretaries, Accountants	2	12
Labourers (skilled)	1	
	114	45

* Including primary school teachers under local contract to the Government of Senegal.

SAMPLE FOR TECHNICAL ASSISTANTS
Distribution by Ministry or Department (DAKAR)
(Based on proposed personnel for 1966, as presented in Table 9, p. 188.)

	Total Tech. Asst.	No. of Interviews
1. Presidency	10	0
2. Foreign Affairs	2	0
3. Justice	23	1
4. Finance	29	1
5. Interior	14	1
6. Labour	2	0
7. Information, Tourism	44	2
8. Commerce and Industry	11	0
9. Development and Planning	26	1
10. Rural Economy	70	3
11. Power	17	1
12. Public Works: Urbanization, Housing	37	2
13. Public Works: Railroads	59	2
14. Public Works: Dakar Port	20	1
15. Public Works: Merchant Marine	13	0
16. Health and Social Services	103	4
17. National Education, Culture		

	Dakar only	All Senegal		
(a) primary ed.	34 ⎫	80 ⎫		4 ⎫
(b) complementary ed.	92 ⎬	144 ⎬ 701		6 ⎬ 20
(c) secondary ed.	95 ⎭	477 ⎭		10 ⎭

Sample of Frenchmen

	Total Tech. Asst.	No. of Interviews
18. Technical Training	319	9
19. Popular Education, Youth and sports	32	2
TOTAL	1,532	50

OUTSIDE OF DAKAR (Teachers only)
Technical Schools, St. Louis: 2 interviews
Secondary Schools, Kaolack, St. Louis: 3 interviews
(Teachers in the Dakar sample are over-represented, because of time and access during the interviewing period.)

Appendix 3. Questionnaire and Frequency Distribution, Jan.–June 1967

Including the basic distribution of responses, both as they appeared on the original questionnaire (with code numbers), or as they were subsequently coded from open responses after the completion of the survey (indicated by '(C)' following the question).

The questions were posed orally by the interviewer in French and responses, both open and pre-coded, were recorded directly on the questionnaire. The results were based on a stratified quota sample of 250 Frenchmen, all of whom answered questions 3–61. The second part of the questionnaire was divided into a number of separate questions for technical assistants and employees in the private sector and liberal professions.

Do not write in the margin

Circle code no.

0–1–2   Number of Questionnaire

		No.	%
3.	*Are you*		
	a French technical assistant	0	17·6
	a military conscript working as a technical assistant	1	4·4
	a member of the private sector with expatriate contract	2	50·4
	a member of the private sector recruited locally	3	16·0
	a member of a liberal profession	4	2·4
	not employed (women exclusively)	5	6·0
	university staff	6	2·0
	others (miscoded employees from private sector)		1·2

		No.	Resps.
4.	*If you are a technical assistant, what is your specific post?*		
	adviser to minister or head of department	0	13
	technical assistant working with Senegalese counterparts	1	12
	teacher—primary school	2	6
	teacher—secondary school	3	22
	university professor or administrator	4	6
	other (specify)	5	1
	no response	9	190

Questionnaire

5. *Are you in the commercial or industrial sector?*   No.   Resps.
 If you are in the commercial sector, are you a (an)

	No.	Resps.
self-employed merchant	0	12
sales clerk or employee in shop	1	10
director of a commercial firm	2	16
executive in a commercial firm	3	9
employee in a commercial firm	4	27
other (specify)	5	13
no response	9	163

6. *If you are in the industrial sector, are you a (an)*

	No.	Resps.
employer	0	3
executive or director	1	23
engineer or other technical profession	2	4
technician	3	26
office employee	4	14
foreman	5	9
skilled worker	6	0
no response	9	171

7. *What level of education have you completed?*

	No.	%
primary school	0	9.6
technical school	1	5.2
secondary school	2	23.6
baccalauréat	3	20.4
university studies	4	5.2
university graduate	5	12.8
doctorate, *agrégation*	6	3.6
advanced technical studies	7	15.2
other (specify)	8	2.8
no response	9	1.2

8. *Age*

	No.	%
under 20 years	0	0.4
20–24	1	8.8
25–34	2	26.4
35–44	3	33.6
45–54	4	21.2
55–60	5	6.8
over 60	6	2.8

9. *Sex*

	No.	%
masculine	0	72.6
feminine	1	27.4

Appendix 3

10. *Marital status*   No.   %
    - married   0   89·1
    - single   1   10·9

11. *Does your spouse*
    - not work   0   32·4
    - work in the technical assistance programme   1   12·8
    - work in the private sector under expatriate contract   2   21·6
    - work in the private sector under local contract   3   10·4
    - work in charitable activities   4   0
    - other (specify)   5   4·8
    - no response   9   16·8

12. *Before living abroad, where have you lived for the longest time in France?*

		%		(C)	
Paris	0	28·0	Other Urban	5	3·6
Marseilles	1	4·4	Other Provincial	6	26·4
Bordeaux	2	4·4	Overseas France	7	4·0
South East F.	3	10·8	Senegal born	8	2·8
South West F.	4	13·2	No response	9	2·0

13.* *Previous to your arrival in Senegal, have you always lived in France? If not, in which countries have you lived?*
    - in tropical Africa before independence   0
      (specify which colony and duration of residence)
    - in tropical Africa after independence   1
      (specify which country and duration of residence)
    - in Indo-China   2
      (specify duration of residence)
    - in North Africa   3
      (specify which country and duration of residence)
    - in France only   4
    - in a foreign country   5
    - no response   9

* Question 13 was recoded as follows:

Questionnaire

13a. *Previous to your arrival in Senegal, have you had any* No. %
    other colonial experience? (C)

	No.	%
no colonial experience	0	67·2
1 to 5 years	1	11·6
6 to 10 years	2	8·4
11 to 15 years	3	5·6
more than 15 years	4	6·4
no response	9	0·4

13b. *In which country would this have been?* (C)

no colonial experience	0	67·2
French West Africa	1	11·2
French Equatorial Africa	2	1·6
both French West Africa and French Equatorial Africa	3	0·8
Indo-China	4	2·4
Algeria	5	3·6
other French Colonies, North Africa	6	6·8
Indo-China and North Africa	7	1·2
other multiples of the above	8	5·2
no response	9	

14. *For how many years have you lived in Senegal?*

less than 3 years	0	16·0
3–6 years	1	18·8
7–10	2	16·8
11–14	3	12·8
15–20	4	19·6
21–25	5	5·2
more than 25 years	6	10·0
no response	9	0·8

Questions 13 and 14 (combined responses of) were recoded as follows:

14a. *What is your cumulative colonial experience?* (C)

less than 3 years	0	10·4
3–6 years	1	12·8
7–10	2	12·4
11–14	3	16·0
15–20	4	24·8
21–25	5	8·0
more than 25 years	6	15·6

Appendix 3

		No.	%
15.	*Since your arrival in Senegal, have you lived*		
	always in Dakar	0	73·0
	almost always in Dakar	1	10·0
	in the large towns of the interior (Rufisque, Thiès, St. Louis, Kaolack, Ziguinchor, Diourbel)	2	15·6
	in the villages of the interior	3	0·8
	no response	9	0·4
16.	*Why did you come to Africa to work?* (multiple response question)		
	I worked with a company in France which assigned me to Africa	0	10·0
	I thought I would find an attractive position, money	1	22·0
	I thought that I would be able to launch a lucrative business	2	1·2
	the possibility of promotion or advancement	3	3·2
	life is more pleasant	4	8·8
	I prefer to live abroad, to get out of the '*cercle*' of France	5	12·8
	my family was already living in Africa	6	14·4
	I was assigned by the Ministry of Co-operation (after volunteering for overseas work)	7	2·4
	Army experience in Africa	8	5·2
	to become acquainted with Africa	9	19·6
	other	x	18·0
	to replace my military service (*militaires de contingent* only)	y	4·8
17.	*Why did you choose Senegal, or Dakar in particular?* (multiple response question)		
	I didn't have the choice (I was assigned)	0	49·6
	the possibility of starting lucrative business	1	2·0
	the possibility of finding an attractive position	2	6·4
	for the climate, the sea	3	6·4
	I liked the country generally	4	2·8
	Dakar is a city with all European facilities	5	7·6
	I had relatives already living here	6	11·2
	I had friends or business associates here	7	7·6
	other (specify)	8	6·4

Questionnaire

	No.	%
demobilized in Dakar after the Second World War	x	4·0
no response	9	1·2

18. *For you, what are the most important advantages in Africa?*
    (multiple response question)

	No.	%
general material or financial gain	0	24·8
possibility of promotion, advancement	1	5·6
opportunity of accumulating savings	2	12·4
long leaves	3	3·6
leisure activities	4	3·6
climate, sea	5	50·8
life is easier and more agreeable	6	22·8
servants in the home (permitting wife more leisure time or opportunity to work)	7	14·4
other (specify)	8	14·8
more responsibility, freedom and diversity in work	x	10·8
no response	9	1·6

19. *What are the disadvantages?*
    (multiple response question)

	No.	%
working conditions	0	9·6
absence of cultural activities	1	18·8
separation from metropolitan life	2	9·2
cost of living	3	2·4
separation from family and friends in France	4	26·8
uncertain future	5	14·4
climate, health problems	6	14·4
difficulty of reintegration in France	7	5·2
lack of contact with the Senegalese	8	4·4
none	9	15·2
other (specify)	x	11·2
educational (or discipline problems) of children	y	4·8

20. *How do the conditions of work for the French in Senegal compare with those in France? If you think that they are better or worse, please state why.*

	No.	%
the same	0	8·0
better	1	48·8
worse	2	26·8
better or worse for different reasons	3	7·2
no response	9	8·4

Appendix 3

21. *Are you a member of a club or social organization in Senegal? If so, do the clubs or other social organizations of which you are a member include*

	No.	%
only Europeans	0	15·6
very few Africans	1	32·4
as many Africans as Europeans	2	4·4
many Africans	3	2·4
not a member of any organization	4	45·2
no response	9	

22. *Do you think that class distinctions among the French in Senegal and those in France are the same*

	0	13·2
more distinct	1	11·2
less distinct	2	70·8
don't know	3	2·0
more marked in Dakar, less in the interior	4	1·6
no response	9	1·2

23. *If you think that they are more distinct or less distinct, please explain why*
    (responses not coded)
    more distinct
    less distinct

24. *Have you any personal contact with the Senegalese outside working hours?*

never	0	23·2
very rarely	1	19·6
rarely	2	13·2
from time to time	3	22·0
often	4	16·0
very often	5	5·6
no response	9	0·4

25. *Have you ever invited any Senegalese to your home?*

never	0	31·2
very rarely	1	13·2
rarely	2	14·8
from time to time	3	28·0
often	4	8·4
very often	5	3·2
no response	9	1·2

Questionnaire

26. *Have you ever been invited to their homes?*

	No.	%
never	0	35.6
very rarely	1	13.6
rarely	2	15.2
from time to time	3	23.6
often	4	8.4
very often	5	2.4
no response	9	1.2

27. *Do you think that in general personal contact between the French and the Senegalese is*

	No.	%
inexistent	0	1.6
very rare	1	11.2
rare	2	51.2
frequent	3	24.0
very frequent	4	2.4
occasional (category not initially included but added at insistence of respondents who felt it was between 'rare' and 'frequent')	5	5.6
no response	9	4.0

28. *Do you consider personal contact between the French and the Senegalese to be important?*

	No.	%
yes	0	65.2
no	1	32.0
don't know	2	1.2
no response	9	1.2

29. *If yes, why?*
    (responses not coded)

30. *If no, why?*
    (responses not coded)

31. *Are there any mixed couples (African-European) among your acquaintances?*

	No.	%
yes	0	62.4
no	1	36.0
no response	9	1.6

32. *Do you approve of such mixed marriages in general?*

	No.	%
yes	0	15.2
no	1	58.8
it depends	2	21.6
don't know	3	.4
don't care: neither for nor against	4	1.2
no response	9	2.8

Appendix 3

		No.	%
33.	*If yes, why?* (C)		
	why not?	0	26·5
	each to his own, I'm not against it	1	34·0
	I recognize difficulties, but don't *a priori* disapprove	2	8·0
	colour doesn't modify marriage	3	11·0
	I approve, but have reservations	4	5·5
	we live in a time when it can work (it creates racial understanding)	5	12·5
	no response	9	2·5
34.	*If no, why?* (C)		
	I am *a priori* against mixed marriages; physical repulsion, ('it's not normal'); a white woman lowers herself in such a marriage, ('she will be asked to do things beneath her')	0	16·5
	Africans are inferior	1	5·0
	differences in ways of life, civilization, (or composite of race, education, and culture)	2	27·0
	African family ties, family milieu, religion (polygamy, attitude to women)	3	8·3
	marriage itself is difficult enough without adding the mixed racial factor	4	5·0
	difference in educational levels	5	2·0
	children of such marriages are unhappy (they are neither black nor white and accepted by neither group)	6	10·0
	they are usually failures in my experience	7	4·0
	It is too difficult in the local context (these marriages are often contracted in France and when the couple returns, the Af. is torn by former friends and family from Eur. wife)	8	7·0
	no response	9	15·2
35.	*If 'it depends', why?*		
	marriage is a purely individual matter	0	20·2
	if the intellectual, educational and social levels of the two partners are the same	2	5·0
	religious differences	3	30·0
	if the African is 'Europeanized' or detached from his family milieu	5	5·0
	I approve of it outside Senegal, because of family problems and women's status	6	9·0

Questionnaire

	No.	%
I am not *a priori* against it, but the high rate of failure and number of problems make me wary	7	18·0
only in exceptional cases, when difficulties can be surmounted	8	4·0
no response	9	9·8

36. *Which daily newspapers do you read regularly?*

	No.	%
Dakar-Matin	0	nearly all
Le Monde	1	30·8
France-Soir	2	13·2
Le Figaro	3	4·4
multiples of the above	4	14·0
none	6	8·0
others (specify)	7	2·8
provincial newspapers	8	2·0
no response	9	2·4

37. *Which weeklies do you read regularly?*
(responses only partially analysed)

	No.	%
Jeune Afrique	0	
Afrique Nouvelle	1	
Moniteur Africain	2	
L'Express	3	
Nouvel Observateur	4	6·4
Canard Enchaîné	5	
Candide	6	
Sélection Hebdomadaire du Monde	7	
Figaro Littéraire	8	
Paris Match, Jours de France	9	25·6
none	x	9·2
several	y	36·0
no response		

38. *Have you read any books on Africa?*

	No.	%
yes	0	84·0
no	1	14·8
no response	9	1·2

39. *If you have, were they mainly*

	No.	%
novels	0	18·0
travel or adventure books	1	11·6
art or anthropology books	2	5·6

Appendix 3

		No.	%
	books on politics or economics	3	9.6
	a bit of everything	4	36.0
	others (specify)	5	4.0
	no response	9	15.2

40. *Could you give me the titles of two books which particularly interested you?*
    (response not coded)

41. *Do you follow political events in France closely?*

	yes	0	55.2
	no	1	44.8

42. *If you were in Senegal at the time of the last French elections, did you vote (by proxy)?*

	not in Senegal	0	6.8
	yes	1	28.4
	no	2	64.8

43. *What is your political preference in France?*

	Communist	0	1.6
	Federation of the Left (P.R.S.–S.F.I.O.), P.S.U.	1	20.8
	Democratic Centre, National Centre of Peasants and Independents	2	7.2
	Gaullist (U.N.R.)	3	30.8
	Independent Republicans, Republican Alliance	4	6.0
	none	5	26.0
	other (specify)	6	3.6
	no response	9	4.0

44. *What do you think of the French policy of 'co-operation'* (C)

	it is necessary	0	6.0
	generally good, very good (France's responsibility to her former colonies)	1	44.0
	good in principle, but weakness of personnel and structure	2	12.8
	it serves the interests of the French in Senegal: I might be vs. it if in France	3	1.6
	money is wasted: it is not controlled	4	13.2
	problems of money, structure and personnel	5	4.8
	good on the French side, but not the African (weakness of structure and personnel)	6	5.2
	'Cartierism': France needs the money more especially in poorer regions	7	4.0

Questionnaire

		No.	%
	co-operation should be internationalized	8	2·0
	generally it is not effective	x	4·4
	no response	9	2·0

45. *What do you think of the effectiveness of the French technical assistance programme in Senegal?* (C)

	No.	%
it is necessary: they do not yet have sufficient personnel, are not capable of running administration	0	12·8
it is generally effective, good	1	28·4
it is generally not effective	2	6·4
good in education, but not in administration	3	4·0
the problem is the type of technical assistant himself	4	23·6
misuse of funds	5	2·8
efforts are not seconded or appreciated by the Senegalese: lost in the stagnation of Sen. institutions	6	8·4
multiples of problems above; good but could be better	7	3·6
some technical assistants are good, others are not	8	4·0
other	x	4·0
no response	9	2·0

46. *Do you think that it is important to follow political events in Senegal closely?*

	No.	%
yes	0	82·4
no	1	15·2
don't know	2	1·2
no response	9	1·2

47. *If yes, why?* (C)

	No.	%
because we live here, interest in the country	0	31·0
to know about the future, if we must leave	1	22·0
to see that stability is maintained: govts. run by Africans are unstable, must watch that Senghor remains	2	19·0
it is for the boss, not me	3	1·0
the economy depends on it, stability of investments	4	22·0
other	5	2·0
no response	9	3·0

Appendix 3

			No.	%
48.	*If no, why?*	(C)		
	uninterested		0	46·0
	there are no real politics, only personalities; it is not serious		1	30·0
	it is unimportant		3	20·0
	Senegal just follows France		4	2·0
	other		8	2·0
49.	*Do you think that Senegalese economic policy is compatible with private investment?*			
	yes		0	43·2
	no		1	34·4
	don't know		2	18·8
	no response		9	3·6
50.	*Do you think that their co-existence is a fruitful and effective base for economic expansion in Senegal?*			
	yes		0	57·6
	no		1	22·4
	don't know		2	15·2
	no response		9	4·4
51.	*If so, why?*	(C)		
	necessary, there is no other source of capital		0	44·5
	yes, but there is a need for more confidence, less socialism		1	13·9
	socialism à la Senghor is not a serious threat—it is liberal		2	6·1
	improved by lower taxes, control of investment		3	3·5
	Senegal in the franc zone		4	0·7
	successes are apparent		5	11·1
	must work with state capital, all one or other would be difficult		6	5·6
	other		8	12·4
	no response		9	2·2
52.	*If not, why?*	(C)		
	discouragement with government policies: no guarantees for investment; potential instability; high taxes and customs		0	35·1
	discouraged by the O.C.A.		1	3·5
	discouraged by waste and mismanagement		2	14·3
	companies only seek their own benefits, are not controlled (from a minority of Tech. Assts. only)		3	7·2
	no response		9	39·9

Questionnaire

53. *What do you think of the future of French private investment and commerce in Senegal? And why?* (C)

	No.	%
optimistic: (unspecified)	0	9.6
optimistic: they always will need private capital (realized the mistake of the O.C.A.)	1	4.4
pessimistic: general malaise in business, shops closing down	2	21.6
pessimistic: lack of local resources, local buying power; political instability, lack of confidence in the future	3	33.6
pessimistic: lack of local personnel or problems	4	3.2
pessimistic: discouragement of high taxes, customs; need for guarantees for private firms	5	13.6
optimistic and pessimistic: for unspecified reasons	6	1.2
optimistic for industry: pessimistic for commerce	7	3.6
no response	9	8.8

54. *Do you think that the Senegalese leaders have grasped effectively the problems of economic development?*

yes	0	38.0
no	1	48.0
don't know	2	9.2
it depends	3	2.8
no response	9	2.0

55. *If so, or 'it depends', can you give a concrete example?* (C)

yes, but the administration is not competent, only Senghor	0	19.0
they know that they need the technical assistants	1	7.4
trying to rectify mistakes (O.C.A., and planning)	2	7.4
Richard Toll, Fleuve development, co-operative improvement, e.g. diversification	3	30.0
fishing industry (tuna) development	4	2.3
tourism development	5	6.2
moderate path of Senghor, not anti-French	6	3.1
other	8	15.5
no response	9	9.1

56. *If not, why?* (C)

only Senghor and a handful have understood, not the rest	0	10.0

Appendix 3

	No.	%
Senegalese not capable of running an economy, lack of technical education	1	12·5
Senegalese are too lazy to carry through projects, ought to work harder	2	5·0
waste of money, disorganized projects, prestige expenditure	3	22·0
corruption	4	10·8
taxes and customs are too high, discourage investment	5	6·7
planning is too short-term	6	9·2
co-existence of public and private economy doesn't work; (O.C.A. discouraged investment)	7	5·0
other	8	13·3
the palaver of politics	x	3·4
élite profits while poor remain poor	y	1·6
no response	9	0·4

57. *Do you think that the Lebanese in Dakar and in Senegal fulfil a useful economic function?*

yes	0	36·4
no	1	43·2
that depends	2	15·6
don't know	3	3·2
no response	9	0·4

58. *If so, why?* (C)

fulfil a role not provided by French, well adapted to the country	0	82·0
fulfil role not provided by Senegalese, the latter are not *commerçant*	1	3·3
both the above	2	6·6
have a good sense of commerce, provide circulation of money and goods	3	3·3
other	8	4·8

59. *If not, why?* (C)

because of their business practices:* cheating, baksheesh, excess credit rates, they are economically parasitic they repatriate capital to Lebanon	0	71·0
they don't hire Africans	1	2·8

* Six respondents attributed this to Levantine racial characteristics.

Questionnaire

		No.	%
	combination of the above	2	5·6
	there are too many of them (they are redundant)	3	2·8
	Africans could take their places	4	8·4
	no response	9	10·4
60.	*If 'that depends', why?* (C)		
	some are good and upright, others are dishonest	0	6·8
	big interests invest, small do not and are redundant	1	34·0
	they bring in capital, but expatriate it again	2	6·8
	they fill a need in the economy, but don't abide by the regulations	3	37·0
	they provide a commercial circuit, but Sens. could take over their jobs	4	6·8
	other	8	8·6
61.	*How do you view Franco-Senegalese relations on a long-term basis?* (C)		
	optimistic—they will stay about the same	0	16·0
	French and Senegalese get on well together: personal affinity; have known each other for a long time; never great shocks between us; we are one 'French family'	1	20·4
	cultural and linguistic ties	2	14·0
	economic links: all investment is directed to France	3	4·8
	they depend on us, need us	4	10·0
	pessimistic—things were better before independence, young Senegalese don't like us, one day we must leave	5	6·0
	unsure after Senghor and de Gaulle	6	12·4
	need for internationalization of aid	7	3·2
	general political chaos in Africa	8	1·2
	gradually they will no longer need us	x	1·2
	no response	9	10·8

THE FOLLOWING QUESTIONS ARE ONLY FOR MEMBERS OF THE PRIVATE SECTOR AND PROFESSIONS (175 RESPONDENTS)

62. *Do you think that there is frequent personal contact between technical assistants and members of the private sector?*

	yes	0	35·7
	no	1	57·7

Appendix 3

	No.	%
don't know	2	4·6
no response	9	2·3

63. *If not, why?* (C)

Lack of work contact means lack of social contact; work together, but leisure time activities are different, different life styles	0	22·0
Tech. Asst. live by themselves, don't buy, save money, live with one foot in France, privileged caste	1	78·0
no response	9	

64. *In your opinion is the output of a Senegalese worker or office employee comparable to that of his French counterpart?*

yes	0	5·1
no	1	88·6
it depends	2	5·1
no response	9	1·2

65. *If not, or 'it depends' how do you explain this?* (C)

it depends on the demands of work	0	2·3
Afs. cannot rise above a certain level of work (e.g. can't organize work as is needed for management)	1	2·9
lack of professional conscientiousness	2	14·3
Afs. are lazy and indolent (owing partly to nutrition and climate)	3	32·0
Afs. don't have ambition, aspirations (*Je m'en foutisme* prevails)	4	11·4
lack of training	5	5·1
Afs. are like big children, need direction	6	4·6
Af. religion inhibits work: Islam is fatalistic; there is a lack of socialization to work in Af. upbringing	7	12·6
Afs. do not have same level of intellect, civilization as Europeans (either biologically inferior, or centuries behind)	8	6·3
multiples of negative responses	x	1·7
no response	9	6·3

Questionnaire

66. *Do you think that accelerated Africanization is advisable in your type of work?*

	No.	%
yes	0	50·3
no	1	45·7
don't know	2	1·7
no response	9	2·3

67. *If you do, will you explain why* (C)

clear yes—this is Senegal after all; it is in the interests of country to Africanize	0	46·8
saves money for co. but poses problems	1	6·8
it is to be hoped for, but not now possible	2	9·2
restricted to jobs of their capacity and ability	3	11·4
for a few only	4	8·0
so long as directed by Europeans	5	3·4
no response	9	14·4

68. *If you do not, will you explain why*

Africans must be surveyed, controlled	0	24·0
not capable of doing the work I do (e.g. commerce)	1	23·0
not trained, not enough cadres or secretaries	2	18·0
not trustworthy to handle money	3	13·0
company has reached a maximum Africanization (imposed on it); now we must wait years—they are not ready	4	17·0
no response	9	5·0

69. *During working hours, do you have more contact with Senegalese or European employees?*

Senegalese	0	37·1
Europeans	1	33·7
about the same	2	25·1
no response	9	4·0

70. *Who defends the interests of the Europeans in the private sector in Senegal?* (C)

No one	0	29·1
Chamber of Commerce	1	6·3
French Embassy	2	10·9
Expatriate Trade Union	3	5·1
Employers' Associations	4	12·0
French Mutual Aid Society	5	4·0
Multiples of the above	6	10·9

Appendix 3

		No.	%
	others	8	1·7
	no response	9	20·0
71.	*Do you think that this person, group or organization has an effective influence on Senegalese economic policy?*		
	yes	0	26·3
	no	1	24·6
	don't know	2	17·1
	no response	9	32·0
72.	*If so, why?* (C)		
	yes, but only a small restricted role (e.g. advice-giving of Chamber of Commerce)	0	20·0
	directors have good relations with the government	1	6·5
	there is a dialogue between the private sector and government	2	17·0
	other	3	2·2
	no response	9	54·3
73.	*If not, why?*		
	mixing in politics is not the role of the French	0	6·8
	no relations with the government	1	6·8
	others (inc. 'they are not listened to')	8	2·8
	no response	9	83·6
74.	*Do you return on regular leave to France?*		
	yes	0	82·3
	no	1	16·0
	no response	9	1·7
75.	*Do you own property (or a flat) in France, or in Senegal?*		
	in France	0	48·6
	in Senegal	1	4·0
	in both countries	2	8·6
	not property owner	3	38·3
	no response	9	0·6
76.	*Do you think that you will remain in Senegal for the longest time possible?*		
	yes	0	59·4
	no	1	33·7
	don't know	2	5·1
	no response	9	1·7

Questionnaire

77. *Do you encourage your children to remain and seek a career in Senegal or elsewhere in Africa?*
    Or, if you had children of working age now, would you encourage them to remain and seek such a career?

	No.	%
yes	0	28·6
no	1	60·8
don't know	2	6·3
no response	9	4·6

78. *If so, why?* (C)

good start, big salaries, responsibility, agreeable life, interesting	0	60·0
my children are here, I prefer that they remain with me	1	18·6
only in specialized work	2	11·2
other	8	10·2

79. *If not, why?* (C)

no future for Europeans in Africa; economic and political chaos	0	36·6
no future—posts must be Africanized	1	21·0
nothing to be learned for young Europeans in Africa	2	5·0
better training in France, better to start off in France	3	13·0
difficulty of being reintegrated into France (professionally), loss of contact with technical aspects of work	5	8·4
other	8	13·0
no response	9	3·0

THE FOLLOWING QUESTIONS ARE ONLY FOR TECHNICAL ASSISTANTS (60 respondents)

62. *Do you think that there is frequent personal contact between technical assistants and members of the private sector?*

yes	0	31·7
no	1	63·3
don't know	2	5·0
no response	9	

Appendix 3

		No.	%
63.	*If so, why?* (C)		
	lack of work contact means lack of social contact; work together, but leisure activities are different, different life styles	0	61·0
	we (Tech. Assts.) are scorned by those in private sector	1	27·0
	mentalities are different	2	2·7
	no response	9	9·3
64.	*Is your work in Senegal different from that which you did before arriving here?*		
	yes	0	26·7
	no	1	48·3
	no response	9	25·0
65.	*If yes, how does it differ?* (responses not coded)		
66.	*During working hours, do you have more contact with the Senegalese in your Ministry (or Department), or with the other technical assistants?*		
	Senegalese	0	26·7
	technical assistants	1	35·0
	about the same	2	36·7
	no response	9	1·6
67.	*What do you think of the efficiency of the Senegalese public service in general?* (C)		
	weak, limited, ineffective	0	26·7
	poor organization, too heavy for efficiency	1	5·0
	it functions at an African rhythm; Af. way of life; parasitic and anti-modern; administrative behaviour is poor—tendency to let things pass	2	26·7
	poor personnel, too many civil servants	3	26·7
	moderately effective, effective in some sectors	4	6·7
	no response	9	8·2
68.	*What do you think is the principal purpose of the French technical assistance programme in Senegal?*		
	to train homologous Senegalese civil servants	0	50·0
	to guide the Senegalese administration	1	6·7
	both	2	23·3
	to supplement the lack of Senegalese cadres	3	8·3
	others (specify)	4	10·0
	no response	9	1·7

Questionnaire

69. *As a technical assistant, what do you think is your role vis-à-vis the Senegalese in your Ministry or Service?* (C)

	No.	%
to direct them	0	8.3
to form homologues, set an example for them	1	36.7
as co-operator, counsellor	2	25.0
to complete their work	3	1.7
I have no relations with Senegalese	4	5.0
other: mainly teachers with no role of formation	8	15.0
no response	9	8.3

70. *Do you think that accelerated Africanization in your type of work is advisable?*

yes	0	26.7
no	1	68.3
don't know	2	3.3
no response	9	1.7

71. *If you do, please explain why*
(responses not coded)

72. *If you do not, please explain why* (C)

lack of cadres, need for further technical training	0	50.2
Afs. work poorly, lack of enterprise, no sense of responsibility	1	13.0
the administration or level of education will suffer	2	23.6
no response	9	13.2

73. *Do you intend to renew your contract or to leave Senegal at the end of your contract? (it being understood, if the government of Senegal requests your service)*

renew	0	63.3
leave	1	23.3
don't know	2	10.0
no response	9	3.4

74. *Why would you like to renew your contract?* (C)

I like it here, work to be done	0	45.5
prefer to live in Africa, rather than France	1	13.5
work, professional conditions more interesting, satisfying	2	21.9
there is no African to take my job	3	5.4
to make more money	4	8.2
no response	9	5.5

Appendix 3

75.	Why would you like to terminate your contract? (C)	No.	%
	children's studies	1	5.0
	career reasons	2	43.0
	discouragement with the milieu	3	21.5
	been here too long	5	21.5
	work is more interesting in France	6	5.0
	no response	9	4.0

Bibliography

ARCHIVES

Archives de la République du Sénégal, Dakar (selected documents).

OFFICIAL SOURCES

Afrique Occidentale Française, Haut-Commissariat de la République, Direction Générale des Services Economiques et du Plan, *A.O.F. 1957, Tableaux Economiques.*

Afrique Occidentale Française, Haut-Commissariat de la République, Direction des Services de la Statistique Générale et de la Mécanographie, *Annuaire Statistique de l'A.O.F. Années 1950–1954*, Vol. V, Tome 1, Paris: Imprimerie Servant Crouzet, 1956.

Afrique Occidentale Française, Haut-Commissariat de la République, *Annuaire Statistique de l'A.O.F., Edition 1949*, Tome 1, Paris: Imprimerie Nationale, 1950.

Afrique Occidentale Française, Gouvernement Général, *Résultats du Recensement des Français d'Origine Métropolitaine et des Etrangers*, Dakar, April 27th, 1946.

Afrique Occidentale Française, Haut Commissariat de la République, Service de la Statistique Générale, *Recensement de la Population non-Autochtone de l'Afrique Occidentale Française en Juin 1951*, Dakar, 1951.

Afrique Occidentale Française, Haut Commissariat de la République, Service d'Etudes et Coordination Statistique et Mécanographique, *Premiers Résultats du Recensement Général de la Population Non-Originaire de l'A.O.F. du 12 Décembre 1956*, Dakar, March 1959.

Afrique Occidentale Française, Haut Commissariat de la République, Service d'Etudes et Coordination Statistique et Mécanographique, *Recensement Démographique de Dakar (1955). Résultats définitifs*, 1er. fascicule, Paris, July 1956.

Dakar, Université de, Bureau Universitaire de Statistique et de Documentation, *Statistiques des Etudiants Inscrits à l'Université de Dakar, Années Universitaires 1961–1966*.

Bibliography

Dakar, Université de, *Organisation et Corps Enseignant*, 10 January 1970.

France (République Française), *Journal Officiel*, on selected topics.

France, Exposition Universelle de 1900, Les Colonies Françaises, Service Locale de la Colonie, *Le Sénégal, Organisation Politique, Administration, Finances, Travaux Publics*, Paris; Augustin Challamel, 1900.

France, Ministère des Colonies, *Le Sénégal et Dépendances: Notice à l'Usage des Emigrants*. Paris: Imprimerie Administrative de Melun, 1900.

France, Ministère de la Coopération, *Cinq Ans de Fonds d'Aide et de Coopération (1959–1964), Rapport présenté par M. R. Triboulet, Ministre délégué, chargé de la Coopération*, April 9 1964.

France, Ministère d'Etat Chargé de la Réforme Administrative, *La Politique de Coopération Avec les Pays en voie de Développement, Rapport de la Commission d'Etude institué par le décret du 12 mars 1963 remis au gouvernement le 18 juillet 1963*. (Jeanneney Report).

Sénégal, République du, Conseil Economique et Social. Letter of P. Bonifay, on behalf of *Comité de Liaison* of the *Conseil Economique et Social du Sénégal* to M. le President de SCIMPEX, February 1 1965.

Sénégal, République du, Conseil Economique et Social, *Note sur la Situation Agricole du Sénégal*, Dakar, 1966.

Sénégal, République du, Conseil, Economique et Social, *Etude sur les Circuits Commerciaux dans l'Intérieur du Sénégal*, Dakar, 1965.

Sénégal, République du, *Journal Officiel*, (on selected topics).

Sénégal, République du, Ministère de l'Enseignement Technique et de la Formation des Cadres, Centre National de Formation et d'Action, *Session d'Information du Personnel de l'Assistance Technique*, Dakar, November 23/24 1963.

Sénégal, République du, Ministère de l'Enseignement Technique et de la Formation des Cadres, Centre National de Formation et d'Action, *Session d'Information du Personnel de l'Assistance Technique*, Dakar, January 16/17 1965.

Sénégal, République du, Ministère de l'Enseignement Technique et de la Formation des Cadres, Centre National de Formation et d'Action, *Session d'Information du Personnel de l'Assistance Technique*, Dakar, February 19/20 1966.

Sénégal, République du, Ministère de l'Enseignement Technique et de la Formation des Cadres, Centre National de Formation et d'Action, *Session d'Information et de Réflexion sur la Coopération Technique au Sénégal*, Dakar, February 4/5 1967.

Bibliography

Sénégal, République du, Ministère du Plan et du Développement, Documents of the thirteen commissions responsible for preparation of the Second Plan, June 1964—April 1965.

Sénégal, République du, Ministère du Plan, du Développement et de la Coopération Technique, Service de la Statistique et de la Mécanographie, *Recensement Démographique de Dakar, 1955, Résultats Définitifs:* 2ème fascicule, Paris, March 1962.

PUBLISHED (BOOKS AND ARTICLES)

Allport, G. W., *The Nature of Prejudice*, New York: Doubleday, 1958.

Amin, Samir, *Le Monde des Affaires Sénégalais*, Paris: Eds. de Minuit, 1969.

Annet, A., *Aux Heures Troublées de l'Afrique Française, 1939–1943*, Paris: Eds. du Conquistador, 1952.

Banton, M., *Race Relations*, London: Tavistock, 1967.

Barot, Dr., *Guide Pratique de l'Européen dans l'Afrique Occidentale*, Paris: Flammarion, 1902.

Bettelheim, B., and Janowitz, M., *Dynamics of Prejudice*, New York: Harper, 1950.

Betts, R., *Assimilation and Association in French Colonial Theory, 1890–1914*, New York: Columbia University Press, 1961.

Boulègue, M., 'La Presse au Sénégal avant 1939: Bibliographie', in *Bulletin de l'Institut Fondamental de l'Afrique Noire* [I.F.A.N.], Vol. XXVII, Nos. 3-4, 1965.

Buell, R. L., *The Native Problem in Africa*, New York: Macmillan, 1928 (2 vols.).

Burns, A., *Colour Prejudice*, London: Allen and Unwin, 1948.

Cartier, R., 'En France Noire', in *Paris-Match*, March 1964, August 11, 18, 1956.

Centers, R., *The Psychology of Social Classes*, Princeton: Princeton University Press, 1949.

Charpy, J., *La Fondation de Dakar*, Paris: Larose, 1958.

Chevallier, J., *Nous, Algériens...*, Paris: Calmann-Lévy, 1958.

Chevas-Baron, C., *La Femme Française aux Colonies*, Paris: Larose, 1929.

Conchon, G., *L'Etat Sauvage*, Paris: Albin Michel, 1964.

Coursin, L., 'Dakar, Port Atlantique', in *Cahiers d'Outre-Mer*, No. 3, Oct.-Dec. 1948.

Cowan, L. G., *Local Government in West Africa*, New York: Columbia, University Press, 1958.

Bibliography

Cros, L., *L'Afrique Française Pour Tous*, Paris: A. Michel, 1928.
Crouzat, H., *Azizah de Niamkoko*, Paris: Presses de la Cité, 1959.
Crowder, M., *Senegal: A Study of French Assimilation Policy*, London: Methuen, 1967 (revised edition).
Curtin, P., *The Images of Africa*, Madison: University of Wisconsin Press, 1964.
Curtin, P., *Two Jamaicas*, Cambridge, Mass.: Harvard University Press, 1955.
Debief, *La Vice en Algérie*, Paris, 1899.
Delavignette, R., *Service Africain*, Paris: Gallimard, 1946.
Delcourt, A., 'La Chambre de Commerce de Bordeaux et la Traite Africaine dans les Dernières Années de l'Ancien Régime (1783–1791)', in Commission de Recherche et de Publication des Documents Rélatifs à la Vie Economique de la Révolution, *Assemblée Générale*, Tome II, Paris: Tepac, 1939.
Delcourt, A., *La France et les Etablissements Français au Sénégal (1713–1764)*, Dakar: I.F.A.N., 1952.
Delmas-Guichenne, R., *Notes et Documents Recueillis pour Servir à l'Histoire du Sénégal jusqu'à l'Indépendance*, Dakar: Private Printing, 1964 (2 vols.).
Deroure, F., 'La Vie Quotidienne à St. Louis par ses Archives (1779–1809)', in *Bulletin de l'I.F.A.N.*, Vol. XXVI, Ser.B., Nos. 3–4, 1964.
Desbordes, J. G., *L'Immigration Libano-Syrienne en A.O.F.*, Poitiers: Imprimerie Moderne, 1938.
Deschamps, H., *Le Sénégal et la Gambie*, Paris: Presses Universitaires de France, 1964.
Didier, H., 'L'Immigration Européenne en Afrique', in *Nouvelle Revue Française d'Outre-Mer*, No. 6, 1953.
Dresch, Jean, 'Villes d'AOF', *Les Cahiers d'Outre-Mer*, Vol. 3, No. 11.
Duchemin, C., 'Les Français à Dakar', in *Europe-France Outremer*, No. 376, 1961.
Dumont, R., *L'Afrique Noire est Mal Partie*, Paris: Eds. du Seuil, 1962.
Exposition Universelle de 1900, *Le Sénégal, Organisation Politique, Administration, Finance, Travaux Publics*, Paris, 1900.
Faidherbe, L., *Le Sénégal*, Paris: Hachette, 1889.
Faucheux, R., 'Premier Voyage à Dakar', in *Lyon Colonial*, No. 80, Nov.-Dec., 1930.
Faure, C., *Histoire de la Presqu'île du Cap Vert et des Origines de Dakar*, Paris: Larose, 1914.

Bibliography

Faure, J.-L., *La Vie aux Colonies: Preparation de la Femme à la Vie Coloniale*, Paris: Larose, 1938.

Flis-Zonabend, F., *Lycéens de Dakar*, Paris: Maspéro, 1968.

Foltz, W. J., *From French West Africa to the Mali Federation*, New Haven, Conn.: Yale University Press, 1965.

Foltz, W. J., 'Senegal', in J. Coleman and C. Rosberg eds. *Political Parties and National Integration in Tropical Africa*, Berkeley: University of California Press, 1964.

Fougeyrollas, P., *Modernisation des Hommes: l'Exemple du Sénégal*, Paris: Flammarion, 1967.

Fougeyrollas, P., 'Phénomèmes d'Acculturation chez les Etudiants de la Cité Universitaire de Dakar', in *Revue Française de Sociologie*, Vol. IV, Oct.-Dec., 1963.

Gorer, G., *Africa Dances*, London: Faber and Faber, 1935.

Gozzini, M., 'Gli Italiani in A.O.F. Ante 1940', in *Affrica*, Vol. VII, Nos. 7–8, 1953.

Greenbaum, J. and Pearlin, L., 'Vertical Mobility and Prejudice', in S. M. Lipset (Ed.), *Class, Status and Power*, Glencoe, Ill.: The Free Press, 1961.

Guillemin, P., 'La Structure des Premiers Gouvernements Locaux en Afrique Noire', *Revue Française de Science Politique*, Vol. IX, No. 3, September 1959.

Hardy, G., *Histoire de la Colonisation Française*, Paris: Larose, 1931.

Hardy, G., *Mise en Valeur du Sénégal*, Paris: Larose, 1921.

Hargreaves, J. D., *Prelude to the Partition of West Africa*, London: Macmillan, 1963.

Hargreaves, J. D., 'Assimilation in Eighteenth Century Senegal', *Journal of African History*, Vol. VI, No. 2, 1965.

Hauser, A., 'L'Emergence de Cadres de Base Africains dans l'Industrie', in P. Lloyd (Ed.), *The New Elites of Tropical Africa*, London: Oxford University Press for International African Institute, 1966.

Hauser, A., *Facteurs Humains Affectant la Productivité des Travailleurs Industriels du Cap Vert*, Dakar: Institut de Science Economique Appliquée, 1963.

Hauser, A., *Les Ouvriers de Dakar: Etude Psychosociologique*, Paris: Office de la Recherche Scientifique et Technique Outre-Mer, 1968.

Hauser, A., 'Quelques Relations des Travailleurs de l'Industrie à leur Travail en A.O.F.', in *Bulletin de l'I.F.A.N.*, Vol. XVII, Series B, 1955.

Bibliography

Hauser, A., Massé, L. and Mercier, P., *L'Agglomération Dakaroise*, St. Louis, Senegal: I.F.A.N., 1954.

Hayter, T., *French Aid*, London: Overseas Development Institute, 1966.

Humbolt, Paul, 'L'Immigration Européenne en Afrique Tropicale', *L'Afrique Française*, April 1952.

Institut de Science Economique Appliquée (I.S.E.A.), *Les Industries du Cap Vert*, Dakar, 1964.

Jacobus, le Dr., *L'Amour aux Colonies Observé Durant Trente Années*, Paris, 1893.

Jahoda, G., *White Man*, London: Oxford University Press, 1961.

Johnson, G. W., 'The Ascendancy of Blaise Diagne and the Beginning of African Politics in Senegal', *Africa*, Vol. XXXVI, No. 3, July 1966.

Jore, L., 'Les Etablissements Français sur la Côte Occidentale d'Afrique de 1758 à 1809', in *Revue Française d'Histoire d'Outre-Mer*, Vol. LI, 1964.

Lannes, X., 'Les Problèmes de Main-d'Oeuvre dans l'Eurafrique', in *Nouvelle Revue Française d'Outre-Mer*, No. 6, 1953.

La Palombara, J. (Ed.), *Bureaucracy and Political Development*, Princeton: Princeton University Press, 1963.

La Salle, A. de, *Notre Vieux Sénégal*, Paris: Challamel, 1909.

Lasswell, H., *Politics: Who Gets What, When, How?* New York: Meridian, 1966 (first published 1936).

Lentin, A.-P., 'La Situation de la Minorité Européenne en Algérie', in *Le Mois en Afrique*, No. 12, 1966.

Loti, P., *Le Roman d'un Spahi*, Paris: Calmann-Lévy, 1935 (first published 1881).

Maddison, A., *Foreign Skills and Technical Assistance in Economic Development*, Paris: Organization for Economic Co-operation and Development, 1965.

Mannoni, O., *Prospero and Caliban: the Psychology of Colonization*, London: Methuen, 1956.

Maunier, R., *The Sociology of Colonies* (Lorimer trans.), London: Routledge and Kegan Paul, 1949 (2 vols.).

Mauny, R., *Glossaire des Termes et Expressions Locaux Employés dans l'Ouest Africain*, Dakar: I.F.A.N., 1952.

Mbaye, K., 'L'Attribution de la Nationalité "Jure Soli" et l'Option de Nationalité dans la Loi Sénégalaise du 7 Mars 1961', in *Penant*, No. 71 (687), 1961.

Mercier, P., 'Le Groupement Européen de Dakar', *Cahiers Internationaux de Sociologie*, Vol. 19, 1955.

Bibliography

Merton, R. K., *Social Theory and Social Structure*, Glencoe: Free Press, 1949.

Mille, P., 'The Black Vote in Senegal', *Journal of the Africa Society*, Vol. I, 1901.

Morgenthau, R. S., *Political Parties in French-Speaking West Africa*, Oxford: Clarendon Press, 1964.

Newbury, C., 'The Formation of the Government General of French West Africa', *Journal of African History*, Vol. I, No. 1, 1960.

Nora, P., *Les Français d'Algérie*, Paris: Julliard, 1961.

NORIA, *Sociétés et Fournisseurs d'Afrique Noire et de Madagascar*, Paris: La Documentation Africaine, 1966 (16th Ed.).

OPTORG, Compagnie de, 'La Compagnie Optorg, un Moteur des Echanges Internationaux', in *Entreprise*, (Company publication), March 1964.

Paillard, J., *La Fin des Français en Afrique Noire*, Paris: Les Oeuvres Français, 1935.

Paillard, J., *Périple Noir*, Paris: Les Oeuvres Françaises, 1935.

Park, R. E., *Race and Culture*, Glencoe, Ill.: The Free Press, 1950.

Pasquier, R., 'Les Débuts de la Presse au Sénégal', *Cahiers d'Etudes Africaines*, No. 7, 1962.

Pasquier, R., 'Villes du Sénégal au XIXe Siècle', *Revue Française de l'Histoire d'Outre-Mer*, Vol. XLVII, 1960.

Patterson, O., *The Sociology of Slavery*, London: McGibbon and Kee, 1967.

Peterson, John, 'The Sierra Leone Creole: A Reappraisal', in C. Fyfe and E. Jones, eds. *Freetown: A Symposium*, Freetown: Sierra Leone University Press, 1968.

Pfeffermann, G., *Industrial Labour in the Republic of Senegal*, New York: Praeger, 1968.

Post, K. W. J., *The New States of West Africa*, London: Penguin Books, 1964.

Powdermaker, H., *Copper Town: Changing Africa*, New York: Harper and Row, 1962.

Prothro, E. T. and Milikian, L. H., 'Studies in Stereotype: Familiarity and the Kernel of Truth', *The Journal of Social Psychology*, Vol. 41, 1955.

Raffenel, A., 'De la Colonie du Sénégal', *Revue Coloniale*, June, 1850.

Ribot, G. and Lafon, R., *Dakar, Ses Origines, Son Avenir*, Bordeaux: G. Delmas, 1908.

Robinson, K. E., 'Senegal: the Elections to the Territorial

Assembly, March 1957', in W. J. M. Mackenzie and K. E. Robinson (Eds.), *Five Elections in Africa*, Oxford: Clarendon, 1960.

Robinson, K. E., 'The *Sociétés de Prévoyance* in French West Africa', *Journal of African Administration*, Vol. II, 1950.

Saint-Lô, Alexis de, *Relation du Voyage du Cap Vert*, Rouen, 1637.

Seck, A., *Dakar*, Université de Dakar, Travaux du Départment de Géographie (Pamphlet) No. 9, 1963.

Seck, A., 'Face Aux Problèmes Sociaux de l'A.O.F.', *Réalités Africaines*, No. 18, 17 August 1956.

Seck, A., 'La Formation d'Une Classe Moyenne en Afrique Occidentale Française', in Institut International des Civilizations Differentes, *Compte Rendu de la XXIX Session*, Brussels 1956.

Senghor, L. S., *Nation et Voie Africaine du Socialisme*, Paris: Présence Africaine, 1961.

Silberstein, F. and Seeman, M., 'Social Mobility and Prejudice', *American Journal of Sociology*, Vol. 65, No. 3, 1959.

Siriex, P. H., *Une Nouvelle Afrique*, Paris: Plon, 1957.

Suret-Canale, J., 'L'Industrie des Oléagineux en AOF', *Cahiers d'Outre-Mer*, No. 11, 1950.

Thibaud, P., 'Dia, Senghor et le Socialisme Africain', *Esprit*, No. 9, 1963.

Thompson, V. and Adloff, R., *French West Africa*, Stanford, Calif.: Stanford University Press, 1958.

Vanlande, R., *Dakar*, Paris: Peyronnet, 1945.

Viard, R., *La Fin de l'Empire Colonial Français*, Paris: Maisonneuve et Larose, 1963.

Villard, A., *Histoire du Sénégal*, Dakar: Imp. Viale, 1943.

Weber, M., *From Max Weber* (trans. and ed. H. Gerth and C. Wright Mills), New York: Oxford University Press, 1958.

Weuleresse, J., *Noirs et Blancs*, Paris, 1931.

Whittlesey, D., 'Dakar and Other Cap Vert Settlements', *Geographical Review*, 1941.

Whittlesey, D., 'Dakar Revisited', *Geographical Review*, 1948.

Winder, R. B., 'The Lebanese in West Africa', *Comparative Studies in Society and History*, Vol. IV, No. 3, April 1962.

NEWSPAPERS AND PERIODICALS CONSULTED

L'Afrique Française (Paris, monthly, published by Comité de l'Afrique Française, 1891–).

Bibliography

L'Afrique Française: Renseignements Coloniaux (documentary appendices).
Afrique Nouvelle (liberal Catholic weekly, Dakar, 1955–).
L'AOF (Dakar, Socialist, Lamine Guèye 1925–60, irregular, 1907–60).
L'AOF Républicaine (Paris, Dioufist, 1932–34).
La Bataille (Dakar, Diagnist, 1932).
Bulletin Mensuel du Chambre de Commerce de Dakar (Dakar, 1910–).
Clarté (Dakar, Ed. Charles Graziani, 1934–35, 1944–47).
Dakar Matin (formerly *Paris-Dakar*, daily 1937–).
La Dépêche de Dakar (Lebanese journal, 1953–55).
L'Echo de Dakar (Independent bimonthly, 1932–33).
Les Echos Africains (Dakar, M. Voisin Ed., 1947–50).
Les Echos d'Afrique Noire (Dakar, Mme. Voisin Ed., 1950–57).
Echos d'Afrique Noire (Dakar, Mme. Voisin Ed., 1957–61).
Echos de France (Dakar, monthly bulletin of Association d'Entr'aide des Français du Sénégal, 1963–).
France-Afrique Noire (Dakar, J. Paillard ed., monthly 1935–37).
La France Coloniale (Dakar weekly, Diagnist, 1927–34).
L'Indépendant (Dakar, European, 1953–58).
L'Indépendant Colonial (Abidjan, European, 1932).
Le Journal de Dakar (Dakar, European weekly, 1930–31).
La Lutte (Dakar, newspaper of the P.A.I., 1957–60).
Marchés Tropicaux et Mediterranéens (Paris, Commercial Weekly, 1945–).
Le Monde (Paris, selected issues).
Le Mois en Afrique (Paris, P. Biairnes Ed., monthly, selected issues).
Le Moniteur Africain du Commerce et de l'Industrie (Dakar, P. Biairnes Ed., weekly 1961–).
L'Ouest Africain Français (Dakar weekly, d'Oxoby Ed., 1919–30).
Le Périscope Africain (Dakar, became *La Rumeur Africaine* 1931–1933, anti-Diagne 1929–31, 1933–36).
Le Réveil (Dakar, G. Etcheverry Ed., 1944–50).
Sénégal Aujourd'hui (Dakar, official monthly, selected issues).
Le Sénégal (Dakar, Ed. A. Goux, 1934–40).
La Voce Italiana di Dakar (Dakar Italian paper, 1932–36).
La Voix de France (monthly, 1966–).
West Africa (London, weekly, 1945–).

UNPUBLISHED SOURCES

Baillet, E., 'Les Etablissements Maurel et Prom', dated 30

Bibliography

September, 1923. Typewritten report obtained from the company archives recounting the foundation and history of its trading activities in Senegal, Communicated Nov. 1966 by the Director-General.

Chambre de Commerce d'Agriculture et d'Industrie de Dakar, 'L'Economie du Sénégal', Dakar (roneo), April 1961.

Chambre de Commerce, Dakar, Importante Réunion à Dakar des Commerçants, Traitants, Cultivateurs Indigènes et Industriels du Sénégal', Dakar (roneo), 29 March 1933.

Collomb, H., Zwingelstein, J. and Picca, M., 'Les Conditions Suicidaires à Dakar en Milieu Non-Africain', Dakar, Centre Hospitalier de Fann, n.d.

Hanna, M. I., 'Lebanese Emigrants in West Africa: Their Effect on Lebanon and West Africa', Oxford University, D.Phil. Thesis, 1959.

Hauser, A., 'Les Problèmes du Travail', Dakar (roneo), 1966.

Hiernaux, G., 'Le Rôle du Grand Commerce Dakarois', Université de Dakar, Faculté des Lettres, Diplôme d'Etudes Supérieures de Géographie, June 1961.

Section Française de l'Internationale Ouvrière, 'Bulletin Intérieur du Parti Socialiste', Paris, June 1955.

Syndicat des Commerçants Importateurs et Exportateurs de la République du Sénégal, (SCIMPEX), 'Compte Rendu des Réunions du Bureau du SCIMPEX du 9 Février 1965 et du 22 Février 1965', Dakar.

SCIMPEX, 'Procès-Verbal de l'Assemblée Générale du 14 Mars 1967', Dakar (roneo).

SCIMPEX, 'Régime des Importations dans la République du Sénégal', Dakar (roneo), 1964.

SCIMPEX, 'Esquisse d'Un Système de Distribution au Sénégal', study by P. Guieysse, Dakar (roneo), April 1965.

Thomas, L.-V., 'Les Fonctions Culturelles de Dakar', Dakar (roneo), 1966.

Union Intersyndicale d'Entreprises et d'Industries de l'Ouest Africain (UNISYNDI), 'A M. le Président du Comité de Liaison du Conseil Economique et Social', Dakar (roneo), February 1965.

Verrière, L., 'La Population du Sénégal', Université de Dakar, Thèse pour le Doctorat des Sciences Economiques, July 1965.

Index

Abidjan (Ivory Coast), 81, 111
L'Abreuvoir (social club for businessmen), 196
Actualités Sénégalaises (cinema newsreel), 15
Aero-Club (Ziguinchor), 235
Africanization, 25, 108, 114, 147–56, 228, in civil service 81, in private sector, 85–7, 147–56, 198, 209, national policy on, 111, French attitudes toward, 148–9, 162 (table), 226, of Chamber of Commerce, 204, at University of Dakar, 254
Afrique Nouvelle, 236
Aid, French, 15, 16, 26, 27, 199, criticism of, 179 (*see also* Technical assistance)
Air-France, 200
Alcoholism in colonies, 89
Algeria, 35, Algerians, 17, white settlers *(pieds noirs)*, 105, 183, 214, 224, war, 104, 105, 231, repatriation of Frenchmen, 112
Amicales (friendly societies), Basque, Breton, Corsican, 232
Angers (France), 89
Arab League, 101
Arabs, 259
Ariège, 56–7, 225, Ariègeois, 226
Armenians, 29
Army, French, 15, 16, 211, recruitment of troops for, 61, ex-servicemen in colonies, 67, cutback (1965), 111, 124, retired officers in Dakar, 224
Assimilation (French policy of), 18, 32, 45–7, 93, 108, and association, 45–7, during wartime, 64–5
Association d'Entraide des Français du Sénégal (Mutual Aid Society), 197, 231, 268
Aude (France), 225
Authority of Senegalese, challenge to, 257–8, 263–4
Aziza de Niamkoko (novel), 237

Bank of West Africa, 200
Banque Centrale (French) in Senegal, 129, 200

Bloc Démocratique Sénégalais (see *Union Progressiste Sénégalaise*), French participation in, 103, 190
Bonifay, Paul, 62, 103, 109, 196, 208, 240
Bordeaux, 17, 30, 55, 89, 215, 225, Chamber of Commerce, 34, 48, trading companies of, 36, 39, 48, families in Senegal, 63
Brazzaville Conference, 67
Buell, R. L. (cited), 51n, 59, 63
Business situation, French attitudes toward, 124, 128, Senegalese attitudes toward, 136

Calvinists, 29
Canard Enchaîné (newspaper), 74
Canary Islands, 111
Cape Verde Islands, migrants from, 240, 265
Cape Verde peninsula (Dakar), 29, 35, 225
Capuchins, 29
Casamance, 145, 224, 235
Catholicism, 29, as factor in race relations, 265
Centre de la Formation Fonctionnelle et Professionnelle (Vocational Training Centre), 154n, 156n
Chamber of Commerce, Senegal, foundational of, 40, protection of French interests, 51, 200, 201, anti-Lebanese campaign, 52–3, 76, 203, Secretary-General, 74, 252, interviews in, 105, and independence, 106, and African socialism, 111, and nationalization, 129, activities and structure, 202–4, ineffectiveness of, 203–4, Africanization of, 204
Chauvenel (company), 116
Chinese, 259, at work, 145
Cinema Club (Dakar), 234
CITEC (company), 122, Bourbel, director of, 199
Civil Service, Senegalese, French attitudes towards, 126–7, 180, persistence of colonial structures and models in, 165, 167, 180, annual running costs, 165, weakness and

314

Index

Civil Service—*cont.*
  inefficiency of, 184, 187, corruption in 187
Class structure among Frenchmen, 72–73, 74, 219–23, 251, as a determinant of racial attitudes, 59, 95, 96, social élite, 66, 72, 220, compared with France, 220
Clubs, European, 232–3, 235
Colin, Jean, 195
Collomb, Dr. Henri, 228
Colonial Service, personnel of, 43, recruitment, 55, of technical assistants, 173, 174n
Colonies, French Ministry of, establishment of, 43
commandant de cercle (district officer), 43
Commerce (*see* Trading companies), difficulties of, 124, employment of Frenchmen in, 133, political influence of, 197–8, circuits in the interior, 208, consumer co-operatives, debate on, 209
Commerce and Industry, Senegalese Ministry of, 168
Common Market (European Economic Community), 110, 121, 179, associate membership for Senegal, 129–130, European Development Fund, 130, 179, internationalization of aid, possibility of, 130
Communes in Senegal, 19, 46, *communes de plein exercice*, 40, 60, non-racial policy of, 59, legal status of, 63, during Vichy, 64–5
Communist Party (French) (see also *Confédération Générale des Travailleurs*), 102
Community, French, 15, 105
Compagnie du Sénégal, 30
Compagnie Française de l'Afrique Occidentale (C.F.A.O.), 49, 78n, 79
Companies, chartered trading, 29–31, British and Dutch, 31
Conchon, Georges, 237
Confédération Générale des Travailleurs (Parti Communiste), 82
Contival, Louis, letter from 88–9
Contracts, expatriate work, in private sector, 140, 147, in technical assistance, 175, local, insecurity of, 230
Coopération (French policy of), 19, 163–4
Crémieux, Pierre, 109
Cultural activities (Dakar), 234–5

Dahomey, 165
Dakar, 27, 40, 67–8, 111, no. of Frenchmen resident, 17, 68, 113, European quality of city, 18, 65, 241, residential areas of, 24, 54–5, 94–5, 216–17, 241, 92, settlement of, 37–8, 54–5, market of, 50, social life and leisure activities in 228, 234–5, wartime, 65, housing problems in, 69, 70, Municipal Council of, 88, centre of commerce, industry, 111, port of, 224, and throughout
Dakar, University of, 22, 170–2, 220, comparison with Ghanian and Nigerian universities, 170, nationality of students, 171, problems of Africanization, 171, absence of staff contact, 255, students and mixed marriage, 273
Decolonization, Constitutional Referendum on, 106, French attitudes toward, 105, 107, effect on commerce and industry, 107
De Gaulle, General Charles, 27, 129, 170, and Second World War, 64, and independence, 106, 107
Delcourt, A. (cited), 30, 34
Delmas, Jean Anselme, 36, 148
Delmas, Robert, 104, 108, 123, 195, family enterprises, 119, 196
Demonstrations, anti-white, 27, 85, 99–100, 106
Depression, Great, effect in Senegal, 51
Development Bank, Senegalese, 116
Dia, Mamadou, 106, 109, 112, 113, 194, Diaists, 147, 201
Diagne, Blaise, 61
Dialogue, Le ('dialogue' between French and Senegalese), 17, 19, 103, 186, 207, 250
Dien Bien Phu (Indo-China), French defeat at, 80, 105
Dieppe, 30
Diop, Birago, 236
Diouf, Galandou, 62
Diourbel (town), 24, 122, 235
Domestic servants, in European household, 243–5
Dumont, René, *L'Afrique Noire est Mal Partie*, 157

Echos de l'Afrique Noire, Les, 74–8, cartoons from, 70–1, 75, 77, on race relations, 99
Echos de France, Les, 201, 232
Ecole Nationale de la France d'Outre-Mer, 55
Economic and Social Council, 190, 196, 199, 202, purpose and functions, 109, activities, 206–10

315

Index

Economic dependence, of Senegal on France, 15, 16, 26, 110, 130, 165
Economic policy in Senegal, French attitudes toward, 126-30, 132 (table)
Economie et Humanisme, 112
Education in Senegal, French contribution to, 22, 166, 168-73, 180-1, manpower planning in, 169, French influence on curriculum, 170, 180-181, vocational training, 172, racial contact in, 254-5
Educational background, Frenchmen, after WWII, 66-7, and occupation, 83, 90 (table), 134, of non-African population, 90 (table), compared with France, 137, 215, and attitudes at work, 146
Élite, Senegalese, psychological dependence of, 16, and assimilation, 18, in trading post, 30, and social life, 58-60, 254, and race relations, 64-5, 97, businessmen, 204, executives, 242, 258, family preoccupations of, 254, and mixed marriage, 266
Empire, French, decolonization in, 104-9
Employers' Associations, 199, 201, structure and activities, 204-6, influence through Economic and Social Council, 208-9, (see also *Syndicat des Huiliers*, SCIMPEX, UNISYNDI)
Employment structure, Frenchmen, 133-40, policy on, 155, compared with other African countries, 133-4, advantages of, 138, in Senegal, (1962), 158 (table), in Dakar (1955), 91 (table), 159-161 (table)
England, competition with France in trade, 34
Estates-General (French Revolution), 33
Etcheverry, Guy, 102, 195
Evolués (African colonial élite), 45
Expatriation, advantages of, 138-40, 223-4, 177, disadvantages of, 227-32
Expeditions, colonial, 35
L'Express, 236

Faidherbe, General L., 37, 38, 43n
Family, French, size of, 69, problems of overseas, 223, 228, 229
Federation of Taxpayers, 76
Folklore, among Frenchmen in Senegal, 214
Fonds d'Investissement pour le Développement Economique et Social (F.I.D.E.S.), 79-80, 165
Force Ouvrière (S.F.I.O.), 82

Franc, C.F.A. (West African currency) parity with franc metro, 80, 138, and inflation, 80
Franc zone, 15, 27, preferential system, 110, 111, price cuts, 114
France, Second Empire and colonial policy, 37, 39, Fifth Republic and constitutional referendum, 106, department of origin of Frenchmen, 190, 215, voting in French elections, 192, 193, Consulate and Embassy of, in Dakar, 231, Ministry of Repatriation, 112, Ministry of Co-operation (Secretariat of State for Co-operation), 164, 167, *Mission d'Aide et de Coopération*, Dakar, 22, 172
France-Afrique Noire, 57, 76, anti-Lebanese articles, 53
Franco-Senegalese relations, 129, 164, 211
Free French Forces, 64
Freemasons, 64
French West Africa, Federation of, 18, 20, 47, 54, 67, 120, 230, Governor-General, 58, letter to, 88-9, taxes in, 76, free trade, 79, wage rates, apprenticeship, 86-7, representative institutions (*Grand Conseil*), 104, market system, 111, 124
Frenchmen in Senegal, future of, 26-7, uncertainty of, 258, and throughout

Galéries Lafayette, 80
Gallenca, Charles-Henri, 123, 202
Gambia, 115
General Council, 39, 63
Geographical origins, Frenchmen, 55-6
Germans, in Senegal during war, 64-5
Ghana, employment structure, 85 (*see* Gold Coast)
Gold Coast, 150, 165
Gorée (island), 29, 30, 33, 34, 36, 38, 39, 40
Graulle, Jean-Baptiste, 225
Graziani, Charles, 103
Groundnuts, for export, 16, trade, 30, 48, cultivation, 17, 36, 145, nationalization of trade, 109, 110, 112-116, refining of, 122, work market of, 126, technical assistance scheme and, 179
Guèye, Lamine, 62, 101
Guide Pratique de l'Européen dans l'Afrique Occidentale, 44
Guinea, independence of, 105, 230
Gum-arabic trade, 30, 34

Habitants (commune residents), 31, 32, *cahier* of, 178-9, 33

Index

Hauser, A. (cited), 9, 134n, 142n, 152n
Hong Kong, 115
Hospital facilities, improvement of, 232

Independence (*see* decolonization), in Africa, 98, in Senegal, 20, 101, 106, French attitudes toward, 128
India, 115, Indians, 259
Indo-China, transfer of capital from, 80, 120, 199, French defeat and withdrawal from, 104–5
Industry, development of, 79, types of, 121–2, problems of investment, 121–2, in politics, 197–8, 205–6
Inferiority, African, belief in, explanations for, 258–60
Inspection du Travail (Labour Exchange), 147
Integration (*see* segregation, race relations) of races in social groups, 92–3, 246, contact between races, 245, 247, 250, 253
Intermediary groups in race relations, 264–6
Interviews, conduct of, 21–6
Investment, French, 15, 26, 27
Islam, importance in social relations, 253, 259, 265, effect on work performance, 144, Ramadan, 144, Koranic teaching, 259
Issa, M., 42
Italians, as labour migrants, 73, 81
Ivory Coast (*see also* Abidjan), French influence in, 128

Japan, 115
Jeanneney Report, 1963, 167
Jeune Afrique, 236
Jews, 29, in colonial service, 64
Job competition, 60, 81, 97–9
Junior Chamber of Commerce, 123, 234

Kaolack (town), 24, 38, 122, 228, 235
Kébémer (town), 225
Kermel (Dakar), 55, 95, 216–17

Labour force, 157–9 (tables)
Labour relations, between Africans and Frenchmen, 20, 84–7, 147–56, job competition, 60, 81, 97–9, apprenticeship system and training problems, 86, 87, assessment of African work performance, 141–6, in France, 148, and race, 241–50, paternalism, 244, complaints at labour exchange, 245
Lafarge, Philippe, 36

Lebanese, early immigration of, 42, development of trading links, 48–51, 113, competition with French, 51–3, 115, 116–19, hostility of French, 51–3, 115, 116–9, in Dakar, 55, 92, anti-Lebanese campaign, 74, 76, 52–3, 203, attitudes of French to, 131 (table), stereotypes of, 118, as intermediary group, 264–5
Lebret, Father, 112
Leisure activities, Frenchmen, 232–6, class divisions of, 219, in Dakar and interior, 229, 234–5, occupational divisions of, 233, lack of racial contact in, 254
Lions Club, 123, 221, 233, 245
Loi Cadre (French West Africa), 104
Lot, Frenchmen from, 56
Loti, P. (cited), 44
Lutherans, 29

Mali Federation, formation of and French views of, 107
Mange-mils, Les (slang for '*colons*' in Senegal), 57
Manpower, training, 20, shortage of Senegalese, 154 planning in technical assistance, 163
Marseilles, 17, 30, 55, 89, 215
Maurel, Hilaire, 36, 37, 48
Maurel et Prom (trading company), 116
Medina (Dakar), 54–5, 95, 216–17, 241
Mercantilism, 29, 34
Mercier, P., (cited), 9, 20, 66, 74, 81
Methodology and procedure of study, 19–24, 239, 240
Métis (mulatto), 31, 38, 39, 40, 92, 237, *métissage*, 33, 93, liaisons, white men, black women, 93, *signares*, 33, *métisse*, families (social élite), 58, 61, 235, 265, children of mixed marriages, 93, 269, and race relations, 264–5
Midi, 224
Migration, Frenchmen to Senegal, 66–9
Militaires de contingent, in technical assistance, 174
Mission d'Aide et de Coopération, (*see* France, Ministry of Co-operation)
Mixed marriage, 240, 265–273, incidence of in Senegal, 265–6, among Senegalese élite, 266, isolation of couples, 266, 272–3, French attitudes toward, 267, education and occupation as a factor in, 267n, Senegalese attitudes toward, 271, failure rate of, 272

317

Index

Mobility, expatriate, social, 218, geographical, 218, 223, and race contact, 257, in employment, 82, 138, 154
Moniteur Africain, Le, 129
Moniteur du Sénégal, Le, 37
Monoprix (company), 80, 104, 120
Montpelier (town), 89
Morocco, independence of, 104
Mutual Aid Society (French), see *Association d'Entraide des Français*

Nantes (town), 89
Napoleon III, 37
National Assembly, French, election of deputy for Senegal (1848), 38, (1871), 39, (1914 and 1919), 61, debate on nationalism, 100
National Assembly, Senegalese, French participation in, 108, 195
Nationality, Senegalese law on, 108–9
Nationalization of groundnut trade, 109, 110, 112–16, 136, 194, 198, French attitudes toward, 112, 201, co-operatives, 113, possibility in other, sectors, 125
Navy, French Ministry of, 35, 36, demise of naval rule in colonies, 43
Négritude, 250
Newspapers, colonial, 41, current, 236
Nice, 17
Nigeria, employment structure, 85
North Africa, 89, 101
Nouvel Observateur, 236

Occupational structure, Frenchmen, 22, 66–7, 68, 72–3, 81–7, 133–40, 159–61 (table), mobility in, 82, 138, 154, company directors, types of, 123, 137, and employment policy, 155, career patterns, 218, hierarchy in French companies, 241, as factor in social contact, 246, 257, 259
Office de Commercialisation Agricole, O.C.A. (Groundnut Marketing Board), 112, 114, 116, 210, French business attitudes toward, 125
Old residents, French, stability and rootedness of, 224–5, stories, attitudes of, 226–7
OPTORG (company), investment of, 80, establishment in Senegal, 120
Paillard, J., 53
Paris, 18, 215, 268, Treaty of 1815, 34
Parti Socialiste Sénégalais, 103
Petersen (company), 116
Petit blanc (roughly 'lower-class' white),
66–89, 95, difficulty of definition, 66, 74
Peyrissac (company), 115, 119
Peytavin, André, 101, 103, 108
Pieds roses (French socialists in administration), 183
Planning, national economic, 113, European business and, 136, 199, 200–1, 213 (table), Ministry of, 168
Plantations, French, absence of in Senegal, 17, failure of, 34–5
Plateau (Dakar), 95, 216–17
Political influence, of business community, 190–1, 197–201, 204–6, 210–11, interest groups (employers' associations), 191, 194–5, impact of technical assistance programme, 182, 185, 200
Politics, electoral (*see also* representative councils) colonial (19c.), 38–40, (1900–1940) 60–4, political clans, 39, 61, 63, 191, 210, 211, European participation in (colonial period), 62–3, 101–9, apathy of Frenchmen after 1945, 101, 102, 190, 192, in France, 191–4
Polygamy, 254
Population, French in Senegal, 17, 26, 68, 69, migration of, 66–9, demographic balance, 69, family size, 69, geographical origins, 215, and mobility, 218, numbers as a factor in race contact, 252
Portugais (migrants from Cape Verde Islands), 265
Poujadism in Senegal, 76, 104
Poverty, among Frenchmen, 231–
Prades (Ariège), 56
Prejudice, in work assessment, 143, 146, 185, 242, in race relations, 256, 259, 263, 273, determinants of, 257, in attitudes to mixed marriage, 267–9
Primary schools, improvement of, 232
Printania (company), 80, 104, 200
Private sector (*see* political influence), 110–129, interviews, 22, 23, Senegalese employees, in, 25, 147–56, Africanization, 85–7, 147–56, 198, and nationalization, 114, Senegalese attitudes toward, 136, protection by French presence in administration, 178
Prom, Louis-Hubert, 36, 48
Puritans, 29

Questionnaire, 281–303, 23, 24, limitations of, 239

318

Index

Quincaillerie Centrale (company), 120

Race relations (*see also* segregation, mixed marriage, racism, prejudice, labour relations), in trading post, 32–3, and politics, 60–1, 100, 102, and job competition, 60, 85, 98, 99, 147, during Vichy period, 64–5, social status and attitudes to, 73, 78, 95–6, 98, 244–6, stereotypes in, 96, 97, 261, 262, generational factors in, 98, 101, 123, 207, 249, 253, 264, in working environment, 143, 146, 185–6, 240–7, contrast urban/rural, 96–7, psycho-social factors, 97–9, occupational distinctions and, 246, 257, 259, 263, paternalism, in, 257, 263, hierarchy of race and culture, 259
Racism, in attitude formation, 256–60, antipathy and prejudice, 256
Rassemblement Démocratique Africain (R.D.A.), 103
Reading on Africa, by Frenchmen, 236–8, prejudice in, 237, stereotypes of race in, 237–8
Reflective Sessions on Technical Assistance, 167
Religion, differences of (*see also* Islam), inhibition to contact between groups, 259, 265, in attitude formation, 261
Repatriation, of poor Frenchmen, 231–2, of colonial officers, 167, Ministry of, 231
Representative councils, colonial, 38, General Council, 39, 63, French participation in, 40, 63, 102–3, 108
Retirement to France, 17
Rhodesia, settlers, 17
Rochelle, La (town), 89
Roles, 18, 19, in administration, 166, in technical assistance, 163, 179–87
Rotary Club, 123, 221, 233, 245
Rous, Jean, 195
Rufisque (town), 29, 38, 40, 122, 226
Rural Economy, Ministry of, 168

St. Louis (town), 24, 29, 30, 32, 34, 35, 36, 38, 39, 40, 41, 42, 43, 44, 57, 58, 231, 235, 254
Salary structure, expatriate, 76, 82, 124, comparisons with Europe, 81, 138
Sample, 277, 280, stratified quota, 21, quotas, 22
Section Française de l'Internationale Ouvrière (S.F.I.O.), 62, 103, 196

Segregation (*see* race relations, racism, prejudice), in social life, 58–60, 233–235, 239, 273, residential, 92, 240, colour bar in South Africa (comparison with), 86, 240, in Central Africa (comparison), 96n, objective factors and factors reinforcing, 240, 253, 250–5, social distance as factor in, 251–2, 260, size of white community as factor in, 252
Sembène, Ousmane, 236
Senegal River, trade on, 30, 35, 38
Sénégal, République du, Ministry of Rural Economy, 168, Ministry of Plan, 168, Ministry of Commerce and Industry, 168, Ministry of Finance, 168–9, Ministry of Technical Education, 181n, 183n, 185n
Senghor, Leopold Sédar, 16, 26, 100, 101, 108, 113, 129, 165, 210, on nationalization, 114, on training at work, 150, on Africanization, 166, as political mediator, 191, on Economic and Social Council, 207, role in politics, 210–12, on negritude, 250
Service de l'Assistance Technique (*see* Technical assistance)
Shopkeepers, French, 50, 112
Slave trade, 30, 34
Social life, French, in the colony, 58–9, differentiation, 66, 72, 73, 78, leisure, 89, 222
Social structure, Frenchmen, homogeneity and diversity in colony, 73, 78, after independence, 217–23, status groups, 221
Social work, among Frenchmen, 231
Socialism, African (of L. S. Senghor), 108, 110, socialist advisers in government, 112
Société d'Assistance Technique et de Crédit Social d'Outre-Mer (S.A.T.E.C.)
Société de Développement Agricole, 179
Société Commerciale de l'Ouest Africain (S.C.O.A.), company, 49, 78n, 79, 115, in SONADIS, 116
Société Electrique et Industrielle de Baol (S.E.I.B.), company, director of, Forrestier, 199
Société Immobilière du Cap Vert (S.I.C.A.P.), (Dakar) company, 95
Sociétés de Prévoyance, 79
SOCOSIM (company) director of, Crémieux, 199
SONADIS (trading consortium), 116, 121, director of, Dupont, 199
Soudan, in Mali Federation, 107
Sow, Amadou, 204

319

Index

Spending patterns, European, 124, African, 125
Suret-Canale, Jean, 103
Syndicat des Commerçants Importateurs et Exportateurs de l'Ouest Africain (SCIMPEX), 115, 205, 208, 209
Syndicat Coopératif Economique du Sénégal, anti-Lebanese, 53
Syndicat des Huiliers, 206
SYNJAMAR (growers' union), 225
Syrians (*see* Lebanese)

Tarn, Frenchmen from, 56
Tarn-et-Garonne, Frenchmen from, 56
Teachers, French, negative stereotypes of, 176, activities of, 180–1
Technical assistance, 163–189, structure and origins of programme, 163, 166, 188–9 (table), absence of objectives, 163, in education, 168–73, Reflective Sessions on, 167, planning commissions for, 172, *Service de l'Assistance Technique*, 172, assessment of programme, 176, 177–9, 185–6, political impact of programme, 182–6, training function in, 184
Technical assistants, interviews and contact, 22, 23, numbers of personnel, 164, 168, 188–9 (table), role unclarity, 163, 166, 179–87, tenure of service, 173, 174n, career patterns, 180, colonial experience, 173, 174n, *militaires de contingent*, 174, social structure and activities, 218, 220, 233
Thiès (town), 24, 235
Togo, 230
Toubab (white man), 29, 103
Toulouse (city), 89
Tours (town), 89
Trade unions, expatriate, organization, activities of, 81–2, limitations of, 140, 193 (*see also* UNISCAMPTA)
Traders, French independent, 36, and colonial policy, 37–8, relations with administration, 42, competition with large firms, 50, difficult position, 51
Trading companies, political activities of, 39, 61, international links of, 79, 115, 120, resistance to Africanization, 86, and nationalization, readjustment, 115, 116, 119, and employment policy, 155

Trading posts, 29–37, personnel in, 30–2
Training problems on the job, 150, 151, 154, compared with British colonial methods, 150, in-service, 153, at executive level, 153, in administration, 185, (*see also* manpower)
Traitants (middlemen), in trade, 49, 51
Traite (trade by barter), 41
Tunisia, 89, 104
Turks, 29

Unemployment, 84–5, 98, 135, 136, underemployment, 87, expatriate, 230
Union, French, migration within, 67–8
Union Intersyndicale d'Entreprises et d'Industries (UNISYNDI), 205, 209
Union Progressiste Sénégalaise (U.P.S.), 16, 147, 204, 209, National Council of, 113, French participation in, 191
Union Sénégalaise des Banques, 204
Union Syndicale des Commerçants Indépendants, 76
United Nations, 15, 195, 237

Vézia (company), 116
Vichy regime in Senegal (1940–42), 64–5, 240
Voisin, Maurice, 76

White settlers, in Africa (*see also* Algeria, Rhodesia), comparison with Senegal, 214
Wolof, 264
Women, French, in sample, 24, in colony, effect on life, 57, 228, employment of, 85, 135, suicide rate, 229, racial attitudes of, 229, 245
Women, Senegalese, exclusion in social life, 253
Work, as field of contact between races, 241, Senegalaise output, estimated by Europeans, 140–6, differing cultural views of, 186–7
Working environment, advantages of for expatriates, in private sector, 139, in technical assistance, 175, 176, contrast of two sectors, 176
World War Two, in Senegal, 64–5

Ziguinchor (town), 24, 235

RENEWALS 458-4574
DATE DUE